The Development and Sustenance of Self-Esteem in Childhood

THE DEVELOPMENT AND SUSTENANCE OF SELF-ESTEEM IN CHILDHOOD

From the Study Group of the Division of Child Psychiatry of
THE CAMBRIDGE HOSPITAL
DEPARTMENT OF PSYCHIATRY
HARVARD MEDICAL SCHOOL
AND THE CAMBRIDGE-SOMERVILLE
MENTAL HEALTH AND RETARDATION CENTER

Edited by

John E. Mack, M.D., and Steven L. Ablon, M.D.

International Universities Press, Inc.

New York

Library of Congress Cataloging in Publication Data

Main entry under title:

The Development and sustenance of self-esteem in
  childhood.

  Bibliography: p.
  Includes indexes.
  1. Self-respect in children. I. Mack, John E.,
1929-   . II. Ablon, Steven L. III. Cambridge
Hospital (Cambridge, Mass.). Division of Child
Psychiatry. IV. Harvard Medical School. Dept. of
Psychiatry. V. Cambridge-Sommerville Mental Health and
Retardation Center. [DNLM: 1. Self-concept—In infancy
and childhood. 2. Child development. WS 105.5.S3

D489]
BF723.S3D47   1983   155.4'18   83-22726
ISBN 0-8236-1255-4

Manufactured in the United States of America

Contents

ACKNOWLEDGMENTS

We are grateful to the family members, friends, and colleagues who have carefully read and criticized this manuscript and made many valuable suggestions. Individual members of the Study Group especially want to thank Dr. Gridth Ablon, Dr. Adele Dalsimer, Dr. James Dalsimer, Dr. Judy Kantrowitz, Ms. Caryle Perlman, Mr. Daniel Givelber, Dr. Nick Browning, Dr. Paul Cotton, Mr. Todd Smith, Ms. Miriam Vale, Dr. Nancy Powell, Ms. Kathleen Linnell, Dr. Thomas S. Geraty, for his critical comments from an educational perspective, Dr. Joseph E. Murray, Chief of Plastic and Maxillofacial Surgery, for the opportunity of working in the Craniofacial Clinic at The Children's Hospital Medical Center, and Dr. Edward Boyd, Director of the Gifford School in Weston, Massachusetts, for his encouragement and support.

We are especially indebted to Shelley S. Ehrlich, M.S.W., for her dedicated and extensive assistance editing and organizing the manuscript. Pat Carr, who has shepherded us through the organizing of drafts and scheduling of meetings, as well as helping to prepare the manuscript, has been invaluable to us. We also want to thank the Psychiatric Service of The Cambridge Hospital and our former Chief of Psychiatry, Dr. Lee B. Macht, who died tragically in April, 1981 at the age of 43.

CONTRIBUTORS

ABLON, STEVEN L., M.D.
Director of Child Psychiatry Training, The Cambridge Hospital
Assistant Professor of Psychiatry, Harvard Medical School
Faculty, Boston Psychoanalytic Society and Institute, Inc.

BELFER, MYRON L., M.D.
Acting Chief, Department of Psychiatry, The Cambridge Hospital
Director of Child and Adolescent Psychiatry, The Cambridge
    Hospital
Associate Professor of Psychiatry, Harvard Medical School

BRAUN, SAMUEL J., M.D.
Clinical Director, Preschool Unit of the Cambridge-Somerville
    Mental Health and Retardation Center
Assistant Professor of Psychiatry, Harvard Medical School at The
    Cambridge Hospital
Consulting Psychiatrist, Cambridge Public Schools

COTTON, NANCY S., PH.D.
Director, Inpatient Child Psychiatry, New England Memorial
    Hospital
Instructor in Psychology in the Department of Psychiatry, The
    Cambridge Hospital, Harvard Medical School

DEMOS, VIRGINIA, ED.D.
Assistant Professor of Child Psychiatry and Pediatrics, Boston
    University School of Medicine
New England Memorial Hospital

GERATY, RONALD, M.D.
Chief of Psychiatry, New England Memorial Hospital
Clinical Instructor in Psychiatry, Harvard Medical School
Medical Director, Fuller Memorial Hospital

GIVELBER, FRANCES, ACSW, LICSW
Social Work Staff, The Cambridge Hospital
Lecturer on Psychiatry, Harvard Medical School
Clinical Instructor, Smith College School for Social Work

HARRISON, ALEXANDRA M., M.D.
Child Psychiatrist, Harvard Community Health Plan, Cambridge,
  Massachusetts
Clinical Instructor in Psychiatry, Harvard Medical School

HUIZENGA, JUDITH N., M.D.
Residency Training Director of Child Psychiatry, Beth Israel Hos-
  pital
Clinical Instructor in Psychiatry, Harvard Medical School
Member, Boston Psychoanalytic Society and Institute, Inc.

JACOBS, DANIEL H., M.D.
Assistant Clinical Professor of Psychiatry, Harvard Medical School
  at The Cambridge Hospital
Faculty, Boston Psychoanalytic Society and Institute, Inc.

MACK, JOHN E., M.D.
Staff Psychiatrist, The Cambridge Hospital and the Cambridge-
  Somerville Mental Health and Retardation Center
Professor of Psychiatry, Harvard Medical School at The Cam-
  bridge Hospital
Chairman, Executive Committee, Departments of Psychiatry,
  Harvard Medical School

MALMQUIST, CARL P., M.D.
Professor of Sociology and Social Psychiatry, University of Min-
  nesota

SCHNEIDER, PAULA, MSW
Assistant Professor of Sociology and Director of the Social Work
  Program, Regis College
Formerly, Clinical Social Work Supervisor, Child Psychiatry Di-
  vision, The Cambridge Hospital
Formerly, Family School Coordinator of the Gifford School, Wes-
  ton, Massachusetts

VAN BUSKIRK, DAVID, M.D.
Staff Child Psychiatrist and Coordinator of Training in Mental Health, Harvard Community Health Plan, Cambridge, Massachusetts
Assistant Clinical Professor of Psychiatry, Harvard Medical School
Graduate, Boston Psychoanalytic Society and Institute, Inc.

WILLS, FRANK, S. G., M.D.
Consulting Psychiatrist, Eunice Kennedy Shriver Center for Mental Retardation, Inc.
Consulting Psychiatrist, Dr. Franklin Perkins School
Clinical Instructor in Psychiatry, Harvard Medical School
Clinical Assistant Professor of Psychiatry, Tufts University School of Medicine

PREFACE

The quest for a sense of personal worth, so critical to small children, remains of central importance for human beings throughout their lives. It motivates much of our activity in seeking personal attachments and meaningful work. Political and religious beliefs and institutions are fashioned to enhance self-worth, and artistic creativity is intimately connected with the need to accomplish something which will give us value. Nothing is more important for the maintenance of well-being. Conversely, no experience is more obviously distressing, or more intimately linked to emotional disturbances of many kinds and, in psychiatry, to various types of psychopathology, than is a diminished sense of worth or a low opinion of oneself.

This book grew out of an ongoing seminar organized by its editors in 1977 to address the question of how self-esteem develops in childhood and adolescence and how it is sustained through childhood and in later years. The examination of this question is its primary purpose. As we pursued our study it soon became apparent that, although a good deal has been written about the psychology of self-esteem from the standpoint of adults, based on the reconstruction of their childhood development, relatively little work has been done based on direct observations of children and their families.

All of the members of the seminar work in the field of child mental health or child development in the Cambridge-Somerville Mental Health and Retardation Center and its affiliated programs.[1] The seminar has included child psychiatrists, child psychoanalysts, psychologists, and social workers who have worked with children in a variety of settings. These settings include child psychiatric and pediatric inpatient hospital units, outpatient clinics, day care centers, private offices, school classrooms for normal and retarded children, and various locations for conducting research. The book includes data obtained from psychotherapy and

---

[1] These are the New England Memorial Hospital, the Harvard Community Health Plan, and The Cambridge Hospital, Department of Psychiatry, at the Harvard Medical School.

psychoanalysis, diagnostic testing, observations on hospital wards, in day care centers, in elementary and high schools, schools for the retarded, and court clinics; from research with infants and their mothers; and from individual and group work with parents or troubled children.

Self-Esteem and Its Development:

An Overview

JOHN E. MACK, M.D.

The inclination of man and his gods to assign value to the universe is present from the start of the Old Testament. In the beginning, God looked at what he had created, including man himself, and decided that "it was good" (Genesis 7:10, 13, 18, etc.). But the matter did not remain so simple. For it was not long before man was disappointing God with his capacity for behavior and emotions to which God assigned an opposite value. No sooner had man begun to increase his numbers and spread over the earth than the Lord noted "that his thoughts and inclinations were always evil." God was "sorry that he had made man on earth, and he was grieved at heart" (5:5–6).

The struggle between the elements in nature to which man has assigned the values of good and evil, especially between those warring "thoughts and inclinations" within himself, constitutes a central theme of human history. Man is forever seeking to find value in himself and his world and to secure the admiration and approval of his fellow human beings. Psychoanalyst Gregory Rochlin (1965) has observed "the timelessness and the universality of conflicts over self-esteem" (p. 4), and has discovered religious rituals in Buddhist and Brahmanic, as well as in Judaic and Christian traditions, which carry a "pleading for special privilege" (p. 5). The claim of the Israelites to being God's chosen people, to having special value in his eyes, is the best known of such pleadings, but fulfillment of man's need to find value in himself and his community is reflected in similar mythologies of special worth among peoples throughout the world and in the endless longing for heroes.

Throughout Western history, with rare exceptions, men and women have looked to some standard or measure outside of themselves, to assess their self-worth. The ultimate agent of this valuing has generally been called God, one of whose principle preoccupations, it would appear, has been to judge the worth of human beings. Among Western philosophers Feuerbach has examined most directly the relationship between man's concern about questions of value, self-worth, and the ideal, and the concept of God. In *The Essence of Christianity* (1843b) Feuerbach argued that man creates God as the representation of the highest image of himself. What is to man "the highest being, to which he can conceive nothing higher—that is to him the Divine being" (p. 38). God, wrote Feuerbach, cannot be conceived of except as man can imagine value within himself: "So much worth as a man has, so much and no more has his God" (p. 32).

Religion serves to empower man's pursuit of the best of which he can conceive for himself by linking it with the power he experiences as pervading the universe. This power is harnessed by means of religious ritual in the service of controlling what is evil or destructive. Indeed, it has traditionally been difficult for man to behave morally by himself, or as a member of a group, without the guiding structures of formal religion. This, of course, is not to deny the fact that groups of men have often turned religion to the service of destruction.

Since *particular* men and women—religious leaders—have usually assumed the responsibility for determining what and whom God values, their criteria have generally favored the groups to which they belong. Value and self-worth derive from membership and good standing in one's own group (including a national group), while evil tends to reside among the members of an outside or alien group. The notion of self-esteem in its *contemporary* sense implies a large measure of reference to internal criteria as well—we judge ourselves in relation to an internalized "sense of who we are," as well as in relation to the community, and are aware of our self judgments, however dependent these judgments may be upon the approval and opinions of others. This book is concerned with how self-judgment develops, and how the assessment of self-worth is organized and sustained in childhood and adolescence.

One of the interminable debates in Judaeo-Christian theology concerns the matter of man's fundamental nature. Much of the

Bible and many later Christian writings take a pessimistic view, the most discouraging being the doctrine of original sin in which the human infant is thought to be burdened at birth with inherited evil passed down from Adam since the time of the Fall. The importance of having an accurate sense of the limits of one's value, especially in relation to the supreme worth of God, is stressed in the Bible and in early church literature. A person may be encouraged (as in the "wisdom literature") to have a just view of his power and ability, but, reveals the Lord, "pride, presumption, evil courses, all these I hate" (Proverbs 8:13). In the medieval church pride heads most lists of deadly or capital sins. In its earliest meaning pride is defined as "a high or overweening opinion of one's own qualities, attainments, or estate; inordinate self-esteem" (*The Oxford Universal Dictionary*). A sense of unworthiness and sin (to be redeemed by good works, including in some interpretations, material success) has dominated Western man's view of himself until modern times, although radical shifts in what society especially values appear currently to be taking place in the United States (Ferguson, 1980; Yankelovich, 1981). The unending search for heroes to worship and follow represents the struggle to transcend the limits of ordinary individual self-worth.

The Puritans of 17th and 18th century New England were especially afflicted with self-doubt and a belief in their unworthiness. As soon as they landed in Massachusetts the Puritans were preoccupied with the notion that they were declining, falling short of their own and God's expectations. Seeking to give each child the best chance to escape damnation and to emerge as one of the elect, they instituted harsh child-rearing approaches, relying on shaming techniques which were devised to break the child's will (Demos, Demos, Binstock, and Levine, 1978).

The Puritans took a view of infancy not far from the notion of original sin and made an effort to stifle evil at the beginning of life (Demos, 1972). John Robinson (1628), an early Puritan educator, allowed that children, "in their first days," may "have the greater benefit of good mothers, not only because they suck their milk, but in a sort, their manners also, by being continually with them, and receiving their first impressions from them" (p. 11). Later on, he wrote, "good fathers" are more important for instilling "virtue and good manners, by their greater wisdom and authority; and ofttimes also, by correcting the fruits of their mother's indulgence, by their severity" (p. 11). Nevertheless, the "spiritual dangers" remain acute "both for nourishing and increasing the corruption which they bring into the world with them; and for diverting them from all goodness. . ." (p. 12).

But it is not only the Puritans, or other harsh self-judgers, who have been concerned with self-worth. The need to feel that one possesses value and worth, is, at least in Western cultures, a kind of psychic bedrock, essential to the existence of the person, analogous to the body's need for air or water. To believe that one is of little or no value, and that this state will not change, is incompatible with the continuing life of the person. Such a psychic state often leads to suicide if the means and the energy exist to carry through the act.

SELF, SELF-ESTEEM, AND PSYCHIC STRUCTURE

Before proceeding further with the discussion of self-esteem, I need to clarify how the term *self* is being used here. What is this entity whose value is under consideration? There is a growing literature in psychoanalysis and related fields aimed at developing a comprehensive psychology of the self. It is interesting to note that this effort, approaching the dimensions of a movement, appears in a time of worldwide political and ecological threats to human survival which have heightened the urgency for individual human beings to take responsibility for their destinies at the individual and community level. Some would argue (and I would include myself among them) that this greater individual responsibility can only follow from greater self-awareness, and perhaps, that this need for greater self-awareness accounts, in turn, for the increasing emphasis in society on self-awareness, self-knowledge, and self-fulfillment (Yankelovich, 1981). In any event, the effort to develop a psychology of the self has apparently resulted from the recognition by psychoanalysts and other clinicians that they are confronting problems in their practices (or at least new ways that their patients present or view personal difficulties) that require, at least for some groups, formulations different from those available in psychoanalytic structural theory. Patients are more likely, for example, to seek help for what they perceive to be problems in the workability of their lives, especially in their relationships with other people, than to present with symptoms or clear-cut mental and emotional disorders that lend themselves to medical diagnosis or structural formulation. "Self psychology" represents an effort to develop new models of psychic organization and functioning that can help us understand these problems In this context, a sense of diminished self-worth has come increasingly to be voiced as a presenting complaint by patients, rather than being offered, as in the past, by the clinician as part of a structural formulation growing out of diagnostic or therapeutic exploration. This phenomenon in itself reflects the increasing self-awareness of our age.

The term *self* is used in several ways in psychology and psychoanalysis. But there is a fundamental, and, it seems to me, inescapable, division of the idea of self into the self as knower or subject, the "I," and the self as known or object, the "me." As William James (1890) wrote, following Kant: "At the basis of our knowledge of our selves there lies only 'the simple and utterly empty idea: *I*; of which we cannot even say we have a notion. . . .' The only self we know anything positive *about*, he [Kant] thinks, is the empirical *me*, not the pure I; the self which is an object among other objects and the 'constituents' of which we ourselves have seen" (pp. 342–343). Wittgenstein (1914-1916) argues in a similar vein. He acknowledges an "object use" of the word *I* as distinct from the knowing or perceiving subject, as in "I have grown six inches" in contrast to "I hear or see such and such." The knowing subject, he states, is not in this world: "If I state I perceive a perceiving I, then I am in error, that is to say I then confuse the I with an object in the world. . . . The I is simply not an object. It is no object for precisely the reason that I cannot stand over against it" (pp. 15–16). In this sense, the I, the knowing or experiencing self, is mysterious, for it cannot be observed—in fact, it disappears when one tries to do so. It is through this I that we become connected with all that is, including other selves and our own selves-as-objects. As psychoanalysts or psychotherapists we engage our patients or clients in a process whereby the I, the "observing ego" or "experiencing self," takes the self-as-object as *its* object.

Otto Kernberg (1980) points to a source of linguistic confusion in Freud's work deriving from his use of the German term *ich*, meaning *I*, to convey both his theory of a mental structure, as an agency, and the more personal, subjective, experiential, 'self' qualities of his concept 'ich' before 1923. A similar distinction between self as subject, or evaluator, and self as a system or structure is contained, he says, in Jacobson's (1964) differentiation of self as person, or knower, and self as an intrapsychic representation, or "self-representation." To avoid confusion with regard to the double meaning of the *self* in *self-esteem* this distinction must be kept in mind. This self is both evaluator—the subjective self evaluating the self's worth—and also the objective self—the aggregate of self-representations whose worth is being evaluated.

Erik Erikson (1980, 1981) recently used the methodology of German "form criticism" to reexamine the Galilean sayings of Jesus in terms of the sense of I. Erikson notes that through the transcendant *I am* Jesus links himself with all others "who share the sense of *I am*" to form a community which connects itself in turn with the Godhead. For Erikson, this subjective self, or *I am*, is at the center of consciousness, "where the light is." It may also be thought of as a form of order, or ordering place. It is represented metaphorically in language as a place of being, a space; and it appears in dreams as a chamber, box, room, or other space-occupying locus. For an infant the emergence of a sense of self or I is a powerful moment in the discovery of being a person.

It is through the experiencing self or *I am* that a person achieves a sense of continuity and cohesiveness, of identity. We speak of another person as having a strong or weak "sense of self"; we thereby suggest that the other person feels sure about his wishes, purposes, and capabilities, and about something more, usually described as a "center" or "core." In this context one is speaking about the self-as-a-whole.

From the perspective of internal experience we do not deal concretely with whole selves. Rather, we experience a group of images by means of which we represent what we mean by *ourselves*. Through these images or self-representations we form a composite out of which we constitute our self-regard (Sandler, Holder, and Meers, 1963; Spruiell, 1981; Grossman, 1983). We see ourselves as tall or short, loving or hating, conscientious or irresponsible, effective or ineffectual. Our level of self-regard depends on how we evaluate these representations in the aggregate. Self-esteem is thus the result of the interplay of the self-as-subject or I, evaluating and experiencing, and the self-as-object, being evaluated or judged by the standards and expectations of the self-as-subject. The affective component, the emotional experience which accompanies the assessment of self-worth, is experienced in the I or subjective self but in relation to the self as object. Self-esteem is a resonance, a constantly shifting interaction between self-as-subject and self-as-object, reflected affectively in altered moods that represent the person's assimilation of new data from the external and internal worlds that bear upon the determination of self-worth.

Psychoanalytic theoretical concepts of psychic organization tend to view the person as a discrete, clearly delimited entity. Although such a view follows naturally enough from everyday empirical observations of human beings in the physical sense, it runs into difficulties when we try to consider the notion of *self*. We often encounter, especially in psychoanalytic writings, the idea of an autonomous ego or self, implying that the self can be truly independent and separate from what is "outside" it.

In recent writings, particularly those by Heinz Kohut and his followers, specific self-structures have been hypothesized, such as "the grandiose self" or "the exhibitionistic self" which represent various configurations of autonomous human functioning. But what are, in fact, the boundaries of self? As soon as we encounter a human being engaged in any particular activity, including thought, we find that he is part of a larger system, with which he is intimately interconnected. Gregory Bateson (1971), who devoted much of his life to the study of organismic systems, put the matter succinctly. The "unit," he wrote, "which processes information, or, as I say, 'thinks' and 'acts' and 'decides,' is a *system* whose boundaries do not at all coincide with the boundaries either of the body or of what is properly called the 'self' or 'consciousness' " (p. 319). The interdependence or interconnectedness of human beings with other persons or selves is perhaps the most obvious example of the limitations of the notion of an autonomous self. Self-help groups such as Alcoholics Anonymous grasp this fact in creating strategies for transcending the conceit of autonomy, our false confidence in the individual's assumed independent or separate functioning, especially in the handling of a powerful chemical force such as alcohol (Mack, 1981). A.A. creates a context which enables the alcoholic to experience his connectedness with the group and with a higher power beyond the limits of his corporal being.

Daniel Yankelovich (1981), an analyst of trends in contemporary American society who is also familiar with psychoanalytic concepts, regards the notion of an autonomous self, which has grown in part out of the atomizing tendencies of psychoanalytic structural theory, as responsible for the self-centered or unrealistic aspects of the search for self-fulfillment in American society. "The root fallacy," Yankelovich writes, "is the assumption that the human self can be wholly autonomous, solitary, contained and 'self-created'" (p. 237). "The self," he observes, "is not an isolated 'object,' a ghost locked in a machine or a mere private consciousness located within a body" (p. 241).

Some contemporary psychoanalytic writers, especially those who have observed infants developing in the setting of the mother-infant dyad, or within the family system, focus our attention upon this fact of interconnectedness. Louis Sander (1979), an observer of infant development, notes that "in the privacy and sameness of the consulting room, it is easy to think of organization as the property of the individual rather than the individual as the property of an active process in an individual-environment system" (p. 10). Sander describes the development in the toddler period of an "intermediate area," which "under favorable circumstances, comes to reside within as a functional configuration characterizing the self—a site of continuing privacy, or continuing integration of inside and outside for the never ending adaptive process" (p. 19).[1]

Child psychoanalysts Gerald Stechler and Samuel Kaplan (1980) have been studying the development of self-awareness and self-organization in infants. They, like Sander, stress the interconnected and transcendent dimension of "self." Stechler and Kaplan

---

[1] George Klein (1976) writes about the affiliative requirements of identity, or *we-ness*. Identity, according to Klein, "must always be defined as having aspects of both separateness and membership in a more encompassing entity." Klein's *we-ness* or *we-go* may be expressed "through familial and societal bonds; or the person may crave surrender to the higher entities of God and Cosmos" (p. 179).

describe "two aspects of the developing self: (1) An autonomous component, as a locus of action and eventually decision; (2) That aspect of self which is a necessary part of a larger unit transcending one's autonomous actions. It is the integration of the 'I' and the 'we' components which spells out a complete entity, i.e., a self or person" (p. 89).

Erikson (1981), in his examination of the sense of I in the Galilean sayings, extends this notion of I-we linkage to the identity of a people or nation. "We come to the conclusion, then," Erikson writes, "that whatever a people's geographic and historical setting, its majority (or its leading aristocracy) must be assured of the reliability of a number of dominant space-time qualities which, in fact, correspond to the requirements of a sense of *I* even as they cohere in a collective *We*" (p. 333). Feuerbach (1843a) realized this communal aspect of self. "The single man *in isolation*," he wrote, "possesses in himself the *essence* of man neither as a *moral* nor as a *thinking* being. The *essence* of man is contained only in the community, in the *unity of man with man*—a unity, however, that rests on the *reality* of the distinction between 'I' and 'you' " (p. 244).

The views of self discussed above contain two basic implications for our discussion of self-esteem. First, we can see that self-esteem is a complex function or relation of functions, and, second, that an understanding of how positive self-esteem develops and is maintained (or, conversely, of what interferes with it) cannot be grasped by the study of the individual in isolation. Just as the beginning sense of being of value grows for the infant out of the shared matrix of loving interactions with its mother, and supportive approval of its efforts to achieve mastery in early exploratory initiatives, so our sense of personal value will always to a degree depend upon relationships with the outside world. It is true, of course, that a core sense of one's worth (or lack of it) may be internalized in childhood and adolescence so that self-esteem will not fluctuate wildly in adult life, like a barometer in the tropics, with each successful or failing encounter with the environment. But at the same time no human being's sense of his value can ever become totally independent of the valuing of other people. This is not to say that there are not those individuals suffering from "narcissistic" disturbances who pathologically fear failure or crave success, or whose self-worth is virtually entirely contingent upon the approval or disapproval of others. But all of our *selves* retain to some degree a dependence upon connectedness with others for validation of our worth; we will never become completely indifferent to the fair acknowledgment of what we have accomplished or honestly given of ourselves. Furthermore, actions which are aimed exclusively at the accumulation of achievements, material goods, or self-fulfillment are, for this reason, unlikely to provide a satisfying sense of personal worth no matter how successful the person may be. It is questionable, indeed, whether human beings can deeply experience positive self-worth except as the result of relationship—through contributing to the welfare of others, communicating in one medium or another, doing creative work, or by connecting in the mutual caring and valuing of loving and being loved. "We all 'know' two truths about the self," Yankelovich (1981) writes "One is that the self is private and alone and wholly encased within one's body. The other is that one is a real self only to the extent that caring and reaching beyond the self continue" (p. 240).

One context in which the participatory nature of self-worth may be observed is our membership in groups. Each child becomes a member of a number of groups beginning with the family. In the mother-infant pair the developing human being learns in the first year of life the "values" of the group, i.e., which actions of his will receive love and encouragement and which will be regarded by the mother, and later by the whole family, as "bad." Self-esteem thus develops in the family, and throughout childhood and adult life it is sustained by the loving support of the family. (Frances Givelber in Chapter 7 and Paula Schneider in Chapter 14 discuss how self-esteem is gained within the family context and how parents can be helped to be more effective in enhancing this critical dimension of their children's development.) When a child begins to participate in other groups, such as clubs and teams, personal self-worth is affected not only by the success of those groups, but also by the group's cohesiveness and alignment with its own values and purposes (morale) and by the child's acceptance within the group. Conversely, rejection by the group or scapegoating can have a devastating effect on self-esteem.

Limit setting by adults in response to aggressive behavior (itself often a reaction to injured self-regard), or in response to the scapegoating of others by physical attack and insults, can be particularly important for the maintenance of high self-regard in children. Children generally feel bad about themselves when their aggression is allowed to run out of control, and of course the victims feel devalued when such assaults are permitted. Scapegoating (Scheidlinger, 1981) represents the projection of unwanted or painful aspects of oneself onto another child who is seen as possessing areas of weakness that are especially threatening to the attacker. The setting of firm limits conveys to all the children the message that the adults love them and care about them enough to protect them, that they are *worth* protecting. Scheidlinger (1981) points out that scapegoating may also serve the members of a group that is injured in *its* self-esteem by ridding it of the painful experience, or by "dumping" the hurt on a vulnerable "outsider."

Kohut (1976) has posited "the existence of a certain psychological configuration with regard to the group" which he calls the "group self." He regards this as "analogous to the self of the individual" (p. 838). I consider this division of the self into an individual and a group self to be artificial, since the self is from the start of life a social entity, defined by its relationships in groups of two or more persons. One might more correctly speak of self at the level of the individual, self at the level of the family, self at the level of the group or the nation.

The peer groups of childhood and adolescence have their adult counterparts in professional organizations and national or ethnic groups. (Examples of the importance of groups for the maintenance of structures serving self-esteem regulation are provided by Samuel Braun in Chapter 12.) It should be stressed that a sense of personal self-worth is very much affected by the perceived fulfillment of values and objectives by an organizational or national group with which an individual is identified. It is perhaps not an overstatement that personal self-esteem rises and falls with the fate of one's nation. This phenomenon is well known to national leaders, who become experts at assessing the national "mood" and in promising accomplishments for a country which would, if realized, raise the self-regard of its populace, whether or not the proclaimed objectives are in any actual sense achievable.

THE DEVELOPMENT OF SELF-ESTEEM

In each stage of development after infancy the achievement of a sense of positive self-worth contributes not only to the child's sense of well-being but also to the quelling of his fears for his actual survival. In the child's eyes, his sense of self-worth is *essential* to his survival. The child who does not experience his value in the eyes of his parents will fear their abandonment and its attendant dangers to his existence. The older child and adolescent may even contemplate suicide. The maintenance of positive self-esteem is so fundamental a task that all of the structures of personality contribute to its organization. Functions of judging and evaluating are assignable to the ego; standards, values, and prohibitions are represented by the ego ideal and superego structures; drives, wishes, and longings, together with their disappointments and frustrations, are experienced in the affective realm. At the same time, self-esteem is affected continuously by experiences in the world as these are represented in the self and interpreted through the above agencies of personality. Many of the character traits which seem to define individual personalities, such as ambition, diffidence, conscientiousness, and the like, have as their underlying motive the maintenance of self-esteem or a compensation for conscious and unconscious doubts about self-worth. Psychoanalysts postulate that there is an optimal balance of need gratification and realistic thwarting in childhood for the creation of later stability in self-esteem regulation. This "optimal frustration," according to Kohut (1977), "provides the storehouse of self confidence and basic self esteem that sustains a person throughout life" (p. 188).

The protection of self-esteem is one of the central development tasks of childhood. Early examples of its expression are seen in the second year, in the protests of the child who denies wrongdoing, or who blames inanimate or human objects in order not to experience the reproaches of his parents. The protection of self-esteem has an important place in Harry Stack Sullivan's theory of interpersonal relations. Sullivan (1953) calls the organization of experience which evolves out of the mother-infant relationship the "self-system," which serves to avoid or minimize anxiety (p. 165). According to Sullivan, "the self-system [is] the vast organization of experience which is concerned with protecting our self esteem . . ." (p. 247).

The central place of self-esteem protection in the organization of personality grows out of the intensity of pain associated with falling self regard, what Kohut (1980) calls "the experiential core of the devastating emotional event we refer to as a severe drop in self-esteem" (p. 503). As Rochlin (1973) writes, "Neither the beloved child nor the favored heroes of legends, any more than a people chosen by God, are spared outrageous trials. The flaw and the virtue in all is in the peril to self-esteem. Its defense may bring the highest honors and justify the lowest violence but its loss risks our extinction" (p. 216).

Each phase of development (as is discussed more fully by Nancy Cotton in Chapter 5) provides particular tasks and arenas of human relationships out of which the sense of self and self-regard emerge. The earliest exchanges between the infant and mother and the earliest forms of physical caretaking provide the context for mutually pleasurable activity between parents and their infants. One might consider the precursor of positive self-esteem to be the good body feeling and the affects of pleasurable excitement and lively interest associated with the mutually loving exchanges, the touching and looking, that occur between the parent and the infant. It is for this reason, one may suppose, that self-esteem remains so intimately linked throughout human life with our valuations of the attractiveness of our bodies and faces ("good looks"), and with physical well-being more generally. It is well known, for example, that the inner feeling of self-worth suffers during bouts of systemic illness, such as influenza or hepatitis, even when there is no significant long-term threat to health or survival.

In each phase of development the child represents internally a multitude of experiences in relation to human and inanimate objects, experiences inevitably linked with the development of his system of self-representations. Some of these experiences are pleasurable and satisfying, others noxious and painful. The maintenance of positive self-esteem depends on the successful integration of positive and negative self-images—Sullivan (1953) called these "good me" and "bad me" (p. 161)—and above all on the establishment of a baseline of positive value or worth which becomes more or less impervious to failure or outside criticism.

Beginning in infancy, and continuing throughout life, the mastery of the special challenges of each developmental stage, together with the inner sense that one has the capacity to repeat the performance when called upon, plays an important part in the establishment of positive self-esteem. Jerome Kagan (1981) has gathered evidence to show that it is in the second half of the second year that the child begins to be able to maintain self-generated goals in relation to specific standards. He distinguishes two types of standards: *normative,* consisting of "representations of actions and events that have been linked with adult approval and disapproval," and *mastery,* consisting of representations of goals which "have not necessarily been associated with adult displeasure or praise" (p. 127). This differentiation is consistent with the dual nature of self-esteem maintenance throughout life—one element deriving from approval by others, the second growing from satisfaction taken in independent, self-generated activity.

The preschool or oedipal period is a time in which psychological structures important in regulating self-esteem, especially the superego, begin to form. At the same time as strong genital impulses and sexual curiosity are prominent in both boys and girls, with emerging masculine and feminine strivings, limits and prohibitions are becoming internalized as superego injunctions. The emotion of guilt is closely related to superego structures and adds its weight to the range of powerful feelings which affect the level of self-esteem. Edith Jacobson (1975) writes: "The standards by which the individual measures his moral attitudes and behavior or his general assets and defects stem from the structure of the superego and the identifications that contribute to it" (p. 172).

Through fantasy and play, especially in combination, small children seek to overcome the continuous hurt to self-esteem that derives from the awareness of their limitations. A boy of five in the first meeting of his psychoanalytic treatment expressed frustration with his parents, especially his mother, who would put him out of her bedroom at night. He was able to use his imagination to feel more powerful and important. He told the analyst that he had Superman, Batman, Mighty Mouse, and Zorro costumes. "When I put on the costume," he said, "I pretend I am actually the one I'm wearing." Religious beliefs, especially ideas about God, begin to develop during this period (Rizzuto, 1979). These ideas serve many functions for the child, but one of them is surely the assurance that derives from the perception of God as a being who, supreme in value himself, nevertheless may love, protect, and value the child as the child wishes. Depending on how religious beliefs have become internalized however, or are imparted within the family, God's esteem may not be given uncritically but may be seen as contingent upon the child's good behavior, or even upon the "goodness" or "badness" of his thoughts.

During the grade-school years the level of self-esteem is further affected by the acquisition of competence and skills (or the failure to do so), especially in school performance, peer relationships, and, to a lesser degree, in athletics. (As Daniel Jacobs demonstrates in Chapter 10, self-regard is deeply affected by success and failure in academic work in school. Ronald Geraty in Chapter 13 further discusses the role of teachers and schools in the development of self-esteem.) Reading is a crucial skill to be gained during these years. Leon Eisenberg (1975) states the relationship between self-esteem and the development of the capacity to read competently: "The 'inevitability' of psychiatric disturbance in the poor reader," he writes, "stems from the pivotal role of success at school for the self-concept of the child. Schooling is, in the first instance, reading. Not only is this the major demand on the child in the early grades, but it is the fulcrum for the rest of his learning. Reading has a multiplier effect, for good or bad, in every academic content area. In the school environment, reading is being. An inadequate reader is, in his mind's eye, an inadequate (that is, bad or stupid) person—and, all too often, in the eyes of his teachers, his parents and his peers as well" (1975, p. 220). The impact of peer review on self-esteem begins during the grade school years, and continues through adolescence and adult life in a variety of forms.

The striving for ideals, and the creation of ideal representations through which the self-as-subject seeks to measure the self-as-object, begins at this time as well, continuing into adolescence. The idealized superheroes and superheroines of the latency years are the precursors of the visionary dreams of personal achievement or romanticized loves which characterize early adolescence. At the same time, the exalted expectations of early adolescents for their parents and other adults, and, one hastens to add, for themselves, must become modified to serve more realistic goals, values, and ideals. The personality structure which crystallizes out of these developmental changes is the ego ideal, which plays a central role in self-esteem regulation throughout life. The ego ideal can trace its roots to the earliest disappointments of childhood. It has been postulated (Freud, 1916; Murray, 1964; Rochlin, 1965) that the ego ideal provides a second chance, a chance to redeem the hurts, losses, and frustrations which inevitably shatter the well-being of childhood wish fulfillment. By contributing something worthwhile to others and pursuing meaningful activities that meet a set of ideal expectations, human beings can recreate the sense of well-being of their childhoods. But in certain adults, usually individuals who have suffered from injuries to self-regard in early childhood, ego ideal expectations retain an unrealistically visionary character. Jacobson (1964) has called these "wishful self images" (p. 203). If such expectations are too unrealistically exalted (grandiose), then their disappointment can be shattering, resulting, in extreme cases, in the turning away from reality or psychosis. More usual are the varieties of mild to severe depressive reactions which accompany the disappointment of ego ideal expectations.

It is in adolescence that the ego ideal becomes consolidated as a structure, a set of standards by whose terms the self is measured (Ritvo, 1971). The issue of personal, especially sexual, attractiveness becomes a sensitive arena for both sexes. Many adolescents find it difficult to handle the awkwardness they perceive in their rapidly changing bodies and selves and shy away from intimate attachments. The pressure in contemporary Western society for early sexual intimacy, for which many adolescents are not emotionally prepared, appears to be heightening the ordinarily difficult problem adolescents face in developing confidence in their self-worth.

The achievement of a manageable degree of separateness from parents is another central task of adolescence. Parents whose own self-esteem, or sense of personal completeness, depends heavily on the presence of the child in the home, may resist and even attack their teenage children verbally or physically as the child tries, often provocatively, to establish greater emotional distance. These parents compound the guilt and self-doubt the adolescent experiences as he tries to achieve greater autonomy and separateness.

Thus, each period of development introduces new arenas or tasks and the accompanying modifications of psychic structures which regulate or determine the level of self-esteem. At each stage the adequacy with which its specific tasks have been negotiated is interpreted by the ego. It needs to be stressed, however, that although new challenges come with each developmental stage, the level of self-esteem continues to be affected by the ongoing handling of demands upon the child or adolescent which carry over from earlier developmental periods. Academic performance, for example, and the achievement of successful individual and group peer relationships continue from the grade school years into high school as important challenges for self-esteem. The loving support of parents remains of critical importance in adolescence, though it must now be conveyed in subtler form, often to a teenager who seems not to "need" anything, rejects parental overtures, and offers little "space" for closeness to occur. As Rochlin (1965) writes, "The condition of self-esteem is not permanently achieved; it requires constant attention for its maintenance" (p. 133). Self-esteem is continually being lost and restored in adolescence and adult life. Its reworking and revision, together with the maturation of the agencies responsible for its regulation, are the central tasks of human life. Of one thing we are certain: "A forfeited, damaged, or decreased self-esteem is an unacceptable condition" (Rochlin, 1965, p. 132).

It must finally be noted that the successful negotiation of the developmental challenges of later stages may make up for or repair the injuries to self-esteem suffered in earlier years. But there is a question as to the degree that this repair can be complete, especially if the early hurt has been severe or prolonged. A person who has, for example, experienced prolonged separations from parents, or rejection by them in the first years of life, may react in later years with marked sadness and self-doubt in the face of minor rebuffs or disappointments, even when there is ample evidence of real success and external approval. While the successful handling of adult tasks, such as parenthood or professional responsibilities, can partially repair childhood injuries to self-esteem, many of these same challenges of adult life may reopen old childhood hurts to self-worth. It is this phenomenon which most frequently brings individuals to psychotherapy. Anna Freud

(1972) has linked what we might now call a core sense of self-worth, or a certain stability of self-confidence, to Freud's concept of primary narcissism and Erik Erikson's notion of basic trust: "The experience of being well loved and highly estimated in early childhood is responsible for 'primary narcissism,' " she writes, "i.e., the child's libidinal investment in himself, [which] creates for all later life an unshakable feeling of security and confidence. We meet the same attributes in the more modern literature under the terms of self-regard, self-esteem or, in relation to the environment, as 'basic trust' " (p. 23–24).

SELF-ESTEEM AND BELONGING

Ana-Maria Rizzuto (1978) tells of a three-year-old child who was abused and neglected by his mother and who turned to her plaintively and asked, "Mommie, am I yours?" A 56-year-old woman returning from the United States to her hometown in Eastern Europe, after being away for 34 years, was asked by another woman while shopping in the town marketplace, "Whose are you?" Throughout our lifetimes the experience of belonging to someone, or of being part of something larger than ourselves, remains an important factor in the maintenance of our self-esteem, a factor apart from how successfully we may have negotiated the developmental stages of childhood. The feeling that one belongs—to a family, a team, a college, a company, a community, or a people—completes an essential part of the self and sustains our sense of worth.

When emotional pain and conflict in the family setting become unendurable in childhood, avoidance defenses may develop which lead the child to distance himself from others in the family unit. Self-esteem may then suffer in adult life as a result of continuing unexplained feelings of social isolation accompanied by a sense of "not belonging." This is illustrated by the analysis of a 36-year-old Jewish professional man from a European country whose baby brother had died unexpectedly when he was five. His parents were plunged at the time into a profound state of grief. The man recalled that he had experienced an intense identification with his parents' grief. He felt great pity for them and responsibility for their sadness. "I was a part of the guilt and responsibility in the family. It was all one," he said. Through his later accomplishments he sought to redeem not only his own oedipal guilt, which was tied to ambivalent feelings he had harbored toward the baby brother, but his parents' unhappiness as well. "Am I not enough?" he asked. The family atmosphere remained, however, one of "doom and gloom," and he tried to escape its oppressive quality by means of an intense identification with his peer group and, later, an idealized connection with the dominant non-Jewish national group of his country. As he became aware of his own family's Jewish identity, and the predominance in the Jewish religion of themes of loss and suffering, he came to associate these elements with the family's pain and his conflict surrounding his brother's death. Thus, in later years, his self-regard suffered not only as a result of unresolved conflicts in his individual development but also because of a continuing experience of alienation from his family and from other groups in his adopted country, the United States.

The family serves as a prototype for ethnic and other group identifications. Impaired participation as a member of the family group can be associated with alienation from subsequent small and large groups in society with serious consequences for the maintenance of self-esteem. The degree to which adults use membership in a particular society or culture to maintain self-esteem is little recognized. This fact is illustrated by the case of a 44-year-old academician from a Middle Eastern country who found himself unexpectedly afflicted with depressive feelings and searching doubts about the value of his work and himself. He was happily married and devoted to his children. He had been highly productive in his work, his writings widely recognized both by colleagues and by others in his field. For the first time, however, he began to fear failure. A careful history did not reveal any immediate factors in his personal life to account for his depression. What his history did disclose, however, was that he was deeply troubled by the civil strife that was tearing apart the fabric of his country. A man of complex ethnic and religious background, his personal integrity and self-worth had been deeply identified with the idea of a harmonious nation, a society in which diverse ethnic and religious groups lived together civilly; and he continued to work toward this ideal. What he had failed to appreciate was the degree to which his fantasies of such a society, and his participation in them, played a central role in maintaining his self-esteem. As violence and loss of civility shattered his image of his society, internal psychological changes occurred. The destruction of his idealized image of his society profoundly altered his view of himself.

Morris Rosenberg (1979) has examined the complex relationship between self-esteem in childhood and adolescence and identification with religious, racial, socioeconomic, and ethnic groups (see also J.W. Klein, 1980). He demonstrates that minority status alone bears a limited relationship to self-regard, for the child tends to see himself as others in his immediate environment see him. According to Rosenberg, it is the individual's relationship of consonance or dissonance with this immediate environment that is more important for self-esteem maintenance than the group's relationship to the larger society. "The individual in the consonant environment," he writes, "is likely to have a feeling of belongingness, the one in the dissonant context to feel strange, 'out of it,' somehow 'wrong' " (p. 125).

The findings of Offer, Ostrov, and Howard (1981) suggest that social and historical change may have a broad impact on self-esteem. Administering to several hundred adolescent boys and girls over an 18-year period a questionnaire designed to elicit their views of themselves (the Offer Self-Image Questionnaire), these authors concluded that "with respect to almost every self-image dimension, teenagers in the 1970's [felt] worse about themselves than did teenagers in the 1960's" (p. 102). The authors speculate as to the social, economic, and political factors which might account for this change, such as the increased responsibilities placed on adolescents in the 1970's, rising unemployment and inflation, the effect of the Vietnam War in the late 1960's and early 1970's, and the disillusioning impact of the Watergate events.

FURTHER THEORETICAL CONSIDERATIONS

Self-Esteem and Narcissism

The concept of narcissism grew out of Freud's (1914) evolving libido theory. Narcissism, at least as Freud originally used the term, represented the investment of libido in the subject's own ego, "ego-libido," which he contrasted with "object-libido," or the investment of libido in another person. Heinz Hartmann (1956), interpreting Freud's usage, refined his definition of narcissism, arguing that the term was used rather loosely by Freud to represent both the investment of libido in the ego *and* in one's own person or self. Noting that *ego* refers to a system of functions, and that the ego also has "tendencies" which "are very frequently object directed," narcissism, Hartmann observed, was better reserved for the "libidinal cathexis" of one's own person or self (pp. 287–288).

The concept of self-esteem has a meaning both broader than that of narcissism, and at the same time narrower and more precise. It is broader in that there are aspects of narcissism which are not immediately related to self-esteem, narrower in referring specifically to the *value* of the self-image among the possible investments of emotion or interest in the self. There are also important dimensions of self-esteem as an ego or affective state which extend beyond the notion of narcissism (Pulver, 1970). (In Chapter 6, Judith Huizenga discusses further some of the relationships between narcissism and self-esteem.)

In the more recent psychoanalytic literature the term *narcissism* has been used more broadly than in Freud's original meaning, appearing to overlap with the definition of self-esteem. In Stolorow's (1975) definition "mental activity is narcissistic to the degree that its function is to maintain the structural cohesiveness, temporal stability and positive affective colouring of the self-representation" (p. 179); while Dare and Holder (1981), in a recent paper, define narcissism as "the sum of positively-coloured feeling states attached to the self-representation" (p. 335). But even with these extensions of narcissism, it remains clear that self-esteem refers to a complex ego state with profound affective, self-regulatory, and self-evaluative dimensions that go beyond the "positive affective colouring of the self-representation" of narcissism. At the same time there are aspects of narcissism, such as the pure love-of-self in the original sense of the Greek myth, and the elements associated with magical thinking and omnipotence, which are only indirectly connected with self-esteem (Spruiell, 1975, 1981).

Self-Esteem and Psychic Structure

There are certain phenomena, on the one hand, so obviously central or pervasive in human mental activity that they are part of our everyday thinking, while at the same time so complex or multidimensional that no theory deriving from a single discipline seems adequate to embrace them. Responsibility, choice, and the need for privacy are such phenomena. Self-esteem appears to be another. Recent psychoanalytic attempts to examine the psychological structures relating to self-esteem reflect a growing awareness of this complexity.

Freud's (1914) ideas about self-esteem or "self-regard" were closely tied to his concept of narcissistic libido. "Self-regard," he wrote, "has a specially intimate dependence on narcissistic libido." Freud considered it to be "an expression of the size of the ego" but regarded as "irrelevant" the "various elements . . . which go to determine that size." "Everything a person achieves," he wrote, "every remnant of the primitive feeling of omnipotence which experience has confirmed, helps to increase his self-regard" (p. 98).

With the development of his structural theory, and the tripartite division of the mental apparatus, Freud could add to his notion of self-esteem as "an expression of the size of the ego" a self-evaluative function which he attributed to the superego or the ego ideal. (Although the relationship between these two agencies was never consistently clarified in Freud's writings, he does state in 1933 that the superego is "the vehicle of the ego ideal by which the ego measures itself, which it emulates, and whose demand for ever greater perfection it strives to fulfill" (pp. 64–65). Discussions of self-esteem in subsequent psychoanalytic writings, most notably those of Jacobson, came to include this self-measuring or self-evaluating function as applied to the self-as-perceived or "self-representation." In her landmark book *The Self and the Object World* Jacobson (1964) writes, "Self esteem is the ideational, especially the emotional, expression of self evaluation and of the corresponding more or less neutralized libidinal and aggressive cathexis of the self representations" (p. 130).

It is through the agency of the ego ideal that the ego measures "its *self*" (Alexander and Friedman, 1980, p. 380). Self-esteem becomes in this view a subjective product of the relationship between ego and ego ideal. But the regulation of self-esteem is a more fluid, more dynamic process than these structural considerations seem to imply. Janice de Saussure (1971), for example, observes that "self esteem, as both a value judgement and an affective state, fluctuates continuously, though not necessarily markedly, expressing the changing relationship between representations of an ideal and a current self. Regulation of this esteem is an ever-present active process" (p. 88). The level of experienced self-regard may fluctuate to some degree from day to day, from hour to hour, or even minute to minute. Neither in ourselves nor in others can we keep up with the complex interplay of outwardly and inwardly focused conscious perceptions and apperceptions reflected in the shifting moods we call self-esteem. Unless we could know in a given instant the web of associated linkages with unconscious images and memories—linkages that move like tectonic forces within and below the earth's surface—we have no way to grasp fully what accounts for the level of self-esteem at any given instant. Beyond this, the state of the self-regard of most children and adults under ordinary circumstances may not be definitively "one way or another." We may feel good about certain human relationships and disappointed about some matter at our place of work. For most healthy individuals a generally positive level of self-regard is maintained more or less impervious to minor disappointments—the barometer does not dip down or soar widely or for long. (In Chapter 8 David VanBuskirk discusses further the relationship between psychic structure formation and the regulation of self-esteem.)

Self-Esteem and Affects

If contemporary psychoanalytic writings generally agree that self-esteem is a complex ego state which fluctuates according to the shifting evaluation and perception of self-representations or self-images by the ego ideal, or by whatever component of the personality organization is considered responsible for the evaluation function, observers also note—and a moment of reflection will show it to be so—that self-esteem is also an affective state (de Saussure, 1971; Stolorow, 1975). Indeed, one cannot speak of fluctuations in self-regard, of high or low self-esteem, without bringing to mind the characteristic emotional experiences which accompany these shifts. Joy, confidence, pleasure, excitement, enthusiasm, and interest are some of the affects associated with high or positive self-esteem, while pain, anguish, doubt, sadness, emptiness, and inertia accompany low self-regard. (In Chapter 1 Virginia Demos shows how these affective states develop from observable beginnings in the mother-infant relationship.) The ability to cope with the range of one's own emotions is essential to mental health throughout childhood, adolescence, and adult life. The achievement of this capacity to master affective states (as Steven Ablon shows in Chapter 2) is accompanied by a particularly strong enhancement of self-esteem and by increased stability of self-esteem regulation.

Fantasies about oneself (Grossman, 1983), or self-images, are powerfully invested with emotion, and singly or in combination, influence the level of self-regard. Sydney Pulver (1970), for example, notes that "when the various self-images become organized into a more cohesive affective picture of the self, we speak of *self-esteem*, with 'high self-esteem' implying a predominance of pleasurable affects and 'low self-esteem' of unpleasurable ones. All of these ego states of affect-self-representation linkages may be either conscious, preconscious, or unconscious, have complex origins, and many defensive and adaptive functions" (p. 334).

Small children are wonderfully communicative when they feel good about themselves. Their positive self-feeling may be infectious. They are, on the other hand, very sensitive to criticism, failures, or disappointments which lower self-regard. They resist the probings of adults that tend to bring them in touch with areas of self-doubt; they may turn away from inquiries which suggest that they have failed to comply with some expectation of the questioner. Shame and guilt are complex emotions associated with diminished self-esteem. Shame seems to develop earlier than guilt and is closer to early narcissism. It grows out of the child's early internalizations of adult expectations of his behavior. It is the emotion which accompanies the acute realization, with or without an external reminder, that these expectations have not been met. Shame is usually felt in the presence of another person, but can linger on in solitude. Shame is more intimately linked than guilt with actual conduct or action. Guilt, on the other hand, is a highly complex emotion which grows out of the internalization of established norms of behavior. Guilt may result from harboring unacceptable conscious and unconscious wishes and fantasies without accompanying "guilty" behavior. The harboring of such hostile or aggressive wishes toward adults to whom the child is attached is especially damaging to self-regard; the guilt is associated with superego prohibitions against such impulses. Guilt is accentuated by external reminders, but is less dependent than shame upon outside confrontations. Both shame and guilt, needless to say, can be devastating to positive self-esteem.

Well-Being and Self-Esteem

Human well-being and the sense of having worth or value are intimately connected. The psychological structures that regulate self-esteem may emerge out of the early positive affective expressions and states of well-being of infancy, but the developmental processes through which this occurs are as yet poorly understood. A moment's consideration will demonstrate that we may speak of an infant as radiating well-being, good feeling, joy, or other positive affective states before it makes sense to speak of a child's possessing positive self-esteem.

The raw materials out of which self-esteem emerge are, however, clearly present in earliest infancy. A baby, we are discovering, is a highly competent and discriminating organism, well equipped to capture his parents' attention and, under most circumstances, to bring about the fulfillment of his needs through a broad range of emotionally toned vocalizations and other communications. We might hypothesize that the capacity to attract the parent, to use relational skills to bring about the fulfillment of needs and wants, is the earliest test of childhood competence and self-worth. The charm of babies for mothers and fathers seems to be an endowment on which they may then build in order to win and hold their parents.

Psychoanalytic writers generally assume that positive self-images emerge out of the mutual good feelings of the mother-infant relationship. Dare and Holder (1981), for example, write that when the mother "smiles and cuddles the infant closely, the emergent self-image will be associated with feelings of warmth, safety

and being cherished" (p. 327). Fenichel (1945) many years ago
made a similar point when he wrote, "The first supply of satisfaction from the external world, the supply of nourishment, is
simultaneously the first regulator of self-esteem" (p. 40). But as
Sander (1979) states "the occurrence and extent of joy and delight
in interpersonal exchange within different dyadic systems has not
been studied longitudinally to discover its longitudinal course or
its essential role in integration" (p. 17)—or, one might certainly
add, to establish its role in the development and maintenance of
self-esteem.

Bodily Feeling, Self-Image, and Self-Esteem

The human newborn has an inherent vitality which is a potential
reservoir of good feeling and, ultimately, of self-esteem. As Freud,
Schilder (1928), Federn (1952), and others stressed many years
ago, the first ego is a body ego and, in Paul Federn's (1952) terminology, early infantile experience may be regarded as "bodily
ego feeling." The rich and complex interactions between the infant and his mother and other providers in the course of feeding,
bathing, playing, fondling, mutual looking, and other caretaking
and caring-for experiences affect profoundly the quality of feeling
associated with the body and its parts. These experiences link up
in incompletely understood ways with inborn capacities for erotic
and other special sensations associated with particular body zones
such as the mouth, other parts of the gastrointestinal tract, and
the internal and external genitalia. These linkages determine the
quality of the images and fantasies associated with various parts
of the body. The infant and small child's intense desire to explore
his own and other people's bodies and their parts augments continuously the body-self–images which emerge. The attitudes of
the adults and other children who are the object of these explorations—loving and accepting, for example, or critical and shaming—will inevitably be incorporated into the child's emerging
sense of self-regard and will affect profoundly the child's self-
esteem.

One need spend only a few minutes with a two- or three-year-
old child to see him make value judgments—*good* and *bad* being
the stock words—about parts or products of his body—the good

(or "yucky") feces, in or out of the toilet, or the bad hand which knocked over a vase. We know that the representation of the self-as-a-whole is much more than the sum of the images of the body parts. As Kohut and others have described, a more fully integrated self-view, a mind-body-self, emerges in the third year of life, similar to what Erikson has called *ego identity*, and possessing a subjective quality of cohesiveness, permanence, and endurance. Nevertheless, the assessment of self—self-regard in its essential aspect—remains throughout life intimately tied to the state of the body and its parts. We can demonstrate this most readily in dreams in which the self is often represented thinly disguised—or with no disguise at all—as a body organ or vessel, with a powerful accompanying affective valence. In depression, or other clinical conditions in which self-esteem is markedly impaired, bodily organs and other parts are perceived as damaged, diseased, or defective, and the self-as-a-whole is negatively identified with the physical self and experienced as repellant or ugly.

Children who have prolonged physical disturbances, suffer from congenital defects (see, especially, Niederland, 1965, and Galenson and Roiphe, 1971), or have other early damage to bodily parts may suffer from special problems of self-esteem (as Alexandra Harrison and Myron Belfer discuss in Chapters 3 and 4). According to Dare and Holder (1981), "babies suffering from severe congenital lesions requiring repeated surgery, infants with neonatal eczema, infants with congenital gastrointestinal complaints (such as fistulae, megacolon, mild pyloric stenosis), or those with feeding disturbances or colic which are not of psychological origin, are examples where the initial experience of the self includes painful affects which give a negative coloring to the earliest self-feelings" (p. 326).

Eleanor Galenson and Herman Roiphe (1971) describe the complex interrelation of the development of self-esteem and sexual identity in a girl born with a congenital defect in the anogenital area: "In this already vulnerable child," they write, "the discovery of the sexual anatomical difference and sexual sensations brought with it overwhelming disappointment and anger at the mother, with loss of self-esteem and the marked inhibited and depressive reaction which continues to characterize her" (p. 214).

Jackson Bate's (1977; see also Mack, 1978) biography of Samuel

Johnson richly documents the lifelong impact of early childhood illnesses and operations, which resulted in defects of sight and hearing, on Johnson's self-esteem. Johnson's struggles to surmount and transform what he called "the paralyzing grip of self-expectation" (p. 26) are reflected in many of his writings. Because and in spite of these conflicts he became one of our greatest writers on the subject of self-esteem and its vicissitudes, and on narcissism more generally.

If the early self is a bodily self it is also a sexual self and remains so throughout life. The importance of eroticism and of perceptions of the genitals in boys and girls for the evolving self-image is well documented in the psychoanalytic literature (Freud, 1905; Kestenberg, 1968; Galenson and Roiphe, 1977; Fast, 1979; Rochlin, 1980). Sexual curiosity and sensation, the discrimination of anatomical differences, the evolution of sexual identity, the perception of genital injury or threat, and the identification of the child with parental sexual models and conflicts all contribute to evolving self-representations and to self-esteem.[2]

Psychoanalysts and other therapists are familiar with child and adult patients for whom the self-image is almost entirely represented by the genitals, especially the phallus in males. In these cases, doubts about self-worth in the sexual area appear to be profound. Reconstruction of the childhood sexual experience reveals that more than usual threat to or discrediting of the child's early genital strivings has occurred. Adolescent and adult failures and injuries in intimate relationships revive childhood sexual hurts and disappointments with a profound sense of injury to self-esteem. The implications of early childhood sexual development for the evolution and regulation of self-esteem await further research.

[2] For further discussion the reader is encouraged to refer to the rich literature on these subjects (Freud, 1933; Deutsch, 1945; Kestenberg, 1968; Stoller, 1968, 1975; Galenson and Roiphe, 1977; Fast, 1979, Rochlin, 1980). Galenson and Roiphe (1977) have shown that there is in boys and girls an "early genital phase" during the second year in which genital sensations are prominent and anatomical differences are discovered with the arousal of intense castration fears and potential threat to later ego development: " . . . the genital zone emerges as a distinct and differentiated source of endogenous pleasure somewhere between sixteen and nineteen months of age, exerting a new and crucial influence upon the sense of sexual identity, object relations, basic mood, and many aspects of ego functioning, such as the elaboration of fantasy and graphic representation in girls and the increased use of the motor apparatus in boys—the latter probably in the service of denial" (p. 54).

Self-Esteem and Mastery

The complexity of self-esteem development derives from its initial dependence upon two separate but interrelated domains—the phenomenon of mastery and the arena of human relationships. (Nancy Cotton discusses these developmental strands more fully in Chapter 5.) Mastery might be defined as the subjective satisfaction which accompanies the achievement of a task that the person considers worth doing.

Mastery takes place in relation to two distinct forms of activity. One of these might be described as delight in the exercise of innate equipment, beginning with the discovery by the infant of the parts of his body and of objects in the outside world and continuing with the enjoyments and frustrations which accompany the application of expanding sensorimotor skills. Kagan (1981) describes what he calls "mastery smiles" that develop during the second year and reflect the child's pleasure in accomplishing planned tasks. He distinguishes between smiles observable in the first year, which are associated with satisfaction in simple motor activity, and "the smile that follows prolonged investment of goal-directed effort which serves a previously generated plan" (p. 57), reserving the term mastery smile for the second sort. The other type of task, as described previously, concerns the ability of the small child to use his communicative equipment to secure the attention, caring, protection, approval, and love of the parent and later of other human beings (Basch, 1976). In this latter case, the infant's pleasure in his autonomous achievements is strongly reinforced by the delight of the parent in those accomplishments. These two initial arenas of mastery—the one more or less autonomous, the other dependent on the response of an object—probably account for the double quality which self-esteem retains throughout life: autonomous, self-regulated, and dependent on the individual's own initiatives on the one hand, while profoundly affected by the approval of a loving or supportive object on the other. Brazelton (1979) describes these two qualities in the baby when he writes that "an inner sense of competence and feeling from a gratifying reciprocity with his environment are necessary to the infant's optimal development" (p. 43).

Self-worth and self-confidence build up gradually out of sequences of "little victories" (a term used by Frank Wills in Chapter

11 with reference to the self-esteem of retarded children, though the concept is not restricted to the development of mentally impaired children). As the child realizes his or her particular skills and talents, continuously experiencing just what expressions of self are valued by the parents and others, the groundwork for later self-expectations is laid. A gradual structuring of values and expectations for the self is internalized in childhood and adolescence and becomes the specific measure by which achievements are gauged. These expectations evolve dynamically, however, in relation to real achievement. Actual accomplishments become part of the data by which the self revises its expectations of what *ought* to be accomplished. This fact may account for the frequently observed phenomenon of individuals with a history of considerable achievement who seem forever, and even increasingly, dissatisfied with themselves. Their achievement arouses, especially among individuals with earlier narcissistic conflicts, demands for even greater performance in order to maintain high self-esteem. Conversely, the experience of repeated disappointment often leads to a downward revision of the level of expectations in order to avoid the pain associated with failure.

William James (1890) grasped long ago the necessity of establishing specific areas of expectation in the maintenance of self-regard, or what he called "self-feeling."

> So the seeker of his truest, strongest, deepest self must review the list carefully, and pick out the one on which to stake his salvation. All other selves thereupon become unreal, but the fortunes of this self are real. Its failures are real failures, its triumphs real triumphs, carrying shame and gladness with them. . . .
>
> I, who for the time have staked my all on being a psychologist, am mortified if others know much more psychology than I. But I am contented to wallow in the grossest ignorance of Greek. My deficiencies there give me no sense of personal humiliation at all. Had I "pretensions" to be a linguist, it would have been just the reverse. . . .
>
> Yonder puny fellow, however, whom everyone can best, suffers no chagrin about it, for he has long ago abandoned the attempt to "carry that line," as the merchants say, of self at all. With no attempt there can be no failure; with no failure no

humiliation. So our self-feeling in this world depends entirely on what we back ourselves to be and do [pp. 295–296].[3]

There are two possible strategies for maintaining positive self-esteem, which might be called the all-the-eggs-in-one-basket approach and the diversification option. The first has the advantage of offering the individual an opportunity to achieve a high degree of competence in the single area chosen, with the disadvantage of possibly catastrophic disappointment should failure occur. On the other hand, to rely on versatility requires a good deal of innate talent, and while providing protection from total failure, runs the risk of limiting satisfaction to that of superficial accomplishment and commitment. It is probably worthwhile for the parent to encourage in each child some degree of versatility, a wide range of potential arenas in which self-esteem may be achieved, while at the same time supporting the development of certain capacities more intensely or in depth. *"If a stable and broad enough base is provided,"* Sander writes, "the infant explores the world, at increasing distances, with investments of attention, and with delight in mastery" (p. 17; my italics). The vital importance for self-esteem of building upon this "broad enough base" is stressed by Kohut (1978): "Mobility and the reliance on several different sources of self-esteem," he writes, "are in the long run safer ways of psychological survival than the maintenance of a rigid narcissistic equilibrium through the employment of a single set of restricted functions" (p. 826).

Self-Esteem and Object Relations

The maintenance of the conviction that one has worth continues to depend heavily throughout life on ongoing human relation-

---

[3] The sociologist Morris Rosenberg (1979), writing 90 years later, describes virtually the same relationship as did James between self-expectations or values and self-esteem: "The differential importance of self-concept components is thus critically significant for self-esteem. Some dispositions or social identity elements rank high in our hierarchy of values—stand at the center of our feelings of worth—whereas others are relegated to the periphery. One person stakes himself on his intelligence but cares little about his savoir faire; for another the reverse is the case. One takes great pride in his social class position, a second in his ethnic background, a third in his race, a fourth in his religious affiliation. A professor may consider himself both intelligent and well-mannered—both dispositions, in other words, are elements of his self-concept—but he may stake himself far more heavily on the former characteristic than on the latter" (pp. 18–19).

ships, especially on the support and love of valued persons and groups, whose approval is sought. In Rochlin's (1965) words, "self-esteem, whether expressed in fact or fantasy or legend, is rarely supported or elevated in the absence of objects" (p. 8).

Kohut (1971, 1978) has developed a further distinction between "true objects," which remain separate from the developing self, and are related to in their own right, and "selfobjects," which "ultimately develop into stable, permanent psychic structures within the ego and superego, under conditions of optimal frustration in infancy and childhood" (Ornstein, 1978, p. 62). Self-objects, in Kohut's view, are essential for the development in early childhood of psychic structure and a cohesive self. Interruption of the structural transformations which depend upon the internalizaton of selfobjects will lead to an "absence of the ability to pursue ambitions, goals, and purposes; of pleasure in various functions and activities; and of reliable self-esteem" (Ornstein, 1978, p. 62)).

Rosenberg (1979) notes in *Conceiving the Self* that the motive to achieve self-worth is "one of the most powerful in the human repertoire." He also notes, however, that "there is no agreement on why this should be so." He suggests that "positive self-attitudes" are "associated with certain pleasurable and rewarding experiences of childhood" (p. 56). But the answer lies much deeper than this. Self-esteem is intimately linked not only with pleasure but with confidence in one's survival. The child psychoanalyst Gregory Rochlin, whose work has been of pioneering importance in this area, documents the intense dread which small children experience when threatened with loss and abandonment, and the relationship of this fear to self-esteem. The nameless anxiety associated with being without an object becomes inseparably associated with "lost self esteem . . . as some maturity of the ego takes place" (p. 15). "With emotional development," Rochlin writes, "the fantasies of being left or abandoned become equated with being worthless" (p. 17). "The belief that there will be one who cares," he observes, "provides a measure of relief from the fears of being abandoned as worthless" (p. 7). Stolorow (1975) also discusses how "object relationships can serve (with varying degrees of success)" to enhance self-worth and how "the loss of object ties can be catastrophic for the self esteem" (p. 183).

What makes this so? How is it that self-worth is so intimately tied to the survival of the self? One answer is suggested in the case of an adult undergoing psychoanalytic treatment. The patient, a 36-year-old man (previously described in this volume), was separated from his wife. Profound doubts about self-worth and the maintenance of self-esteem were central issues in his treatment, although he generally functioned at a high level. He had formed a relationship with another woman, herself divorced, with whom he would from time to time have arguments in which she threatened to leave him. These involved his plans to travel to another city to visit his wife and small child. Following one such argument he had a nightmare: He is with a woman to whom he feels attached. She tells him she is going to go back to her husband. He is overcome by a feeling of utter terror and wakes up and tries to shake it off. He tells himself it is only a nightmare, but the terror of abandonment persists. Associating to the dream, he noted that he had experienced before fears of being destroyed, cut up, attacked, but nothing like the nightmare in which he felt "a terror from within," as if "my self was broken into a thousand pieces, utterly shattered." He had learned that his wife, to whom he did not intend to return, had found another man, not only closing the door on the marriage but possibly endangering visits with his daughter. Further associations led him to recall the birth, when he was three and a half, of a baby brother, which he experienced at the time as the "loss" of his mother. He felt then a sense of intense helplessness, one that was recreated in the dream. Looking further, he saw that this feeling related to his mother and that he had felt no power to hold on to her. At age five, when his baby brother, then one and a half, died, he had felt the same helplessness, compounded now by sadness and guilt. The terror in the dream was linked with feelings of worthlessness. Not only would he be left, but he was not worth being found. The danger was of being too worthless to matter to a caretaking woman. No one would care for him and no one else would take the place of the woman who had abandoned him. He had previously protected his self-regard by means of pride and by not committing himself to a woman. Yet when threatened with being left by his partner, conflicts from early childhood relating to self-worth and the threat of abandonment were revived in the context of the therapeutic relationship. The nightmare linked together in highly condensed form the threat of loss in the present, the terror of abandonment in early childhood, the danger of worthlessness, and the compounding problem of guilt and responsibility. It also demonstrated the disorganizing terror that is experienced when feelings of worthlessness become linked with the threat of abandonment.

Having value or worth in the eyes of a caretaking object is the only assurance the small child has that he will not be abandoned. It is this linkage at the deepest psychological level with abandonment and survival that makes self-esteem a "dominant motive" in the human "motivational system" (Rosenberg, 1979, p. 54). Conversely, to be left or abandoned conveys to the child that he is powerless to hold the object. It is a statement of his failure that he is not worth being or staying with. The experience of abandonment, especially if repeated, is internalized in the form of diminished self-worth, as intense conflict in the realm of self-esteem. Clinicians repeatedly observe that children and adults who have an unusual degree of anxiety in relation to separation from love objects have considerable doubt about self-worth. The separation represents not only the loss of a protective, need-satisfying object, but also the confirmation of diminished self-worth and the pain and danger associated with it.

Aggression and hostility toward the object are a continuously threatening complication for the child's precarious self-esteem. Each period of development contains its characteristic hurts and disappointments, to which the small child responds with hatred and rage toward the object. Hostility occurs when a caretaking person fails to feed, comfort, be with, protect, admire, love, or value the child as he expects to be fed, comforted, valued, etc., and is itself threatening to self-worth. Small children tolerate poorly their hostility toward an object to whom they are attached through love; and in such situations readily redirect aggression against themselves in accidents, hypochondriacal preoccupations, and self-destructive behavior. Fear of retaliation adds additional anxiety. Guilt, emanating from the superego, is closely associated with aggression and serves to control it. But guilt also diminishes self-esteem, as Rochlin (1965, 1973) has stressed. At all costs "the object must be spared" (1965, p. 27), even though the self is placed in danger from its own attacks and from the self-reproach and penance demanded by the superego. Thus aggression is multiply threatening to self-esteem. It risks retaliation by the object and thus intensifies the threat of abandonment; it endangers, at least in fantasy, the object itself; it results in the child's own hostility being redirected against the self in order to spare the object; and, as personality structures crystallize in the oedipal period, threatens attacks by the superego.

These observations imply that it is a central task of childhood to achieve, to whatever degree possible, a stable and enduring sense of self-worth, or, stated differently, to develop the assurance of protection against severe lowering of self-esteem. This is accomplished in the following ways: (1) through the development of real skills and mastery in a broad range of activities; (2) through the establishment of the capacity for stable and enduring human relationships, which in turn depends on; (3) the internalization of positive or loving self- and object representations; (4) through the evolution of flexible superego and ego ideal structures; (5) by achievement of the capacity to modify, soften, or otherwise transform hostile impulses toward valued objects; and (6) through affiliation with meaningful cultural subgroups to which the child knows that he belongs.

SELF-ESTEEM AND PSYCHOPATHOLOGY

It has often been the case in psychology, as in medicine, that our knowledge and theories of the normal and everyday derive from experience with the extremes, with psychopathology. So it is with self-esteem. The recognition by Freud (1915) that "a lowering of the self-regarding feelings" was a central feature of clinical depression, or melancholia, distinguished this condition from ordinary mourning and opened the way to the study of the structure of self-esteem and self-esteem regulation. The condition we call *depression* occurs when, for whatever reason, there is a marked subjective lowering of the sense of self-worth, accompanied by a sense of hopelessness, i.e., a prediction that the future will not be different. Depression results when a loved or needed object (especially a person or group experienced as essential for the maintenance of self-esteem) is experienced as withdrawing love or is *lost* in fantasy or reality. The intertwining cycles of loss, hostility, fear of abandonment, guilt, diminished self-esteem, reduction of psychic energy, and self-destruction that characterize depression are familiar to those who work with adults. In children many of the same psychodynamic forces operate but may be expressed differently because of the immaturity of the psychic apparatus.

Most important among the immaturities of psychic organization and functioning is the poor tolerance by children of the painful affects associated with narcissistic injury and lowered self-regard. Thus the picture of depression in childhood may be different from that of adults, characterized by hypochondriacal symptoms, accident proneness, overactivity, withdrawal from friendships (and activities), school failure, drug taking in adolescence, suicide threats or attempts, or other behaviors which are propelled by the need to avoid or escape from the emotional pain associated with diminished self-esteem. (Carl Malmquist in Chapter 9 discusses further the relationship between self-esteem and depression in childhood.)

As William Meissner (1978) has shown, conflicts relating to self-esteem play an important part in the psychology of paranoia. Mechanisms of projection and externalization may be used to spare the individual unbearable emotional pain associated with a devalued self-image and low self-worth. Through blaming others the self is relieved, at least temporarily, of the burden of self-reproach. Someone else is responsible, someone else is at fault. Paranoid projections also serve to protect the child or adult from the danger of hostility toward objects who have withdrawn their love or threatened abandonment, and from the injuries to self-esteem associated with a host of hurtful childhood experiences. In order to redeem the loss and protect the object, the child internalizes aspects of the parental figures. But now new dangers arise as "the previously loved object is then perceived as directing criticism, reproach, and hate against the self" (Meissner, 1978, p. 141). Through projection and externalization the object can be spared and the subject relieved of the pain associated with severely diminished self-esteem.

The need for revenge, for the righting of earlier wrongs to self-esteem, bears a close relationship to paranoia. Through the acting out of hostility—felt to be justified on personal, historical grounds—slights, insults, abandonment, and other hurts to self-esteem seem to be redeemed, however much new conflicts and dangers to the self may be created.

Increasingly, conflicts related to self-regard and self-esteem regulation are coming to be seen as central elements, if not the etiological basis, of a number of conditions which come to the attention of clinical psychiatrists and psychoanalysts. Most prominent among these in the recent literature are the so-called narcissistic personality disorders, in which pathology in self-esteem regulation is seen as lying at the root of the disorder. In such characteristically troubled individuals, according to Annie Reich (1960), "unsublimated, erotized, manic self-inflation easily shifts to a feeling of utter dejection, of worthlessness, and to hypochondriacal anxieties. 'Narcissists' of this type thus suffer regularly from repetitive, violent oscillation of self-esteem" (p. 224). De Saussure (1971) writes of adult patients who experience disturbances of self-esteem regulation and use magical beliefs and archaic or unrealistic idealization of the self and objects to offset the injury and pain associated with lowered self-regard. Offer, Ostrov, and Howard (1981) have documented lowered self-esteem among delinquent adolescents and in a variety of other pathological adolescent conditions.

The reconstruction of the early childhood parenting experience of adolescents and adults suffering from disturbances of self-esteem regulation has consistently demonstrated emotional hurt or injury to the developing child resulting from the relative lack of adequate empathic mothering. Extensive clinical observations corroborate these findings. Their value in developing a theory of pathogenesis and psychic structure formation is limited, however, by the fact that we have, as it were, only one side of the story, namely that of the patients. Increasingly, however, we are learning from the direct observation of family relationships and mother-infant pairs that the infant, through his or her own initiatives and emerging personality, plays a major role in creating the quality of the mother-child relationship and in setting the tone of the interaction (Brazelton, 1979; Stechler and Kaplan, 1980). Realistically, moreover, the inevitability of disappointment is built into the mother-infant relationship. As Sander (1979) states, the infant soon discovers "the mother's limits, the extent of her availability to his specific and intentional demands" (p. 17). The unfolding of health and pathology will probably depend more on how the family handles the hurt, emotional pain, and the hostility (or *narcissistic rage* in Kohut's terminology) associated with the child's experience of these limits than upon the initial disappointments and frustrations themselves. (Virginia Demos in Chapter 1 describes some of the emotional characteristics of mother-infant reciprocity in the early months of life and considers how these experiences might bear on the later establishment of self-esteem and self-esteem regulation.)

Although depression and certain character problems are the conditions most intimately associated with disturbances in self-regard, conflicts relating to self-image and self-esteem may play a role in almost any troubling or troubled emotional state. Virtually all maladaptive defensive patterns in childhood, adolescence, and adult life have as at least one major purpose protection from the pain associated with lowered self-esteem. As Rosenberg (1979) points out, "certain depth psychologists have gone so far as to contend that self-esteem problems are at the heart of the neurotic process" (p. 54). Whether or not this claim can be substantiated, most child and adult psychotherapists would, I think, agree that conflicts relating to self-esteem constitute an important part of their current work, including the treatment of neurotic or less severely disturbed individuals. In part this may result from our increased recognition of the centrality of problems with self-esteem in the development and organization of troubled emotional states. It may also reflect a cultural shift, a making conscious of the need of the individual to find relationships and work which give his life meaning and value. It is possible that the need for self-worth remained unconsciously assumed (and therefore not explicit) in human life by virtue of the confirmations of self, place, or worth afforded by family, work, religious, national, and other community and institutional structures. Perhaps, as these structures break down, or change, the need for self-worth or self-fulfillment becomes a more conscious, hence a more prominent, element in modern life.

REFERENCES

Alexander, J., & Friedman, J. (1980), The question of the self and self-esteem. *Internat. Rev. Psycho-Anal.*, 7:365–374.
Basch, M. F. (1976), The concept of affect: A re-examination. *J. Amer. Psychoanal. Assn.*, 24:759–778.

Bate, W. J. (1977), *Samuel Johnson*. New York: Harcourt Brace Jovanovich.

Bateson, G. (1971), The cybernetics of "self": A theory of alcoholism. In: *Steps to an Ecology of Mind*. New York: Valentine Books, 1971, pp. 309–337.

Brazelton, T. B. (1979), Behavioral competence of the newborn infant. *Seminars in Perinatology*, 3:35–44.

Dare, C., & Holder, A. (1981), Developmental aspects of the interaction between narcissism, self-esteem and object relations. *Internat. J. Psycho-Anal.*, 62:323–338.

Demos, J. (1972), Character and the social order in Puritan New England. In: *Main Problems in American History*, Vol. 1, 3rd Ed., ed. H. H. Quint, M. Cantor, & D. Albertson. Homewood, Ill.: Dorsey Press, pp. 1–21.

——— Demos, V., Binstock, W., & Levine, R. (1978), Presented by J. Demos at a workshop on Child Rearing and the Self, Boston Psychoanalytic Society & Institute, November 14.

Deutsch, H. (1945), *The Psychology of Women*. New York: Grune & Stratton.

Eisenberg, L. (1975), Psychiatric aspects of language disability. In: *Reading, Perception, and Language*, ed. D. D. Duane & M. B. Rawson. Baltimore: York Press, pp. 215–230.

Erikson, E. H. (1980), The "I" in religion. Presentation, Wellfleet, Mass., August 22.

——— (1981), The Galilean sayings and the sense of "I". *The Yale Review*, Spring, pp. 321–362.

Fast, I. (1979), Developments in gender identity: Gender differentiation in girls. *Internat. J. Psycho-Anal.*, 60:443–554.

Federn, P. (1952), *Ego Psychology and the Psychoses*. New York: Basic Books.

Fenichel, O. (1945), *The Psychoanalytic Theory of Neuroses*. New York: Norton.

Ferguson, M. (1980), *The Aquarian Conspiracy: Personal and Social Transformation in the 1980's*. Los Angeles: Tarcher.

Feuerbach, L. A. (1843a), Principles of the philosophy of the future. In: *The Fiery Brook: Selected Writings of Ludwig Feuerbach*. New York: Anchor Books, 1972, pp. 175–245.

——— (1843b), *The Essence of Christianity*. New York: Blanchard, 1855.

Freud, A. (1972), The widening scope of psychoanalytic child psychology: Normal and abnormal. In: *The Writings of Anna Freud*, Vol. 8. New York: International Universities Press, 1981.

Freud, S. (1905), Three essays on sexuality. *Standard Edition*, 7:135–243. London: Hogarth Press, 1964.

——— (1914), On narcissism: An introduction. *Standard Edition*, 14:73–102. London: Hogarth Press, 1957.

——— (1915), Mourning and melancholia. *Standard Edition*, 14: 243–258. London: Hogarth Press, 1964.

——— (1916), Some character-types met with in psychoanalytic work: The "exceptions. *Standard Edition*, 14:311–315. London: Hogarth Press, 1964.

——— (1933), New introductory lectures on psycho-analysis. *Standard Edition*, 22:5–182. London: Hogarth Press, 1964.

Galenson, E., & Roiphe, H. (1971), The impact of early sexual discovery on mood, defensive organization, and symbolization. *The Psychoanalytic Study of the Child*, 26:195–216. New York: Quadrangle.

——— (1977), Some suggested revisions concerning early female development. In: *Female Psychology: Contemporary Psychoanalytic Views*, ed. H. P. Blum. New York: International Universities Press, pp. 29–58.

Grossman, W. I. (1983), The self as fantasy: Fantasy as theory. *J. Amer. Psychoanal. Assn. 30:919–937*.

Hartmann, H. (1956), The development of the ego concept in Freud's work. In: *Essays on Ego Psychology*. New York: International Universities Press, 1964, pp. 268–296.

Jacobson, E. (1964), *The Self and the Object World*. New York: International Universities Press.

——— (1975), The regulation of self-esteem. In: *Depression and Human Existence*, ed. E. J. Anthony & T. Benedek. Boston: Little, Brown, pp. 231–277.

James, W. (1890), *The Principles of Psychology*, Vol. 1. Cambridge, Mass.: Harvard University Press, 1981.

Kagan, J. (1981), *The Second Year: The Emergence of Self-Awareness*. Cambridge, Mass.: Harvard University Press.

Kernberg, O. F. (1980), Self, ego, affects, and drives. *J. Amer. Psychoanal. Assn.* 30:893–917.

Kestenberg, J. S. (1968), Outside and inside, male and female. *J. Amer. Psychoanal. Assn.*, 16:457–520.

Klein, G. S. (1976), *Psychoanalytic Theory: An Exploration of Essentials*. New York: International Universities Press.

Klein, J. W. (1980), *Jewish Identity and Self-Esteem: Healing Wounds through Ethnotherapy*. New York: American Jewish Committee.

Kohut, H. (1971), *The Analysis of the Self*. New York: International Universities Press.

——— (1976), Creativeness, charisma, group psychology: Reflections on the self-analysis of Freud. In: *The Search for the Self: Selected Writings of Heinz Kohut: 1950–1978*, Vol. 2. New York: International Universities Press, 1978, pp. 793–843.

——— (1977), *The Restoration of the Self*. New York: International Universities Press.

——— (1978), *The Search for the Self: Selected Writings: 1950–1978*, Vols. 1 & 2. New York: International Universities Press.

——— (1980), Reflections on *Advances in Self-Psychology*. In: *Advances in Self-Psychology*, ed. A. Goldberg. New York: International Universities Press, pp. 473–554.

Mack, J. E. (1978), Psychoanalysis and biography: A narrowing gap. *J. Phil. Assn. Psychoanal.*, 5:97–110.

——— (1981), Alcoholism, A.A., and the governance of the self. In: *Dynamic Approaches to the Understanding and Treatment of Alcoholism*, ed. M. H. Bean & N. E. Zinberg. New York: Free Press, pp. 128–162.

——— Hickler, H. (1981), *Vivienne: The Life and Suicide of an Adolescent Girl*. Boston: Little, Brown.

Meissner, W. W. (1978), *The Paranoid Process*. New York: Aronson.

Murray, J. M. (1964), Narcissism and the ego ideal. *J. Amer. Psychoanal. Assn.*, 12:477–511.

Niederland, W. G. (1965), Narcissistic ego impairment in patients with early physical malformations. *The Psychoanalytic Study of the Child*, 20:518–534. New York: International Universities Press.

Offer, D., Ostrov, E., & Howard, K. I. (1981), *The Adolescent: A Psychological Self-Portrait*. New York: Basic Books.

Ornstein, P. H. (1978), Introduction to *The Search for the Self: Selected Writings of Heinz Kohut: 1950–1978*, Vol. 1. New York: International Universities Press, pp. 1–106.

Pulver, S. E. (1970), Narcissism: The term and the concept. *J. Amer. Psychoanal. Assn.*, 18:319–341.

Pine, F. (1981), In the beginning: contributions to a psychoanalytic developmental psychology. *Internat. Rev. of Psycho-Anal.*, 8:15–34.

Reich, A. (1960), Pathologic forms of self-esteem regulation. *The Psychoanalytic Study of the Child*, 15:215–234. New York: International Universities Press.

Ritvo, S. (1971), Late adolescence: Developmental and clinical considerations. *The Psychoanalytic Study of the Child*, 26:241–263. New York: Quadrangle.

Rizzuto, A. (1978), The patient as hero. Presented at Tufts University Department of Psychiatry, April 28.

——— (1979), *The Birth of the Living God: A Psychoanalytic Study*. Chicago: University of Chicago Press.

Robinson, J. (1628), Of children and their education. In: *The Work of John Robinson, Pastor of the Pilgrim Fathers*, Vol. 1. Boston: Doctrinal Tract and Book Society, 1851, pp. 242–250.

Rochlin, G. (1965), *Griefs and Discontents: The Forces of Change*. Boston: Little, Brown.

——— (1973), *Man's Aggression: The Defense of the Self*. Boston: Gambit.

——— (1980), *The Masculine Dilemma: A Psychology of Masculinity*. Boston: Little, Brown.

Rosenberg, M. (1979), *Conceiving the Self*. New York: Basic Books.

Sander, L. W. (1979), Development as creative process. Presented as the first Ellen B. Stechler Memorial Lecture. Published by The Boston University Medical Centre.

Sandler, J., Holder, A., & Meers, D. (1963), The ego ideal and the ideal self. *The Psychoanalytic Study of the Child*, 18:139–158. New York: International Universities Press.

Saussure, J. de (1971), Some complications in self-esteem regulations caused by using an archaic image of the self as an ideal. *Internat. J. Psycho-Anal.* 52: 87–98.

Scheidlinger, S. (1981), On scapegoating in group psychotherapy. Prepared for Presidential Address, American Group Psychotherapy Association, February 12, 1982.

Schilder, P. (1928), *Contributions to Developmental Neuropsychiatry*. New York: International Universities Press, 1964.

Spruiell, V. (1975), Three strands of narcissism. *Psychoanal. Quart.*, 44:577–595.
———— (1981), The self and the ego. *Psychoanal. Quart.*, 50:319–344.
Stechler, G., & Kaplan, S. (1980), The development of the self: A psychoanalytic perspective. *The Psychoanalytic Study of the Child*, 35:85–106. New Haven: Yale University Press.
Stoller, R. J. (1968), *Sex and Gender*. New York: Aronson.
———— (1975), *Perversion: The Erotic Form of Hatred*. New York: Pantheon.
Stolorow, R. D. (1975), Toward a functional definition of narcissism. *Internat. J. Psycho-Anal.*, 56:179–185.
Sullivan, H. S. (1953), The interpersonal theory of psychiatry. In: *The Collected Works of Harry Stack Sullivan*, Vol. 1. New York: Norton.
Winnicott, D. W. (1965), *The Maturational Processes and the Facilitating Environment: Studies in the Theory of Emotional Development*. New York: International Universities Press.
Wittgenstein, L. (1914–1916), In: *The Essential Wittgenstein*. New York: Basic Books, 1979.
Yankelovich, D. (1981), *New Rules: Search for Self Fulfillment in a World Turned Upside Down*. New York: Random House.

CLINICAL AND THEORETICAL
CONSIDERATIONS

1

A Perspective From Infant Research on

Affect and Self-Esteem

VIRGINIA DEMOS, Ed.D.

This paper will draw on concepts and data from infant research to explore the relationship between affect and the development of self-esteem in children. Before focusing on this topic, however, I should like briefly to describe my approach to affect and to the role of affect in development. The more specific role of affect in relation to self-esteem will then be addressed.

My approach owes much to the work of Silvan Tomkins (1962–1963), who postulates that affects constitute the primary motivational system of the personality. The inadequacies of the drive-reduction theory of motivation are by now widely recognized (Arnold, 1960; Bowlby, 1969; Sroufe, 1979; and others); but Tomkins goes further than others in offering affect as a viable, comprehensive alternative. The link between affective expressions and particular motivational dispositions toward the environment was first expressed by Darwin in 1872. He argued that particular affective displays evolve primarily because of their value as preparatory acts; and secondarily because of their communicative value. For example, the act of baring the teeth, an expression of anger in primates, represents primarily a preparation for biting and secondarily a threat signal.

Tomkins expands Darwin's original idea by positing the existence of innate affective patterns of response that are experienced as motivated states. He designates nine primary affects. Listed in their mild and intense form they are: interest-excitement, enjoyment-joy, surprise-startle, fear-terror, distress-anguish, anger-rage, shame-humiliation, contempt and disgust. Tomkins postulates that discrete affects, with the exception of contempt and disgust, are activated by variations in the density of neural firings or stimulation, where density is defined as the product of intensity and the number of neural firings per unit time. There are three classes of variations: stimulation increases, stimulation levels, and stimulation decreases. The organism is thus capable of responding to anything that is changing or staying the same at non-optimal levels of stimulation. Differing rates of stimulation-increase activate startle, fear, or interest (in a descending order of suddenness). Differing non-optimal levels of stimulation activate distress or anger (in an increasing order of intensity); and differing rates of stimulation-decrease activate laughter or the smile of enjoyment (in a descending order of suddenness). Shame is activated when positive affect (e.g., interest) is interrupted and attenuated, without being completely reduced.

The discrete affects evoked in this way act as amplifiers, reproducing by means of facial, vocal, bodily, and autonomic patterns an analogue of the gradients and intensities of the stimuli, and imprinting immediate behavioral response with the analogue: "An excited response is accelerating in speed whether in walking or talking. An enjoyable response is decelerating in speed and relaxed as a motor or perceptual savouring response" (Tomkins, 1981, p. 322). In this way, "affect either makes good things better or bad things worse by conjointly simulating its activator in its profile of neural firing and by adding a special analogic quality that is intensely rewarding or punishing" (1980, p. 148). In this model, the organism is biased to prolong and maximize positive affect, and to try to change and minimize negative affect. Tomkins argues that the motivational role of affects derives from their greater generality ("one can be excited about anything under the sun"), their independence from physiological needs, and their freedom to amplify in an abstract and urgent manner a wide range of "events" (physical, cognitive, drive states, etc.).[1]

This formulation reverses the usual tendency to treat affects as epiphenomena, i.e., as passive reactions of the individual to her/his (hereinafter referred to as "her") experiences, or as drive derivatives. It insists that affects are themselves the primary motivators

---

[1] This brief summary cannot do justice to the complexity of Tomkins's theory. For a full account the reader is referred to Volume 1 of *Affect, Imagery, Consciousness*, particularly Chapters 1–9.

and are intricately involved in shaping experiences. While emphasizing the motivational function of affect, the theory also recognizes the communicative importance of affective expressive behaviors. Indeed, in early infancy, before the advent of language and other symbolic forms of representation, the infant's affective expressive behaviors are probably the only reliable and valid indication of the saliency of events for the infant, and thereby constitute the primary medium of communication and meaning in the infant-mother system. In articulating the role of affect in development it is possible to argue that the motivational and communicative functions of affect are not contradictory or even unrelated, but are functional aspects of an integrated biological system. One possible integrated view of these functions might be the following. Affective expressive patterns represent an amplified, qualitative analogue of the rates and levels of stimulation experienced by the organism from whatever source; and as such, they regulate exchanges with the external world by priming the organism to *act* in analogical ways, and thereby reflect the *saliency* of an event for the organism and act as a *communication* to the caregiver.

Given this formulation of the role of affect in development, it is now possible to ask how affect relates to the development of the self and self-esteem. What is meant by "self-esteem" and "self?" It is generally assumed that self-esteem is a subjective value judgment that the individual makes about herself (e.g., Mussen, Conger, and Kagan, 1974). As such, it consists of a combination of affective and cognitive components that result in the experience of positive thoughts and feelings toward the self, and the overall experience of cohesiveness and well-being. The self is then the phenomenological experience of inner continuity and coherence in the face of rapid developmental changes in neurological organization, physical growth, and hormonal balance. From a theoretical point of view, the self is probably best understood as a construct designed to account for this continuity of experience. As such it is seen as a gradually evolving psychological structure that possesses organizational and integrative properties. If the self is understood as an organizing structure, then it too probably consists of a combination of affective and cognitive components that have formed on the basis of at least the following three aspects of experience: judgments of one's competence versus incompetence; trust in one's inner states versus mistrust; and judgments of one's relatedness to others versus one's isolation. (There are of course other aspects of experience that are relevant to the contents of self structure; to focus on these three is to highlight them as important but not exclusive aspects.) To the extent that the self is experienced as relatively competent, trustworthy, and related, positive self-esteem can be maintained.

What is the role of affect in influencing these aspects of the self and, by extension, the capacity of the individual to experience positive self-esteem? To explore the interaction of affect and the self-organization in a developmental context, it is necessary to articulate the developmental processes relevant to each of these organizational systems.

DEVELOPMENT OF THE SELF

Several authors, in describing the development of the self, refer to a dual process of development that includes both what goes on within the infant and young child and what goes on between the child and the caregiver. Stern (1980) writes of the polarity between the child's emerging representations of self and other and the representations of "being with" the other, and articulates three ways of "being with" the other, namely, self-other complementing, mental-state sharing or state tuning, and state transforming. Sander (1980) describes the necessity, in the life of the developing child, both for "open spaces," which are segments of experience free from internal or external pressures for adaptation, and for the occurrence of the ongoing negotiations of a "fitting together" with the caregiving environment. G. Klein (1976) and Stechler and Kaplan (1980) discuss the "I" and "we" aspects of the self and their simultaneous development. Stechler and Kaplan, building on Klein's concept of incompatibilities (which is seen as a broader concept that encompasses the narrower psychoanalytic concept of conflict), specify that development involves a dialectical process whereby the infant is continually challenged by incompatibilities (e.g., wanting to perform two incompatible behaviors at once, or an empathic failure between infant and caregiver). When the challenge is within the infant's integrative capacities, the infant creates a new solution to the problem and the self is strengthened. When the challenge is beyond the infant's integrative capacities, the infant either persists and continues to struggle or she wards off and defends against the negative experience. In the latter case—of warding off and defense—the self is weakened. This dialectical process is thought to begin at birth and to proceed as the infant gradually constructs a self structure consisting of these accrued experiences of challenges that either add to the evolving structure or weaken it. All of the above formulations assume that the creation and integration of self structure are occurring during both "I" and "we" experiences, that both kinds of experiences are necessary (indeed are probably inevitable), that they are mutually enhancing, and that there should therefore be a more or less equal and simultaneous development of these two aspects of the self in order to promote optimal adaptation and to avoid an overcompensation in either direction.

These formulations differ from Kohut's (1971, 1977) proposal of the development of the bipolar self. The mirroring and idealizing aspects of the bipolar self, as described thus far in the literature, can perhaps best be understood in the present context as differing aspects of "we" experiences. As such, future researchers might well find it helpful to relate them to Stern's three ways of "being with" the other. Kohut's formulation does not seem to acknowledge the importance of the "I" experiences. Or to phrase this statement somewhat differently, Kohut's reconstruction of early experience relevant to the development of the self does not seem to take into account the possibility that learning and structure building might occur in those moments when the infant or child is essentially alone, unpressured by either drive or social demands, and is free to respond to her own motivational urges. To stress the importance of "I" experiences, however, is not to claim that the young child can do without a caregiver. Self and self-other, or "I" and "we," experiences are intricately interrelated and interdependent and both occur within the context of a social system. Further, when observing a child, it may be difficult to know with certainty at any given point in time which aspect of self experience is occurring. Nevertheless, the distinction is useful theoretically and forces researchers to sharpen and articulate their behavioral criteria.

DEVELOPMENT OF AFFECT

All affective experiences can be conceptualized as involving
three components: the triggering event or stimulus, the affective
experience per se, and a two-fold response to the affective experience, involving both the recruitment in memory of past experiences and motor responses. Although innate factors play a
role, learning and therefore development occur in relation to all
three components. An example will help to clarify the kinds of
learning involved. As a young child looks at, approaches, and
reaches for a pair of scissors, she is indicating *simultaneously* her
affective state of interest, the focus of that interest on the scissors,
and her response of approaching and reaching toward the object
of her interest. Whatever the outcome of this affective moment,
it provides the child with information about all three components
of the experience. If no one intervenes, and the child hurts herself
with the scissors, she learns that scissors can lead to pain and
distress, that interest can lead to pain and distress, and that approaching, reaching, and touching objects can lead to pain and
distress. If a parent, trying to prevent injury, distracts the child
away from the scissors by presenting another, safer object that
evokes the child's interest, then the child learns that interest can
lead to more interest, that scissors can lead to other interesting
objects, and that approaching and reaching toward can lead to
more approaching and reaching toward. On the other hand, if
a parent removes the scissors and scolds the child, also in an
attempt to prevent injury, the child learns that interest can lead
to distress, that objects of interest, such as scissors, can disappear,
and that approaching and reaching toward objects of interest can
lead to distress.

The learning that occurs in any particular moment can be generalized to other similar moments in a variety of ways. For example, with frequent repetitions of the last sequence described
above, a child may learn to inhibit her interests generally, or to
inhibit her interest in scissors and other "similar" objects, or to
inhibit her response of approaching and reaching toward interesting objects, or to inhibit her response only in the presence of
her parents, etc. According to Tomkins (1978), this generalization
involves a magnification of affect across situations perceived by
the individual to be similar, where the similarity is created by

perceiving analogues or variance (that is, a repetition with a difference) from one situation to another. Moreover, because each individual creates unique analogues and variance, the consequence of any particular affective moment—which elements in the experience will prove to be lasting or formative—depends as much on what follows as on what happens and is impossible to predict. This magnification process is thought to begin at birth, although because of the infant's immature cognitive apparatus it is possible that similarities may be based more on perceiving variance than on perceiving analogues in earliest infancy.

The variety of ways in which learning can occur in relation to affect becomes even more extensive when the three components of affective experience are explored in more detail. The first component of affective experience refers to the triggering event or stimulus. Development involves an expansion of the number and kind of stimuli that can evoke particular affects. Initially this relationship between the stimulus and the affect may be innate, e.g., a sharp pinprick activates distress, a loud noise produces startle, a bitter taste evokes disgust, a human face activates interest, etc. And gradually as the child's experiences become diversified, some mediated by the caregiver and others not, and as she perceives similarities across the diversity, she builds up expectations for an ever-increasing array of situations. For example, Sroufe and Wunsch (1972) describe a developmental sequence for laughter that progresses from quantities of stimulation in the neonatal period to the content of stimulation by the third month of life. Once again, there are presumably no limits to the kinds of expectations that can be built up. As Tomkins (1968) has said, one can learn to be afraid of, angry at, interested in anything under the sun. An optimal outcome of this aspect of socialization would produce a wide range of events associated with positive affects.

The second component, the affective experience per se, refers primarily to the distinctive punishing or rewarding quality of each affect. This distinctive quality partially depends on the innate biological programs for each affect described by Tomkins. Although these are assumed to remain constant throughout life, they are subject to modification. Therefore, the distinctive quality of each affect is also partially dependent on these learned modifications such as controlling the facial expression of affect, the range of intensity, duration, and density of each affect, the recruitment of past experiences of affect, and affect-affect interactions such as blends and sequences of affects.

The modulation of affect, once it has been triggered, can occur through learning to control and manage the innate facial and vocal expressions of affect. Tomkins describes the innate patterns of facial expression for each affect. Ekman (1972, 1977) and Izard (1971) demonstrate the presence of these patterns in various non-Western and Western cultures, arguing for their universality. There is less extensive work describing vocal expressive patterns for each affect. Ekman (1978) has produced an atlas of facial movements and developed a precise notational system for analyzing all movements that occur on the face, including those that pertain to affect and others that do not. He describes three major ways of managing and controlling affective expressions: (1) One can qualify an expression by adding a further expression which functions as a comment on the expression one has just shown, e.g., smiling right after an angry expression. Such a qualification of anger usually conveys the message: "I'm angry, but I've got it under control." (2) One can modulate the intensity of an expression to show either more or less than is actually felt. This can be done by varying the number of facial areas involved, the duration of the expression, or the strength of the muscle action. (3) One can falsify an expression. This can be done by simulating an expression, e.g., showing a feeling when none is felt, by neutralizing an expression, e.g., showing nothing when feeling something, or by masking an expression, e.g., covering one expression with another expression. All cultural, social, and familial groups require their members to control and manage their expression of affect, and thus all members of human groups learn some or all of the three major ways described above. Although little is known about the precise learning processes involved, some imitation probably occurs, as well as individual adaptations to particular environmental or internal pressures. I have described elsewhere (1982a) idiosyncratic expressive patterns already observable on the faces of infants by the end of the first year of life. Presumably optimal development involves learning the socially appropriate expressive rules or conventions without overcontrolling or undercontrolling one's affective expressions and by implication one's affective experience.

The intensity, duration, and density factors in affective experience, while constituting only part of what needs to be managed, are perhaps the most troublesome, since they remain throughout life not entirely under voluntary control. We are talking here primarily about troublesomeness in regard to negative affects, for we assume that the experience of pure, positive affect, even at high density levels, is not toxic, and therefore not troublesome, except perhaps in a social sense where expressive rules about appropriateness are involved. Hence, although control of the intensity, duration, and density of negative affect is never altogether reliable, nevertheless, in most circumstances adults are able to produce partial, modulated, economical responses—a developmental achievement when compared to the whole-body involvement of the infant's responses. Even infants possess some capacity to modulate their negative affective states at a low level of intensity; but as the intensity level rises, they tend to continue to escalate, thereby compounding intensity with duration and producing a high density of negative affect. Infants are therefore dependent on caregivers to modulate, soothe, and maintain them at more moderate density levels. The ease or difficulty that a particular infant-mother pair experiences in trying to regulate the intensity, duration, and density of the infant's negative affective states is influenced both by the infant's characteristics (e.g., vigor, threshold for stimulation, capacity to achieve smooth transitions between states, etc.) and by the mother's characteristics (e.g., calmness, soothing skills, ability to dose the quantity of stimulation, etc.). Thus both constitutional factors and environmental factors make a contribution. We assume there is an optimal density of negative affect that is neither too low nor too high but that ranges from moderate to moderately high. A successful developmental adaptation in this area involves an increase in the child's capacity to sustain her affectivity within this optimal band of density and leads to the child's increasing trust in the reliability of her own inner experiences. The risk of failure in this area is that the child will come to mistrust and to fear her negative affective responses because of their high density, unmanageableness, and her past experiences of having been overwhelmed, surprised, or disorganized by them. This can lead to a general inhibition of negative affect alternating with explosiveness, or to the selective inhibition of a particularly troublesome affect.

The recruitment from memory of past experiences of similar affect, although mentioned earlier as a response to affect, can also modulate the qualitative experience per se by either attenuating or magnifying the experience. For example, if an experience of joy recruits a memory of a similar joyful experience, but one that ended in disappointment, the present experience may be attenuated in anticipation of a similar consequence. By contrast, if the affect recruits a memory of pure joyfulness, the present experience is magnified. Past affective experiences, recruited because of their similarities in quality to the present, can also modify the present qualitative experience by adding their subtle nuances to the experience. Gradually, over time, complex associational networks are built up, so that the recruitment of past experience makes possible an ever-increasing elaboration of current emotional experience.

The relations between affects may result in the gradual acquisition of affect sequences (e.g., interest followed by enjoyment, or interest followed by shame) or in the gradual acquisition of affect blends (e.g., of distress and anger so that the experience of the one without the other becomes rare). The acquisition of a characteristic affect sequence may be influenced both by innate affect-affect dynamics and by environmental factors. For example, the affect distress may continuously re-evoke more distress in a positive feedback loop until a level of stimulation is reached that innately triggers anger. If such an affective sequence becomes magnified over time through repetitions of situations that are similar but different—that is, through either variance or perceived analogues or both—then even mild distress can become a learned trigger for anger. Or, a child's fear could be ridiculed by family members in a variety of situations, thereby creating, primarily through environmental factors, a fear-shame-distress sequence. The occurrence of blends is more controversial and less clear. Some argue that blends are the predominant experience and that discrete affects occur only rarely (Lewis, 1980); however, I have reported elsewhere (1982a) that at least from six months to two years of age discrete affects occur with a greater frequency than blends. If the experience of discrete affects is more common, and the occurrence of blends represents a mixture of discrete qualities triggered by a compound stimulus (e.g., an enjoyable surprise, or a distressing surprise), then there are probably several ways for a blend to become habitual. The triggering events might be chronically or characteristically compounded, or an experience may chronically recruit a particular affect so that the blending occurs as a result of the past and the present experiences co-occurring in consciousness. In such cases the child might find it difficult to experience either affect as discrete and apart from the blend. There is presumably no limit to the kinds of sequences and blends that could occur.

These affect-affect interactions are, strictly speaking, responses to affect, e.g., learning to feel shame as a response to one's fear, and should be part of the discussion of the third component of affective experience. But because they can become substitutes for, or blend with, the original affect, they relate directly to the qualitative experience per se, and thus are discussed in this section rather than with the other behavioral responses to be discussed below.

The third component of affective experience, namely, the response to the affect, refers to what one learns to do with one's anger, distress, joy, etc. (as distinct from the immediate facial and vocal expression of the affect). This response is two-fold, and involves both the recruitment of past experiences already discussed and behavioral responses. It was argued earlier that an affective experience is a motivational experience and primes the individual to act in a way that is analogically similar to the triggering stimulus. Thus "an excited- response is accelerating in speed, whether in walking or talking" (Tomkins, 1981, p. 322). The innate relationship between the stimulus and the response operates at an abstract and general level and has a very brief duration in time. Therefore, one can learn a wide variety of discrete behaviors as responses to a particular affective state. For example, when experiencing anger one can learn to kick the nearest object, or to yell at someone, or to destroy a favorite object, or to count to ten, or to bite one's knuckles, etc. Or, to stay with the affect excitement, which, as mentioned above, predisposes one to respond in an accelerated manner, one could learn to talk faster and louder, to jump up and down, to clap one's hands, to pound the table or a person, to spin around, to somersault, to throw one's hat in the air, to run, etc.; or one could learn an equally diverse

range of behaviors to tone down or to suppress such predispo-
sitions. Some of these responses are shaped by cultural norms for
children and adults, or males and females. In our own culture,
children and females are expected to jump up and down, squeal,
and clasp their hands when excited, while men are expected to
keep their feet on the ground and smile broadly, except for professional athletes who are allowed to jump up and down, yell, and
pound each other on the back when points are scored. Theoretically, there is no limit to the kinds of behaviors that can be learned
in response to a particular affect, although presumably behaviors
that go against the innate analogic quality of the affect would be
harder to learn, e.g., learning to relax the large striated muscles
throughout the body as a response to anger. Optimal development
in this realm would involve learning behaviors that are within
one's cultural norms and that lead to more or less constructive
outcomes for the individual.

AFFECT AND SELF-ESTEEM

   To review briefly, I am suggesting that the child's capacity to
experience positive self-esteem rests on the degree to which she
feels competent, reliable, and related to others. These strengths
represent at least three important components of self structure
that accrue through the simultaneous growth of "I" and "we"
aspects of the self. And finally, the development of affect is a
process involving three factors—the triggering stimulus, the affect
per se, and the response to the affect. The task now is to relate
the development of affect to the development of self-esteem.

   The infant's capacity to modulate affect and to sustain negative
affect within an optimal range relates directly to the development
of both the "I" and "we" aspects of the self. This capacity grows
out of the countless experiences of successful mutual regulation
of state that occur between the infant and its caregiver from the
moment of birth on. Stern (1980) describes this kind of experience
as one of his three ways of "being with" the other, namely, as state
transforming, and argues that it represents an anaclitic experience
for the infant—a transformation of self via another. He relegates
the importance of such experiences to the development of physical
intimacy. It seems likely, however, that the repeated experience

for the infant of building up and coming down from states of distress and anger, without losing control, gradually enables the infant to trust her inner responses, and thereby to tolerate moderately intense affective states. The growing trust and tolerance are important psychological components of the infant's capacity to engage in both "we" and "I" experiences; for only as the child learns to feel that her inner states are reliable will she continue to be free to risk becoming affectively aroused either in transactions with another or while pursuing her own goals. From birth on, the development of the capacity to tolerate moderately intense negative states is likely to lead gradually to a trusting of one's inner experience, which represents a basic component of the capacity for positive self-esteem.[2]

Beyond the issue of developing a tolerance for negative affect, the role of affect in promoting "we" experiences in infancy has been conceptualized in various ways. Kohut (1971, 1977) refers to the mirroring function of the caregiver in infancy as providing a validation and a sharing of the infant's affective states as well as of the infant's exhibitionistic wishes. Through relatively good empathic mirroring, the infant can develop healthy grandiosity. Stern (1980), drawing on infant observational data, describes two additional self-other experiences in infancy—self-other complementing and mental-state sharing. Mental-state sharing is the more relevant concept for the development of self-esteem. It involves the aim of providing for or inducing the other into a similar state or experience. Stern argues that these shared moments provide the infant with an early sense of the commonality of experience, of a relatedness whereby the infant first begins to see her distinct experiences as part of shared human experience. This intersubjectivity includes both the affective and the cognitive elements of the experience (although the affective elements probably predominate in early infancy), and relates to the capacity for intimacy and self-esteem. Stern is careful to specify that while, in theory, such moments may risk blurring the distinction between self and other, they derive their power from the experience of a separateness being shared. To the extent that the infant can tolerate the affectivity of "we" moments, these shared experiences are likely to contribute to her growing sense of relatedness versus isolation and thereby increase her capacity for self-esteem.

[2] See Chapter 2 for a similar point of view in relation to older children.

The role of affect in fostering "I" experiences can be understood in several ways. "I" experiences are moments in which the infant is alone, free of internal drive pressures and external interactional pressures. As such, they provide an opportunity for the infant to experience her own inner wishes in stark relief, and to follow their lead, e.g., to consolidate and practice newly acquired skills, or to explore new actions and ideas in relation to objects, her own body, etc. Sander (1980) refers to these moments as "open spaces." This experience may also be close to what has been called the conflict-free sphere of the ego for somewhat older children. Affect plays a role in three important ways. First, affect provides the motivational thrust, the interest, excitement, and enjoyment that promote exchanges with the world and that shape behavioral and cognitive activities toward the world. Since this is a biological given, these affective programs will be activated in the absence of other competing stimuli. Second, negative affect can disrupt "I" experiences, so that the infant must be able to manage or regulate the intrusion of negative affect into such moments. For example, if low-level fatigue or hunger begins to activate distress or if the activity proves to be difficult and begins to activate anger, the infant must be able to prevent the escalation of the negative affect in order to sustain her interest and activity, and to use the anger constructively to focus and to mobilize her efforts. This means she must have developed a tolerance for the presence of negative affect, derived from past experiences of successfully modulating these affects and from knowing that they do not always escalate and get out of control. Third, and apart from the presence or absence of negative affect, the infant has to be able to sustain her interest-excitement and enjoyment-joy. The growth of this capacity depends on experiences with the other of the mental-state sharing kind, which involve the sustained sharing of interest and enjoyment. These experiences impart to the positive affects a value—the infant appreciates their importance—and thereby contribute to the infant's capacity to sustain the affects. It is through the gradual expansion of the infant's interests that basic components of positive self-esteem.

In this formulation of the role of affect in the development of self-esteem, the capacity to tolerate and modulate negative affect is of paramount importance, and is seen as a basic requirement for the full participation in "we" and "I" experiences. In the discussion of the "I" experience, however, we see clearly that the management of negative affect is not the whole story. The development of the capacity to sustain positive affect—in particular, interest-excitement and enjoyment-joy—is equally important. This capacity does not develop merely in the absence of disruption from negative affect. Interest and enjoyment are positive affects with motivational properties, and they require nurturance and support from the caregiving environment in order to develop into enduring motivational structures, capable of supporting self-esteem. To illustrate this point, the final section of this paper will describe two infant-mother pairs representing two styles of the socialization of interest and enjoyment.

INFANT-MOTHER TRANSACTIONS: AN ILLUSTRATION

The segments of behavioral interaction to be described here are drawn from a larger body of data that was collected in the homes of the subjects. Each family was visited once a month, over a six-month period, and their ongoing daily routine was videotaped. The two infant-mother pairs described in this paper include two male infants, between the ages of 19 and 24 months. A 10-minute free-play session was selected for each pair, from their total three-hour corpus of data. Free play is defined as a time when both infant and mother are together and when no maintenance tasks, such as feeding, bathing, or housework are occurring. These free-play segments have been microanalyzed (see Demos [1982b] for a more complete description of this study and its findings). The present discussion will focus on the first three minutes of the two 10-minute segments.

The comparison of the first three minutes of these two play sessions is instructive because both involve the activity of coloring; in both cases the mothers do not seem very interested in coloring, both mothers suggest changing the activity at nearly the same point in time (2' 40" for mother C and 2' 47" for mother D; see Exhibits 1 and 2), and both children use the crayons in non-standard ways, e.g., mouthing them, banging them, and throwing them. Yet despite these similarities the transactional styles of pair C and pair D differ. Pair C manifests a transactional style char-

Exhibit 1
Pair C

Child		Mother	
		0.0	Or shall we play with your number game?
2.8	Right there.		
5.0	Mommy put crayon.	7.0	What do you want mommy to do?
11.0	Write.		
12.6	Mommy write de way.	14.6	What do you want me to write?
21.8	Write.	22.4	What shall I write?
22.6	Write.		
24.2	This. This. Moon.	28.0	Well I did a moon. Can I do something else?
30.2	Yeah.	30.6	What else can I do?
32.0	Hmm. This (holds up doll).	34.8	I know, do you want me to draw a man?
36.6	Yeah.		
41.0	This?	42.0	Hmm?
42.8	Lady.	44.0	Do you think it's a lady?
45.6	Man.	47.2	Well, it's a lady.
49.0	Man.	50.2	(laughs) Do you think it's a man?
		52.2	With long hair like yours.
54.0	Ah.	54.8	Yes.
		58.6	What are you doing?
59.6	I put hat.	1 00.8	Hat?
		1 11.8	Benjamin, can you make a pretty picture here? Let's take these other pieces of paper away. (Sorry [spoken to cameraman].)
		1 16.4	Let's see if you can draw a nice picture. Here.
1 19.2	(vocalizes)	1 19.8	Now you make a pretty picture. Can you pick up . . .
1 21.8	Mommy pretty picture.	1 23.6	Well mommy will do one pretty picture and Benjamin do one pretty picture.
		1 27.2	How's that?

1 29.4	Bow Bow.	1 31.0	You do one pretty picture there, and I'll do one here.
1 35.2	Bow.		
1 45.4	Here. This one.	1 47.8	Are you going to do one? You do one.
1 50.4	You do it.	1 51.0	No, you do it.
1 52.2	Mommy do it.	1 53.0	I did it. Look, I've done three.
1 56.4	Mommy do it.	1 57.8	You do it.
1 59.0	Mommy do this.	2 00.4	No, Benjamin going to do it.
2 01.6	Mommy do it.		
		2 06.6	Here, what color is this?
		2 09.8	Pretty hard to tell, isn't it?
2 11.8	Brown.	2 13.0	No.
2 13.6	Brom.		
2 15.2	Blue.		
2 17.8	Bluegree.		
2 19.8	Blue.		
2 22.2	Baboo.		
2 27.6	Here.		
2 31.1	Mommy, here.	2 31.0	(burp)
2 33.2	Brown.		
2 36.2	Truck.		
2 37.8	Truck.	2 37.8	Truck outside, yes.
		2 40.0	I think it's a garbage truck. Let's put your crayons away and do something else, because I'm tired of crayoning and you're not crayoning.
		2 46.8	So I'm going to put them away.
2 50.0	Are you take the writing?	2 51.8	Well, are you going to do some writing?
2 53.2	Yeah.		

Exhibit 2
Pair D

Child		Mother	
1.0	Oh color. (puts crayon in mouth)	2.8	Yeah, and no eating it. You color . . . No. I shouldn't even have said that should I.
15.0	Color.		
17.6	Color.		
20.0	Color.	21.8	O.K. Go ahead. What are you going to color?
		25.4	Huh?
		27.0	Remember, you have to hold the paper. Yeah.
31.6	Color.	33.0	Yeah, come on.
35.2	Color.	36.0	And use your other crayons too, if you want.
42.6	Color.		
43.6	Color.		
51.4	Color.		
55.0	eah-da, sca . . .		
59.6	(vocalizes)		
1 04.0	(sneezes)		
1 05.4	Mmmm color.		
1 08.0	(sneezes)	1 09.0	Bless you.
1 10.4	Mmm color.	1 11.8	Bless you.
1 22.8	Color.		
1 29.4	Oh, de color.		
1 33.0	Color.		
1 34.0	Color.		
1 35.4	Color.		
1 37.8	Oh, color.		
1 41.6	eeeah-h-h . . .	1 44.8	What?
1 46.2	Color.		
1 48.4	Color.	1 49.8	O.K. Color on the paper.
		1 53.8	You want some different crayons?
		1 56.8	Maybe we'll find a nice bright yellow.
2.00.8	Color, color.	2 02.8	Billy, I don't believe you're eating these.
		2 06.2	That's when we take them away though, huh?

		2 12.2	Yellow (as she places crayon on tray).
2 13.0	(puts crayon in mouth)	2 15.0	No!
		2 16.8	Or I'll take them away.
2 16.0	(uses crayons)	2 19.4	Well, I think you're going to be left-handed.
2 21.0	(knocks paper and crayons on floor)	2 22.2	Ah!
		2.23.2	Oh oh.
2 24.0	(writes on tray of high chair)	2 25.2	No. On the paper.
2 27.6	(vocalizes)	2 28.4	On the paper.
		2 29.6	Here (puts paper and crayon back on tray).
2 32.4	(vocalizes)	2 33.8	Huh.
2 35.0	(throws crayon)	2 36.0	O.K. We'll trade. I'll give you a brown for a yellow (retrieves crayon, puts it away, places another one on tray).
2 45.6	(vocalizes)	2 47.0	I think you're all through coloring.
		2 49.8	Looks like it.
2 52.2	Mmm color.	2 55.0	Mmm.
2 56.0	Mm mmm e . . .		
2 59.8	Color.		

acterized by the goal of maintaining mutuality, which involves minimizing the differences between mother and child in size, authority, knowledge, and experience; and maximizing the child's opportunities to express and pursue his interests. Pair D, by contrast, manifests a style characterized by the goal of maintaining a standard of behavior in the child, which involves, when necessary, stressing the mother's authority and power, emphasizing structure and rules, and being alert to "misbehavior." The child's interests are not consistently supported. In order to specify the particular ways in which each child's expressions of interest and enjoyment are handled, and the various modes of expression for both mothers and children, the first three minutes of the transactions will be described in detail.

Perhaps the first thing to note in comparing the two records is the mother's physical distance from the child. Mother C is seated at a child-size table, on a small chair, across from her child, and within arm's reach throughout the three-minute segment. Mother D, by contrast, has placed her child in a highchair and has seated herself several feet away at the kitchen table, coming in closer on occasion to retrieve a dropped crayon or to arrange paper and crayons for the child. Thus, from the very beginning, the physical arrangements suggest different maternal conceptions of the situation, with the first seen as a joint activity and the second as a child activity with mother nearby.

Next it is important to examine the speech behaviors of each pair. A verbatim record for the three minutes of transaction is presented in Exhibit 1 for pair C and Exhibit 2 for pair D. Pair C is engaged in a reciprocal conversation, characterized by fairly regular turn-taking and by a focus on the present ongoing activity. According to Snow (1976), these characteristics are typical of infant-mother speech for infants of this age. Snow argues that mothers, even long before their children possess adequate linguistic skills, use a conversational model with their young children in which reciprocity is a major goal. She describes several tactics mothers employ to get their children to take their turn in conversation and to keep conversation going, e.g., ceding a turn to the child, accepting any reasonable attempt at a word by the child, following the child's shifts in topics, using questions frequently, filling in for the child when he misses his turn, and repeating or changing her own utterances until they elicit a response. Mother C utilizes most of these tactics, and her child responds by taking his turn appropriately. Only once, in the middle of the segment, when she is trying to get him to do a "pretty picture" and he changes the subject (at 1′ 29.4″, "Bow Bow") does she fail to follow his shift in topic. Even toward the end of the segment, when she clearly wants to end the coloring, she responds to his reference to the truck before suggesting that they put the crayons away.

Pair D, by contrast, shows an inability to achieve this conversational, turn-taking pattern. The mother does not use the interrogative as frequently as Mother C. She imparts information using declarative or imperative grammatical forms, neither of which invites or requires a response from the child. When these utterances are combined with negative content, they are even less likely to invite a response. In the beginning of the segment mother D does invite a response from her child, but she does not persist in trying to obtain a response from him. Indeed her goal does not seem to be to establish reciprocity and conversation, but rather to make sure that he colors properly. Perhaps this is why she goes on to ignore most of his subsequent verbalizations, interpreting them as indications that he is busy coloring. She responds to his sneezes, and to his denotative vocalization (at 1′ 41.6″); but once again the majority of her statements do not invite a response from her child and a reciprocal verbal exchange does not develop.

These different patterns of verbal exchange are important because they provide one channel through which affect is socialized, and one way, in particular, that a child learns to express interest. In working toward a goal of reciprocal conversation, focused primarily on the child and his actions, mother C communicates her interest in the child as well as encourages him to express his interests verbally and to share them with her. To the extent that this conversational reciprocity develops in the context of the child's involvement in a task, he will come to experience his utterances as communications and to feel that both his *experience* of having been engaged and interested in something and his *conversation* about it are important and valued. In such circumstances, a child's capacities to use and sustain his interest, to resist distractions, and to communicate it to others are likely to be enhanced. To the extent that conversational reciprocity does not develop, as with pair D, the child may come to feel that neither his experience of involvement nor his verbal expressions are important or valued; and his capacities to persist and to develop his interests may be diminished. As noted above, however, verbalizations are only one channel through which interest can be experienced and expressed. These mothers and children were also doing things as they talked, and we will now shift to examining their actions and gaze patterns during these two three-minute segments.

Pair C

Pair C begins by discussing what parent and child might do together, in an exchange that lasts about 50 seconds. It is striking how the mother continually involves the child in the decision-making process, seeking out his ideas by asking him questions in response to his requests that she draw, rather than simply deciding for herself and imposing her own ideas. Even when he holds up a doll for her to draw and his intent is obvious, she phrases her response in the form of a question (at 34.8″). We have already discussed how the use of questions encourages a reciprocal conversation, but in this exchange it also involves the child in the decision-making process. Moreover, this mother goes one step further by acting on his suggestions and drawing the things he suggests. The mother is, in effect, purposely toning down the differences between them in authority, knowledge, and experience, and treating her child in both word and deed as a collaborator. And the child is receiving through a variety of channels the message that his own interests, wishes, and ideas are valued.

Near the end of the first minute, pair C engages in a playful discussion of whether the mother is drawing a lady or a man. The mother is amused by the child's idea that it is a man because it has long hair like his own. She smiles and looks at his face, and he begins to engage in playful antics. Her uninterrupted gaze and approving smile last for roughly 20 seconds; and the child responds by continuing his silly antics, e.g., putting the crayon in his hair, banging it on the table, etc. Thus the playfulness is shared by both mother and child, and shared in a nonverbal manner, for the mother does not comment on their mutual enjoyment. The mother decides to end the silliness, and she does so by trying to redirect the child's interest and enjoyment and get him involved in coloring (at 1' 11.8"). In making the transition, she avoids any negative comments intended to stop his playful behavior. Thus, use of redirection at this point can be seen as an attempt to preserve and validate the child's affective state of interest and enjoyment while shifting it to something the mother considers more appropriate. Her efforts succeed in focusing his attention back on the coloring, but the child still wants the mother to do all the coloring.

The mother continues to try to get the child involved in the coloring by structuring their activity, e.g., rearranging the paper and crayons, etc., and then by trying to bargain with him: She will do a picture if he will do one too (1' 16" through 1' 31"). But the child asserts his counterwish that she color and persists in his noncompliance by naming a color and offering the crayon (1' 29.4") to her. Both mother and child repeat their attempts to persuade the other, without success, and a 10-second period follows during which nothing is said. The child handles crayons, and the mother picks one up and uses it. The issue is unresolved. The child then offers her another crayon saying, "Here. This one" (1' 45.4"), thereby reasserting his position. The mother looks at his face briefly as she takes the crayon; then she puts it down forcefully on the table while asking in an irritated tone of voice, "Are you going to do one?" She then sits back in her chair, folds her arms across her chest, looks him in the eye, and says, "You do one." They get into a back-and-forth exchange—"You do it"—"No, you do it"—that continues for 14 seconds. During this period the mother remains with her arms folded in a non-participatory stance and looks directly at the child's face. He, by contrast, seems to avoid looking at her face, as he maintains his part of verbal standoff, and continues to offer crayons. It is the mother who finally gives in, takes the crayon, and begins to color. She then makes a gesture to restore good feelings between them by asking, "Here, what color is this?" The child responds with a small smile of relief, reestablishes eye contact, and then proceeds to name colors and offer her crayons.

This sequence illustrates once again the mother's intention to allow the child scope for his own point of view. She could, at any time, have overridden his refusal to color. She allows herself to become irritated, but that is as far as she goes in exerting negative pressure. And, as she ends the skirmish, she once again refrains from scolding or criticizing the child for his refusal. Nor does she try to articulate for the child the experience they have just shared. The squabble ends without comment and with an effort to reestablish a positive exchange. Thus she maintains mutuality and reciprocity even in the context of a disagreement.

For the next 25 seconds the child continues to name colors, to vocalize, and to make suggestions as he offers his mother more crayons. The mother does not speak during this period (from 2′ 13″ to 2′ 37.8″), but she does share his interest by receiving each crayon and by using it for a brief obligatory moment before setting it down. At this point in the transaction the mother gives up arguing with the child and trying to convince him to color, and by her actions indicates that she will do the coloring. Thus, although she is not much interested in coloring, she upholds her part of the settlement by responding in this reciprocal and obligatory manner. But when the child's interest momentarily shifts to the garbage truck outside (at 2′ 36.2″), the mother first responds to his inquiry, albeit in a perfunctory tone of voice, and only then takes advantage of this interruption to suggest that they put the crayons away and do something else, explaining that she is tired of it and he is not doing it. At the same moment she picks up the crayon box and begins to put the crayons back in. This is another example of the mother's use of structuring comments and actions to redirect the child's interest. This time she succeeds, for a few seconds later the child complies by joining her in putting the crayons away. The three-minute segment ends here; but mother and child proceed to get out the number-sorter, and for the rest of the 10-minute session, he plays with the number-sorter, and other toys, as his mother participates by offering suggestions, encouragements, and praise.

Pair D

Child D begins by expressing his interest in coloring and watching his mother as she arranges the crayons and paper for his use. She responds to his interest with a negative suggestion in the form of a prohibition, "Yeah, and no eating it." This statement seems to interrupt his interest in coloring, and direct it to her negative suggestion. He responds by playfully putting the crayon in his mouth, and she immediately responds with a "No." The child looks away and the mother goes and sits down at the table and begins to read, leaving him to color in his highchair.

A few seconds later, when the child again expresses his interest, his mother initially ignores him, then responds in an irritated tone of voice, and, finally, in a perfunctory tone of voice, structures the situation by urging him to color and reminding him to hold the paper. He complies on both counts. This set of exchanges shows how little it can take sometimes for the mother to support the child's interest. Even the most perfunctory or irritated responses seem to be sufficient. It also illustrates how reciprocity can be obtained by a combination of verbal utterances and actions. Child D tends to respond to his mother's speech with behavior rather than with words. We have already discussed how his mother's speech does not seem designed to elicit verbal responses.

At 41 seconds, the child again invites a response from his mother by looking at her, by making a gesture toward the crayons lying on the table, and by verbalizing his interest. His mother shows no sign of noticing, and this lack of response to his expression of interest creates an uncertain moment for the child, during which he partially retracts his arm and his behavior is temporarily inhibited.

At 48 seconds, the child begins, once again, to handle the crayons and to verbalize and vocalize, and he continues to do so for roughly 30 seconds before he seems to lose some vitality and focus. He stops handling the crayons and sits, staring into space with a blank look, for six seconds; then he recovers from this state, without intervention from his mother, and resumes verbalizing and handling the crayons for another 22 seconds. Throughout this entire 58-second period, the only response the mother makes is to his sneezing; and the child, for his part, no longer seems to try to invite a response from her. He is left to his own resources during this period and is able to sustain his interest for nearly half a minute before there is a lapse.

At about one minute and forty-one seconds the child again invites a response from his mother by emitting an unusual vocalization and by looking at her. Three seconds later she responds with a question, and a look, and when he replies, she responds, at first only with a perfunctory tone and a structuring comment with which he complies. But then she seems to get more involved, and in turn invites a response from the child by offering him more crayons. When he expresses interest in this idea and reaches toward the crayons his mother is now holding, the mother introjects a negative suggestion in the form of a criticism. The mother's criticism in response to her child's positive expression of interest illustrates again how she interrupts his involvement and substitutes a negative suggestion. This leads to the same predictable sequence that occurred at the beginning of the segment. As soon as she places the crayon on the highchair tray, he picks it up and puts it in his mouth, while looking directly at his mother and smiling. She responds immediately with a forceful "No!" and follows this with a warning.

The child loses out in these exchanges. His own expressed interest is interrupted. When he picks up on his mother's negative suggestions, he obtains some momentary mischievous pleasure, not shared by his mother, and then must face her disapproval. How can he pursue his interests and enjoyments and receive any confirmation or support for them? At this point in the transaction, child D shows mild signs of frustration (2' 19"). He begins to color with more force than usual, which results in the paper falling on the floor. The mother's response is ambiguous: mock surprise and a teasing "Oh oh." The child responds with a playful gesture, knocking some crayons onto the floor, smiling, and writing on the tray, but the mother now clearly indicates her disapproval, verbally. Then, as she moves toward the child to retrieve the paper and crayons and rearrange them on the tray, he expresses apprehension by grimacing and retracting his arm.

For the remainder of this three-minute segment, crayons continue to be thrown or knocked off the tray. The mother stops retrieving them, sits back, and says quietly that maybe he is all through coloring; but she takes no action to end the coloring. The child does not comply with this indecisive statement. As the mother remains in her non-participatory posture, the child continues to express interest in the crayons and produces a playful invitation at the end of the three-minute segment that is not shared by his mother. The record ends here, but the mother goes on to say: "That's not funny . . . even though it's fun to do." And so the mother continues to minimally support the child's expressions of interest, to substitute negative suggestions followed by disapproval, to disengage from his playfulness, and to communicate ambiguous and indecisive messages about putting the crayons away. The issue is finally resolved later in the 10-minute session when the mother removes the crayons and the child has a temper tantrum.

SUMMARY OF FINDINGS

The model of affective development set forth earlier, in which three components of the child's affective experience were specified, namely, the triggering stimulus, the affective state per se, and the response to the affect, is pertinent here. It was argued that these components are present in all affective moments, and that whatever the adult response, it provides the child with information regarding all three. It may be helpful to restate the differences in the transactional styles of pair C and pair D in these terms.

Mother C, who was described earlier as pursuing a goal of mutuality with her child, consistently responds in a positive manner to her child's expressions of interest and enjoyment; she produces statements and behaviors that serve to sustain, enlarge, and prolong these affective states. She creates reciprocal conversation using frequent questions, following the child's shifts in topic, etc. She participates in his activities by coloring and by sharing his expressed interest and enjoyment through her words and facial expressions; and she deemphasizes the power differential between them, enabling him to stand his ground in a disagreement. When she wishes to change the focus of his interest and enjoyment, she does so by redirecting his focus through the use of structuring comments and actions, and refraining from negative statements or actions that would dampen or discourage these affective states. She persists in these behaviors even in the face of a disagreement and when her own interest wanes. On the latter occasion, it was noted that while the quality of her response is perfunctory, she nevertheless feels obligated to produce it. All these behaviors serve to enhance her child's capacity to sustain and to enlarge the boundaries of his interest and enjoyment. On two occasions, however, this mother does not make use of another technique of enhancement: She does not articulate the child's experience for him when the affect shared by the two of them is somewhat more intense than usual, e.g., when he is acting silly and when they get into a verbal tug-of-war.

Mother D, by contrast, was described earlier as pursuing the goal of maintaining a standard of behavior. In so doing, she attends primarily to her child's behavioral responses. When she wants to change those behaviors, she expresses disapproval; and when she wants to encourage them, she structures the situation and leaves the child to proceed on his own. She does not encourage a conversational reciprocity, nor does she participate in his activities either by coloring or by sharing his expressions of interest and enjoyment with her own expressions of these affects. Although she attends primarily to the child's behaviors, her responses also affect the child's expressed states of interest and enjoyment. From this point of view, her responses are inconsistent, sometimes supporting those states briefly, sometimes ignoring them, sometimes substituting her own negative suggestions, and sometimes discouraging them directly by criticizing and prohibiting. In such a social context, the child's capacity to sustain and enlarge the scope of his positive affects is not being enhanced. Moreover, he is gradually learning to inhibit his behavior, at least in the presence of his mother, which will further diminish the likelihood of his freely exploring and discovering the environment and developing his skills.

How do these contrasting styles of responding to positive affect relate to the development of self-esteem in these two children? Thus far we have looked at the effect on each child's capacity to sustain and enlarge the scope of his positive affects. This capacity relates directly to how the child gradually builds up skills, information, and experience, or stated differently, how the child develops competence. The dialectical model of Stechler and Kaplan (1980) described earlier in this paper, when applied to the present cases, suggests that mother C always manages to keep the degree of incompatibility confronting her child well within his capacities to resolve. For example, the issues of what would be drawn, when to stop the silliness, and who should do the drawing all represent moments in the transaction when there is a conflict of agenda between the mother and child. These are negotiated successfully, without a break in the child's experience of positive affect, primarily because of the mother's skill in allowing the child a role in the negotiations. Thus we assume that the child in these exchanges experiences himself as competent and effective and that his self structure is thereby strengthened.

Mother D, by contrast, seems to present her child with incompatibilities without allowing him the scope to resolve them successfully, e.g., how the crayons should be used, when to be playful, and how to retain his mother's involvement. The child's solutions to these issues are not accepted, are sometimes ignored, or are overridden. We assume that, in these exchanges, the child experiences himself to be relatively powerless and incompetent, and that his self structure is thereby weakened.

Although the long-term outcome for these two children is not known, there is at least some contemporary evidence to support the claim that the interactional styles of the mothers were affecting their children's capacities to sustain positive affects and to develop competence during the 10-minute observational period. Several measures were used in order to assess these capacities. Two levels of involvement with objects were scored for both children. The highest level was "using" an object, and was defined as using a toy or object appropriately (e.g., spinning a top, stacking a stacking toy, etc.), which presupposes some prior experience with the toy and the prior acquisition of the necessary skills. The next level down was "handling" objects, and was defined as actively manipulating objects, as opposed to holding them passively. During the entire 10-minute period, child C *used* toys for a total of three minutes and forty-one seconds, as compared to twenty-five seconds for child D. The amount of time spent handling toys was more similar for the two children: two minutes and eight seconds for child C, and one minute and fifty-eight seconds for child D. When the total time spent engaged with objects was calculated, once again child C came out higher with nine minutes and fifty seconds, as compared to six minutes and eighteen seconds for child D. The direction of the child's gaze was also analyzed, and the results indicated that although both children spent the majority of their time and produced their longest gazes looking at objects, child C was somewhat more focused and less distractable than child D. And finally, the number of times the child was "victorious" with a toy was calculated. In order to obtain a victory, or non-victory, score, the child had to demonstrate some effort and persistence in trying to perform a task. This measure was an attempt to represent the child's tendency to try things at the limits of his ability and his persistence when things got difficult. These qualities are related to skills needed in school, where children are often required to confront and stay with tasks which they are not initially able to understand or master. Child C produced a ratio of 10:6 victories versus non-victories, while child D produced a ratio of 2:0. The difference in the sheer number of instances is most noteworthy, reflecting both the greater involvement with objects shown by child C and his willingness to try tasks that he had not yet mastered. All of these differences are considerable, and consistently indicate that child C's capacities to pursue his interests and continue to develop his skills are greater than those of child D.

There is also another way in which the two contrasting styles of interaction relate to the development of self-esteem. The three-minute segments involve primarily "we" experiences for the children, although the middle portion of child D's record probably involves an "I" experience as well. In describing the behaviors of pair C, terms such as mutuality, reciprocity, and sharing are often used. It is likely that much of what child C experiences in this particular segment could be encompassed by Stern's notion of mental-state sharing. It was argued earlier that this kind of "we" experience contributes to the child's growing sense of relatedness rather than isolation. Thus an important value of these shared moments, in addition to their role in prolonging and enlarging the scope of the child's positive affects, is their role in providing the experience that one's inner feelings, ideas, and intentions can be understood and shared by another person. Under such circumstances, we assume that the child's capacity for positive self-esteem is enhanced and feelings of isolation are minimized. By contrast, much of what child D experiences can be understood as "we" experiences that do not include a sharing of his mental state. Such occasions, at the very least, are missed opportunities, and are possibly experiences of isolation or emptiness that work against the child's capacity for positive self-esteem.

No direct evidence supports this interpretation of the possible effects of the different "we" experiences of child C and child D, although indirect evidence suggests that these two children differ in the quality of their expressions of positive affect and in the context and form of their distress expressions. We will present this evidence briefly. All of the facial expressions the children produced during the home visits throughout the six-month period of observation and videotaping were analyzed using a variant of Ekman's (1972, 1977) system for coding facial movement.

In comparing the positive expressions, we note the following differences (see Demos [1982a] for a fuller description of these results). Child C produces a variety of smiles, all of which are relaxed and smooth and two-thirds of which are full and intense (i.e., involving a cheek rise and lower eyelid rise). He also shows a versatile use of his eyebrows and mouth as facial signals serving a variety of functions (e.g., raising the brows when asking a question, etc.). By contrast, nearly half of child D's smiles include an element of tension (a clenched jaw) and/or uncertainty (an upper-lip rise). This combination give his smiles a somewhat forced or fake quality, an impression that is enhanced on several occasions by the addition of a forced laugh. This kind of laugh is unique to child D's record and contrasts strikingly to his own spontaneous laughter at other times. He also produces an unusual enjoyment-anger blend. Roughly 80 percent of his smiles involve the lower face only, as opposed to the fuller, more intense smiles of child C. It is not possible to conclude that child D's capacity to experience enjoyment has been impaired, for he is capable of spontaneous, relaxed expressions in certain contexts, e.g., on the playground and when interacting with peers. Yet it must be said that child D is the only child out of 12 in the study whose expressions of enjoyment were so frequently mixed with tension, uncertainty, and anger. At the least, perhaps it is possible to say that many more situations for this child evoked mixed or attenuated enjoyment.

The form and context of their distress expressions differ in the following ways. Child C's distress occurs when his mother is absent and usually involves the full face, e.g., both mouth and brows, but no vocalization. Child D's distress occurs in situations of struggle or "incompatibilities" with his mother, and almost always includes a vocalization, e.g. fussing, whining, or crying, and sometimes efforts to deintensify the vocalization. The difference in contexts is striking and is consistent with the view of these two pairs obtained from the three-minute segments. The absence of vocalizations in child C's record indicates that the distress is probably relatively mild and that the child is successfully modulating it in the presence of the cameramen. The type of vocalization produced by child D, however, seems to suggest a partial inhibition of the vocal expression of distress in the presence of his mother. Again, it is not possible to conclude from these data that this child's capacity to express his distress freely was impaired, but only that the situations that evoked distress for him also required an attenuated expression.

CONCLUSION

This paper attempts to integrate a model of the development of affect—drawn from the work of Silvan Tomkins—with several models of the development of the self—drawn from infant research—in order to explore the variety of ways in which affect relates to the development of self-esteem. Two examples of mother-infant interactive style, drawn from my research, are described in detail to illustrate the importance of the development of positive affects and to explore the possible effects of contrasting styles on the development of self-esteem. Throughout the discussion, statements and conclusions are offered tentatively, and evidence is presented to demonstrate the contemporaneous effects only. The long-run effects are unknown. Indeed, one of the major issues confronting infant researchers is how to begin to conceptualize and study the ways in which children gradually structure their experience and the forms and variety of transformations these constructions undergo during the course of childhood.

REFERENCES

Arnold, M. (1960), *Emotion and Personality*, Vols. 1 and 2. New York: Columbia University Press.
Bowlby, J. (1969), *Attachment and Loss*, Vol. 1. New York: Basic Books.
Darwin, C. (1872), *The Expression of the Emotions in Man and Animals*. Chicago: University of Chicago Press, 1965.

Demos, V. (1982a), Facial expression in young children: A descriptive analysis. In: *Emotion and Early Interaction*, eds. T. Field & A. Fogel. New Jersey: Erlbaum. pp. 127-160.

———— (1982b), The role of affect in early childhood: An exploratory study. In: *Social Interchange in Infancy Affect, Cognition, and Communication* , ed. E. Tronick. Baltimore: University Park Press. pp.79-123.

Ekman, P. (1972), Universal and cultural differences in facial expression of emotion. In: *Nebraska Symposium on Motivation*, Vol. 19, ed. J. R. Cole. Lincoln: University of Nebraska Press, pp. 207–283.

———— (1977), Biological and cultural contributions to body and facial movement. In: *Anthropology of the Body*, ed. J. Blacking. London: Academic Press.

————Friesen, W. (1978), Manual for the *Facial Affect Coding System*. Palo Alto, California: Consulting Pychologist Press.

Izard, C.E. (1971), *The Face of Emotion*. New York: Appleton-Century-Crofts.

Klein, G. S. (1976), *Psychoanalytic Theory: An Exploration of Essentials*. New York: International Universities Press.

Kohut, H. (1971), *The Analysis of the Self*. New York: International Universities Press.

———— (1977), *The Restoration of the Self*. New York: International Universities Press.

Lewis, M. (1980), The socialization of affect. Presented at the workshop "Infant Affective Displays and Physiological Correlates during Normal, Disturbed and Manipulated Social Interactions" of the Mailman Center for Child Development, Miami.

Mussen, P. H., Conger, J. J., & Kagan, J. (1974), *Child Development and Personality*. New York: Harper & Row.

Sander, L. (1980), To begin with—reflections on ontogeny. Presented to the symposium "Reflections on Self Psychology" of the Boston Psychoanalytic Society and Institute, Boston.

Snow, C. E. (1976), The development of conversation between mothers and babies. *J. Child Lang.*, 4:1–22.

Stroufer, L. A. (1979), The ontogenesis of emotion in infancy. In: *Handbook. Infant Development*, ed. J. Osofsky. New York: Wiley.

———— & Wunsch, J. (1972), The development of laughter in the first year of life. *Child Devel.*, 43:1326–1344.

Stechler, G., & Kaplan, S. (1980), The development of the self: A psychoanalytic perspective. *The Psychoanalytic Study of the Child*, 35:85–105.

Stern, D. (1980), The early differentiation of self and other. Presented to the symposium "Reflections on Self Psychology" of the Boston Psychoanalytic Society and Institute, Boston.

Tomkins, S. (1962–1963), *Affect, Imagery, Consciousness*, Vols. 1 & 2. New York: Springer.

————(1968), Affects—primary motives in man. In: Humanities, III, pp. 321–346.

———— (1978), Script theory: Differential magnification of affects. In: *Nebraska Symposium on Motivation*, Vol. 25, ed. J. R. Cole. Lincoln: University of Nebraska Press, pp. 201–236.

———— (1980), Affect as amplification: Some modifications in theory. In: *Emotion: Theory, Research, and Experience,* Vol. 1. New York: Academic Press, pp. 141–164.

———— (1981), The quest for primary motives: Biography and autobiography of an idea. *J. Personal. & Soc. Psychol.,* 41:306–329.

2

Affect and Self-Esteem

STEVEN L. ABLON, M.D.

When a child says, "I feel bad," he may be talking about his self-esteem as well as how he feels. To say "I feel bad," the child has to be able to stand at some distance from himself, observe and verbalize how he feels. After age two, children increasingly develop the capacity first to name and subsequently to describe their feelings (Demos, 1974). By the time a child can do this, his ego has formed in a sophisticated, complex way, sufficient to serve as a basis for judgments about self-esteem.

The statement "I feel bad" also underscores the idea that self-esteem is closely related to an affect state. Affects are indicators of self-esteem and self states—a child does not have a fall in self-esteem without an affect, and feelings about oneself are much more than value judgments. In the case of lowered self-esteem a child might feel pain, anxiety, anguish, helplessness, shame, or humiliation. A child might say he feels bad, rotten, or no good. The nature of affective states that embody self-esteem is poorly understood, and the fundamental adaptive aspects of positively colored affect and self-esteem need to be clarified. This paper does not attempt to explore these questions except in an indirect way. It focuses on how the successful mastery of affect states has a positive effect on self-esteem, and it attempts to outline a way of thinking about how self-esteem and affect mastery are progressively related during a child's development. From this outline we can explore therapeutic implications for the development and maintenance of self-esteem.

DEVELOPMENTAL PERSPECTIVES

Different affective states are present as early as the newborn period (Sander, 1962, 1964; Rexford, Sander, and Shapiro, 1976;

79

Emde, Gaensbauer, and Harmon, 1977), as expressed in tension and relaxation (Piaget and Inhelder, 1969), crying, quiescence, smiling, fearfulness (Emde, Gaensbauer, and Harmon, 1977), pleasure and unpleasure (Freud, 1911). Observers have noted that infants have unique temperaments and ways of expressing affect (Rexford, Sander, and Shapiro, 1976). The recognition, tolerance, and channeling of expression, and the eventual cognitive understanding of feeling states, are ego functions. Beginning at birth, ego development can be measured by how effectively an infant uses behavioral patterns to express his distress, his wishes, and his needs (Brenner, 1974; Basch, 1976); moreover, the recognition of affect in others has important self-preservative and adaptive value for the child (Modell, 1968; Basch, 1976). Spitz (1975) stresses that affective exchanges precede all other psychic functions, adding that pleasure and unpleasure (frustration) are vitally important in stimulating activity and reality testing. Stechler and Carpenter (1967) also emphasize and clarify the adaptive or ego functional aspects of affect. They explore how "emotion arises as part of the adaptive process when there is a major discrepancy between the attempt (wish) to act on a perception and the ability to do so" (p. 173). This adaptive process effectively utilizes inner affective responses even when realities in the outside world cannot be changed. Signal anxiety, frustration tolerance, and impulse control are examples of this process.

Children develop the capacities to acknowledge, tolerate, and put their feelings into perspective progressively, beginning with the dyadic relationship between the infant or small child and his caretakers. As many observers have noted, affect is communicated in a reciprocal exchange between the mother and child, by means of eye contact, the way the child is held, posture, molding, sensory input, and differential responses during play and stress between the mother and the child. Smiling at three months and stranger anxiety at eight months indicate to many observers the increased social meaning of moods and affects (Spitz, 1975; Piaget and Inhelder, 1969; Emde, Gaensbauer, and Harmon, 1977).

The mother's responsiveness and sensitivity to the infant and child's needs and feelings have been conceptualized by Winnicott (1965) in terms of a "holding environment" and by Hartmann (1939) in his concept of an "average expectable environment."

One way self-esteem starts to develop is in the effective reciprocal communication of affect, of feeling between the infant and the important people in his life. When the infant or child's affective messages about what he is feeling are not responded to, he experiences a discordance with the environment that heightens his tension and anxiety. If the anxiety and confusion become unmanageable, they overwhelm his developing ego and undermine the eventual development of a sense of basic confidence and competence (White, 1963) in affective communication with others. There is an interference with the ego's ability to effect reciprocal communication of feelings. The resulting helplessness is an important precursor of a sense of low self-esteem (Bibring, 1953). In older children, unacknowledged feelings are experienced as wrong and denied in favor of trying to follow or support the prevailing feelings of the mother or environment (Spitz, 1975; Winnicott, 1965). (I am referring of course to children under the age of five. After that age, the child begins to evaluate his level of self-esteem in terms of judgments of himself made in relation to his superego or, in adolescence, in relation to his ego ideal.)

If, in the first year of life, the mother confirms and validates the child's feelings, in the second year, she helps the child gain an increased capacity to tolerate his feelings—which leads, in turn, to an increased sense of competence and a more adaptive use of affect—by setting protective, loving, and consistent limits (Coopersmith, 1967; Meyersburg, Ablon, and Kotin, 1974). Limit-setting also gradually helps the child modify his omnipotent strivings, increase his reality orientation, and experience himself as a separate person—crucial steps for the development of self-worth. Mahler (1966) emphasizes the relationship between self-esteem and the gradual modification of the child's omnipotence: "The two pillars of early infantile well-being and self-esteem are the child's belief in his own omnipotence and his belief in the parents' omnipotence of which he partakes; these beliefs can be replaced only gradually by a realistic recognition of, belief in and enjoyment of his individual autonomy and by the development of object constancy" (p. 162). If these omnipotent views persist, they lead to deficiencies in reality testing and to defensive avoidance of affect and impaired mastery of affect.

Omnipotent ideas of restitution or rageful fantasies undermine the capacity to tolerate disappointment and associated painful affects such as sadness and anger. This is seen when the child struggles with distressing situations in which he is or feels helpless. In this regard, Bibring (1953) has emphasized the importance of the ego's awareness of its own helplessness, sadness, and anger. The growth of the ego's capacity for such awareness is impaired when trauma in the child's life is extensive or when the mother does not provide the necessary emotional security; the child cannot tolerate his feelings of helplessness. In these situations active-passive reversals are common (Meyersburg, Ablon, and Kotin, 1974). In order not to feel helpless about the absence of the mother, for example, the child reverses the situation, making the passive painful experience an active one, by viewing himself as having caused the parent to disappear: "You did not leave me, I left you." This bears directly on the psychopathology of perfectionism (Meyersburg, Ablon, and Kotin, 1974; Greenson, 1978), which involves just such problems with affect and self-esteem and just such active-passive reversals. A person who is not loved enough as a child feels bad and deficient. The child then turns his rage at not being loved inward and feels bad about himself all over again, but now in an active way, in response to his own rageful feelings. This, in turn, supports his original view that he is not loved because he is bad and deficient.

At the same time as the parent sets appropriate limits, the "holding environment" confirms and contains such painful affects as anger, sadness, and helplessness. In this way primitive violence and rage are gradually neutralized and the capacity to be sad and to grieve increases. As Zetzel (1970) points out, antedating self-object differentiation, the mother's responsiveness in an intuitive, relatively unambivalent way is essential, for it helps the child gain confidence that his feelings are valid. Subsequently children and adults know that it is possible to feel sad or angry without feeling dysphoric or bad about oneself. Herein lies the difference between sadness and depression. Depression is used to *avoid* sadness, anger, helplessness, or other painful affects. It reflects a *lack* of competence in handling sadness and grief. This lack of competence then contributes to lowered self-esteem in turn. Of course, a person can have lowered self-esteem and not be depressed, since affective issues represent only one aspect of a person's self-esteem. But because competent handling of affect is so important, it is unusual for a person to be depressed and not suffer lowered self-esteem as well. In "Mourning and Melancholia" (1917), Freud describes the relationship between low self-esteem and depression in terms of the superego. But these issues are also present before the internalization of the superego.

During the period of separation-individuation, particularly in the second half of the second year of life, the child is at the height of his struggles about assertiveness, aggressiveness, and autonomy. Conflicts over toilet training take center stage. The mother is involved in helping the child acknowledge and bear his aggressive feelings. When affective communication between the child and the parents has been defective in a substantial way, attempts to control aggression verbally and symbolically are unsuccessful. As a result, defenses such as splitting, projection, passive-active reversals, withholding, and withdrawal are mobilized. These defenses interfere with both self-worth and self object differentiation; the ensuing sense of helplessness and lack of competence weigh on the side of lowered self-esteem, even before the formation of the superego. Later, in the phallic-oedipal period, the inability to acknowledge and tolerate anger becomes one of the superego's reason for judging the child to be "bad;" and the anger itself comes to serve the part of the punitive, self-hostile superego. The developmental failure to gain mastery of a sense of phallic assertiveness also contributes to lowered self-esteem.

CASE 1

Clinical examples illustrative of some of these ideas are necessarily limited by the fact that much of the development of competence in handling affect occurs in preverbal eras. Since the present example comes from psychotherapeutic work with an older child, the dangers of extrapolation and reconstruction must be kept in mind.

The case I will present exemplifies three aspects of relatively successful handling of affect: acknowledging, bearing, and putting feelings into perspective. It describes work with anger, sadness, and the defenses against these affects, and explores the implications for therapeutic interventions and for improved self-esteem.

Katherine was first brought for evaluation when she was almost five years old because of difficulties in several areas. She had repeated nightmares in which an ugly witch put her in jail and would not let her out. Her parents were divorced, and Katherine saw her father for a month in the summer and then infrequently the rest of the year; this arrangement upset her. She often retreated to her blanket, sucked her thumb, and wet her bed at night. She had gained 12 pounds over the past year. Her teachers described Katherine as intelligent and curious but not interested in learning basic word and number skills. She got along with the other children but was sometimes withdrawn and had no close friends. At times Katherine sat by herself, seeming preoccupied, sad, and angry. Katherine's infancy had been stressful. She had had colic until she was six months old; by age three she had experienced significant losses in relationship to her mother and other primary caretakers. At 18 months Katherine entered a day care program, and when she was two-and-a-half, her father moved out of the home. Katherine's mother was depressed and preoccupied about losses in her own family.

Katherine was seen weekly in psychotherapy for one year. During this time Katherine's mother was seen every other week and her father approximately every six weeks. Katherine was at first reluctant to come and to acknowledge her feelings, which she felt were dirty and unacceptable. She was also wary of becoming involved in another relationship with comings and goings that seemed unpredictable to her. During her treatment an effort was made to have Katherine see her father on a regular basis and for her to develop a stable, consistent relationship with both parents. Even when fairly clear arrangements were possible, however, the situation was still confusing to her.

Katherine was a large-boned, stocky, sad, and stolid-looking girl with short brown hair cut in severe, somewhat harsh lines. She was bigger than the average five-year-old and dressed in a neat but drab manner. From the first interview, her sad, controlled style and her rejection of her hungry and aggressive feelings suggested issues of low self-esteem. She externalized her feelings about herself by insisting that coming to therapy made her have bad dreams, feel bad, and feel that nobody liked her: "If I didn't have to come here, I wouldn't have any worries." By the fifth meeting she could begin to acknowledge that maybe she had some feelings that worried her and came in sucking her thumb and carrying a baby doll previously left in the waiting room.

This interview will be described in some detail because it illustrates how Katherine's hungry and angry feelings were expressed in her early sessions. While straightening out the dollhouse furniture, she told about not liking a scary bird in a schoolbook and the bad witch in the *Wizard of Oz*. She played a car game with many accidents; people were injured and had to be rescued. Katherine repetitively and intensively played a superwoman game in which the superwoman rescued a baby who cried, "Help, a robber's after me." Then Katherine said that the robber was dead, that the superwoman left and the baby hid. Katherine found a larger baby doll; giving the baby a bottle, she put it to sleep. Katherine became annoyed that the baby slept too much and kept waking the baby. At this point Katherine said she had a car at home with diamonds but she could not bring it because it would get dirty. She said she was hungry and sadly said that hot dogs are bad for you and that she is not allowed ice cream for lunch. She asked if the therapist's children had a mother. She said she could not see the therapist every week because maybe her mother was moving and she would be with her father. The therapist acknowledged the sadness that the parental divorce caused in Katherine's daily living and how she wished she could be with both parents. The interview touched many of the themes that were discussed subsequently.

During treatment Katherine gradually became more comfortable with opposite feelings such as "angel love" as she cared for the baby doll and "shooting, killing" feelings as she played darts or fighting games. Katherine felt her "shooting, hitting, breaking" feelings made her like a dirty car that could never be washed clean and be part of the car family. She described not only how the car never got clean, but how it had to be kept away from other cars because it would dirty them. The dirty car also got tickets for going through red lights. She put people in the trunk of the car like luggage. In this play Katherine and her therapist came to understand how she felt about being sent from one parent to another like luggage, as if no one wanted her because she was bad and dirty. Her anger made her feel even more bad and unwanted.

Katherine began to understand how her aggressive feelings made her feel bad about herself. This moved her to play games of Geronimo in which she was Geronimo, shouting, snorting, playing "breaking" and "hungry piggy" games. Katherine said sadly that she wanted a big family with a mother, father, brothers, and sisters. She expressed longings for her father to stay with her for 20 years or for her therapist to be her father. At these times she would threaten to shoot the therapist with the darts if he said the interview was over. Katherine's helplessness contributed to her sense of low self-esteem. She felt angry both that she did not have the kind of family she wanted and that she did not live with her father. Feeling guilty about this anger, she once asked her mother to stab her. Her guilt undermined the effectiveness of Katherine's ego and also resulted in lowered self-esteem.

Katherine explored how hungry she was for love and talked about her "piggy" feelings. She played many restaurant games, being the waitress and writing down the therapist's order and her own. Very excited, she would eat fast, making gulping, snorting noises. She talked about where she ate with her father on weekend visits, how hungry she was for him, and how being with him was "home sweet home."

Treatment ended after a year when Katherine's mother found a good position in another city. Katherine was no longer having nightmares or wetting her bed; her schoolwork and friendships were progressing well. Her parents were cooperating so as to make better living arrangements for Katherine; she now saw her father on a regular, predictable basis. Saying goodby to her therapist, Katherine was able to share her anger, disappointment, loneliness, and sadness; themes of her therapy were reviewed again. Katherine now seemed more easily able to acknowledge, tolerate, and put into perspective her angry and sad feelings. Her self-esteem had improved; she looked happier and more confident and was more energetic and effective both at home and at school. Katherine no longer played the dirty car game and no one in her play felt isolated or left out. She spoke happily of her friends at home and those she met visiting her father. She seemed to feel reasonably confident about making new friends although she was anxious about the new school and neighborhood. When the therapist clarified some of her statements about the sadness of moving and not seeing her therapist and her school friends, Katherine sadly added, "That's life, we have to make the best of it." Around the same time, after saying that a woman her father was seeing should be in the zoo, Katherine talked about her aunt who got married. Katherine said she didn't want her aunt to get married, but that it was okay.

About a year after Katherine was last seen, her father came to visit the therapist while in New England on business. He said that Katherine was doing well, had adjusted to her new home and school, and was involved with friends and school activities. Her symptoms had not recurred.

Therapeutic work on affective issues had helped Katherine with her self-esteem in a number of ways. From ages one to three Katherine had had painful losses: Her babysitter had left, her mother had been depressed, preoccupied, and less available to her, and her father had left the home. In therapy, Katherine was helped to acknowledge, bear, and put into perspective her angry and sad feelings about her current relationships with her mother and father. These current feelings reverberated with the unresolved earlier losses, which now could be reviewed in therapy and mastered. At the same time, the therapist began to help Katherine with the defenses she used to avoid these painful feelings, including denial, externalization, displacement, reaction formation, withdrawal, ego regression, and passive-active reversals. At first Katherine's self-esteem seemed related to the value she attributed to her genital and ano-urinary areas, as symbolized by the car she had at home with diamonds that she could not bring because it would get dirty. During treatment Katherine began with regressive concerns about being dirty and being fed, and then progressed to developmentally more age-appropriate oedipal issues which increased Katherine's self-esteem. Concurrently, Katherine's self-esteem improved as she became more comfortable with her "shooting, killing," her "Geronimo," and her "hungry piggy" feelings. She was able to master some of her magical thinking and omnipotent ideas about the danger of these feelings, leaving her free to resolve the active-passive reversals that led her to feel bad and deficient, like a "dirty car" or "luggage." Correcting the active-passive reversals allowed Katherine to feel the anguishing helplessness of her losses. As Katherine increased her capacity to tolerate helplessness and to grieve for the lost "angel love" and "home sweet home," her expectations became more realistic. She could sadly accept her father's potential marriage and the end of her therapy, saying "That's life, we have to make the best of it." As Katherine became more accepting of her own feelings, particularly her anger, she did not turn her rage upon herself. She was less self-critical and judgmental, lessening her sense of being bad and unlovable. Structurally, Katherine's self-esteem benefited from this softening of her super-ego as well as from the expansion of her ego capacities. The growth of her ego in its increasing awareness of affects and greater capacity to tolerate and to communicate affects, and the changes in her defenses, enhanced her self-esteem. At the end of treatment Katherine's defenses included displacement and reaction formation, but also greater neutralization and sublimation in school and with friends. There was also cognitive growth in understanding reality. Of course, the ability of Katherine's parents to provide an increasingly consistent and empathic family situation, despite the unavoidable disruptions, was of crucial importance for Katherine and her therapy.

As Katherine's treatment suggests, we need to consider the developmental issues of affect and self-esteem in our therapeutic work. The ability to acknowledge, tolerate, and put feelings into perspective allows the child to feel a sense of competence in handling and communicating affect. This competence develops in a stage-specific way. The "holding environment," limit-setting, gradual modification of omnipotent fantasies, tolerance for helplessness, and elimination of active-passive reversals and other defenses promote neutralization, sublimation, and self-esteem. In the process of therapeutic work the interconnected developmental stages of affect and self-esteem can be experienced and reworked.

REFERENCES

Basch, M. F. (1976), The concept of affect: A re-examination. *J. Amer. Psychoanal. Assn.*, 24:759–777.
Bibring, E. (1953), The mechanism of depression. In: *Affective Disorders*, ed. P. Greenacre. New York: International Universities Press, pp. 13–48.
Brenner, C. (1974), On the nature and development of affects: A unified theory. *Psychoanal. Quart.*, 43: 532–556.
Coopersmith, S. (1967), *The Antecedents of Self-Esteem*. San Francisco: W. H. Freeman.

Demos, E. V. (1974), *Children's Understanding and Use of Affect Terms*. Unpublished doctoral dissertation, Harvard University.

Emde, R., Gaensbauer, T. J., & Harmon, R. J. (1977), *Emotional Expression in Infancy: A Biobehavioral Study*. [*Psychological Issues*, Monogr. 37.] New York: International Universities Press.

Freud, S. (1911), Formulations on the two principles of mental functioning. *Standard Edition*, 12:213–226. London: Hogarth Press, 1958.

―――― (1917), Mourning and melancholia. *Standard Edition*, 14:237–258. London: Hogarth Press, 1957.

Greenson, R. R. (1978), *Explorations in Psychoanalysis*. New York: International Universities Press.

Hartmann, H. (1939). *Ego Psychology and the Problem of Adaptation*. New York: International Universities Press, 1958.

Mahler, M. (1966), Notes on the Development of Basic Moods: The Depressive Affect. In: *Psychoanalysis: A General Psychology. Essays in Honor of Heinz Hartmann*, ed. R. M. Loewenstein, L. M. Newman, M. Schur, & A. J. Solnit. New York: International Universities Press, pp. 152–168.

Meyersburg, H. A., Ablon, S. L., & Kotin, J. (1974), A reverberating, psychic mechanism in the depressive process. *Psychiatry*, 37:372–386.

Modell, A. H. (1968), *Object Love and Reality*. New York: International Universities Press.

Piaget, J., & Inhelder, B. (1969), *The Psychology of the Child*. New York: Basic Books.

Rexford, E., Sander, L. W., & Shapiro, T. (1976), Introduction. In: *Infant Psychiatry: A New Synthesis*. New Haven: Yale University Press, pp. xv–xix.

Sander, L. W. (1962), Issues in the early mother-child interaction. *J. Amer. Acad. Child Psychiat.*, 1:141–166.

―――― (1964), Adaptive Relationships in Early Mother-Child Interaction. *J. Amer. Acad. Child Psychiat.*, 3:231–264.

Spitz, R. A. (1975), *The First Year of Life*. New York: International Universities Press.

Stechler, G., & Carpenter, G. (1967), A viewpoint on early affective development. In: *The Exceptional Infant*, Vol. 1:163–189, ed. J. Hellmuth. Seattle: Special Child Publications.

Tomkins, S. S. (1962–1963), *Affect, Imagery, Consciousness*, Vols. 1 & 2. New York: Springer.

White, R. (1963), *Ego and Reality in Psychoanalytic Theory*. [*Psychological Issues*, Monogr. 11.] New York: International Universities Press.

Winnicott, D. W. (1948), Reparation in respect of mother's organized defense against Depression. In: *Through Pediatrics to Psychoanalysis*. New York: Basic Books, 1975.

―――― (1965), *The Maturational Process and the Facilitating Environment*. New York: International Universities Press.

Zetzel, E. R. (1970), *The Capacity for Emotional Growth*. New York: International Universities Press.

3

Body Image and Self-Esteem

ALEXANDRA M. HARRISON, M.D.

At each stage of psychological development body image influences self-esteem in stage-specific ways. The term "body image" refers to the mental representation of the body and the complex set of experiences, feelings, and fantasies which revolve around it. The role of the body in psychic development was stressed by Freud (1923), who thought of the early ego as developing around a core of body experience. Schilder (1956) elaborated this idea in his classic book about body image development. Since then many papers have addressed the issue of body image both as a theoretical construct (Dowling, 1977; Lichtenberg, 1978) and in terms of its relation to physical deformity (Tisza, Silverston, and Rosenblum, 1958; Longacre, 1973; Macgregor, 1974; Viederman, 1979). In this paper, case material from the psychotherapies of two five-year-old girls with body defects will demonstrate the effect of each child's defective body image on her developing self-esteem.

A body defect can affect self-esteem directly, by causing negative feedback about appearance, and indirectly, by interfering with the developmental process. Interference with mastery of developmental tasks occurs when the body defect serves as the organizing factor for all the child's feelings of defectiveness. Conflicts about the body defect become intermingled with developmental conflicts about badness or defectiveness. Thus intermingled, the two sets of conflicts present an overwhelming problem to the child, and instead of being resolved, are repressed. The child is deprived of the sense of mastery associated with successful accomplishment of a developmental task and is left with a sense of failure.

I would like to thank Dr. Joseph E. Murray, Chief, Division of Plastic and Maxillofacial Surgery, The Children's Hospital Medical Center, for making it possible for me to work with patients undergoing plastic surgery and for stimulating my thinking about body image and self-esteem.

In a similar way, the continuing development of the whole family is affected by the presence of a child with a body defect. All family members are tempted to project their own feelings of vulnerability and defectiveness onto the "defective" child. These projections distort perception of the child's true strengths and weaknesses. They also interfere with other family members' attempts to deal with their own feelings of defectiveness.

The symbolic power of the body defect derives in part from its association with badness. At a primitive cognitive level an equation is made between good and beautiful, bad and ugly. Literature is full of examples of physical defects as symbols of evil—obvious instances are Shakespeare's Richard III and the Old Testament's Cain, branded with "the mark of Cain." One way of understanding this equation is to postulate a universal aesthetic such as that proposed by Arnheim (1966), in which harmonious interaction between the visual image and the viewer is given a positive value. Discordance in the visual image or in the response of the viewer to the image produces a negative response. Arnheim's theory incorporates another relevant factor—internalization of societal values, such as the negative values a society places on weakness, obesity, or deviations.

Body image development affects self-esteem in normal children as well as in children with body defects. Short stature, mild obesity, even objectively unrecognizable physical problems can become the focus for low self-esteem. Because of the associations between good and beautiful, bad and ugly, even children without objective physical deformities often focus their feelings of badness on some physical attribute. In this way an adolescent struggling with a negative identification with one parent may seek a rhinoplasty as an unconscious way of eradicating the bad parent in them by getting rid of "mother's nose."

We can trace the effect of body image on self-esteem from infancy to the preschool, or oedipal, years. Although little is known about how the infant experiences his body, we can assume that the infant builds his body image from his growing awareness of his body and from the ways the parents reflect back to him their feelings about his body. The literature includes discussions of how parents of a defective child find it difficult to deal with the normal ambivalence which parents have toward their infants

(Anthony, 1968); it is probable that parents consciously or unconsciously communicate their feelings about a defective body part through their handling of the infant's body and their remarks about it.

Recent papers concerned with gender identity development (Galenson and Roiphe, 1976; Kleeman, 1976) pay particular attention to the second half of the second year of life as a time when three important developmental processes converge: an increasing interest in the genitals, a growth in cognition permitting labeling and classification, and a critical stage of separation-individuation. At this stage—Mahler's (Mahler, Pine, and Bergman, 1975) practicing and rapprochement subphases of separation-individuation—the child is particularly sensitive to loss of the mother and may displace this fear of loss to part of his or her body. Some observers describe a mourning reaction in little girls who associate their feelings of greater separateness from, or loss of the mother, with their lack of a penis (Galenson and Roiphe, 1976). Depression may result if earlier experiences of loss or deprivation have complicated the girl's separation from her mother (Galenson and Roiphe, 1976). At this stage in development, a body defect, especially involving loss of a body part, is often used as an organizing factor for feelings of narcissistic injury. The fantasy themes characteristic of the age, such as loss of precious body products or parts, and the concurrent appearance of explosive rage give symbolic representation to these feelings.

As development proceeds, the child moves through a stage in which he seeks to gain approval by exhibiting his body. Kohut's (1971) notion of the grandiose self is particularly relevant to this stage of body image development. According to this theory, age-appropriate "mirroring responses" from the parents are required for the integration of the grandiose self, a primary narcissistic structure, into the growing psyche. A body defect may interfere with the mirroring process and thereby constitute a trauma to the developing self.

The penis has particular narcissistic importance during this stage. The body defect may be displaced and experienced as a defective genital. In the girl, the sense of narcissistic injury from a body defect—or from any other source—may be understood symbolically as the lack of a penis. She envies her father and brother for having what she does not have. Envy of her mother for possessing other things she wishes for, such as a husband and baby, further lowers her self-esteem.

Proceeding into the oedipal phase, the little girl who is burdened by incompletely resolved conflicts from earlier stages is at a serious disadvantage. Her exaggerated envy and feelings of defectiveness, both testimony to earlier developmental conflicts, interfere with her ability to make a positive identification with her mother. Deprived of the usual means of resolving the oedipal conflict and missing the chance to consolidate her sexual identity, the little girl may be left with major problems in self-esteem development.

CASE 1

For Sarah, born with an extra thumb, issues of self-esteem were expressed in the theme of specialness. Her parents dealt with their feelings about her congenital deformity by treating it as "special." Her mother told Sarah that "when she came around, God thought she was extra special, so He gave her something extra." Sarah did think of herself as special: She insisted on dressing in ruffled dresses and ribbons, she loved to put on dances for her father and other admiring adults, and when Sarah drew pictures she paid little regard to the natural colors of the objects in the pictures, preferring to be "different" even in her choice of colors. Although she got along well with neighborhood children, she had a tendency to be bossy. With her mother, a warm and sensitive woman, she had a basically good relationship. But in the year before her hospitalization for a fifth surgical procedure on her hands, there had been increasing antagonism between mother and daughter.

A few weeks before this hospitalization, Sarah was brought for psychiatric consultation to prepare her for the surgery. Sarah's mother had been with her during the previous hospitalizations, all of which had gone well, except the fourth, shortly after the birth of Sarah's sister, when Sarah was three years old. During this pregnancy Sarah's mother had learned that Sarah's deformity was inherited and that a second child might have the same problem; she was anxious and depressed. Things had gone well, however, and Sarah's parents were relieved to have a "perfect baby." Although she had a new baby, Sarah's mother was with Sarah during most of her fourth hospitalization. Still, this admission had been painful for both mother and daughter, since Sarah was fearful and clung to her mother whenever she left.

The therapist tried to prepare Sarah for the upcoming hospitalization to remove the extra thumb. In the first interview Sarah proudly drew a picture of a "flower," a circle with many lumpy projections around the circumference which looked more like a primitive hand with lots of fingers. She then became anxious and drew more and more "flowers," covering both sides of the paper. Themes of anxiety about the hospitalization itself, with its separations, and also fears and excitement about what the God-like doctors were going to do to her in the operating room emerged. One fantasy was that something important would be taken away from her; she spoke of a doll she had lost during a previous hospitalization.

The therapist was present when Sarah's dressings were first removed after the surgery. Sarah was surprised and sad when she saw that her extra thumb was gone. After the surgery Sarah changed in her play with the other children on the ward, suddenly losing friends because she could not bring herself to share her toys with them. She was conflicted between her desire to keep friends and her need to keep all the toys for herself. She also became bossier. Her mother noticed that Sarah seemed sad, referring to herself as "ugly" or "dumb," and she requested follow-up visits with the psychiatrist after discharge. In these sessions Sarah was very controlling. At the beginning of each, she suggested that she and the therapist divide all the toys evenly, but then she would ask the therapist to return what she considered the "pretty" toys one by one until the therapist had only the pigs and the black and brown Magic Markers. Sarah, acknowledging with embarrassment the therapist's remark about her feeling that she "needed all the pretty things," said that she had lost something in the operating room—her doll. In a previous surgery Sarah had taken a favorite doll, a transitional object, into the operating room with her, and the doll had been lost in transit. The therapist thought that the doll symbolically represented to Sarah the lost thumb and the loss of her mother in separation. It might also represent the loss of Sarah's "specialness," that quality which exempted Sarah from the limitations tolerated by ordinary people.

During these sessions there was also play in which a little boy doll kept trying unsuccessfully to get the other children to play with him. The other children finally sent him away with a remark like, "Go play with the pigs!" Sarah appeared not to know why the little boy was reprehensible, saying only that he was "ugly" and a "jerk." When the boy turned into a robber wanting to steal jewels from the little girls, Sarah explained that the other children didn't want to play with him because he was "bad." The therapist thought that Sarah had reversed the real wish of the little girl to steal the boy's jewels. She told Sarah that the little boy might feel like stealing things if he felt he didn't have what he needed to feel good. Following this intervention Sarah stopped calling herself "ugly" and "dumb." Sarah was making a connection between the sense of defectiveness she felt after her surgery and her own "bad"—unacceptable—robber fantasies and impulses. A connecting fantasy might have been that the removal of her special thumb was a punishment for her greedy wishes for someone else's possessions—her mother's baby, her father's penis.

In school Sarah was confronted with other children's reaction to her deformed hand and also with the anatomical difference between the sexes. She did well in her kindergarten work, and got along well with teachers and peers. She brought home pictures in which the grass was colored green and the skies blue. Another period of therapy began in the middle of the school year because of phobic symptoms and a compulsive kind of sexual exploration with a boy cousin. She also began to have trouble with her playmates again, was extremely provocative to her mother, and talked about hating herself. Her phobic fears included fears of being kidnapped by strange men and being taken away from her mother. In therapy the theme of separation from her mother was again linked to the loss of a body part, first of a tooth (a recent event), then to the loss of her thumb, and finally to her concern about the sexual differences. The theme of specialness was symbolized by a glorious Tooth Fairy, whom Sarah colored with all the colors of the rainbow and decorated with many projecting feathers. This seemed to express a wish that the Fairy (perhaps the therapist herself) would restore to Sarah the lost tooth, thumb, penis, i.e., her specialness. Sarah elaborated the fantasy of being punished for her competitive wishes toward her mother (and her competitive wishes toward men) by her mother or by the doctor who had deprived her of her specialness. The therapist interpreted this fantasy to Sarah. The specialness of an extra thumb was clarified as coming from the imagination of Sarah and her parents. After all, a thumb is just a thumb. The sadness had to do with finding out that something special in her imagination was not real. The real satisfactions in Sarah's life were her accomplishments at school, her good relationships with her family, and the adult satisfactions she had to look forward to. As Sarah integrated this, her phobic symptoms disappeared, as did her driven sexual exploration. Sarah's mother reported that she was happier and seemed to have recovered her self-confidence.

CASE 2

For Mary, who had lost the tip of a finger in an accident, the issues of self-esteem were again focused on competition. Competing with her mother for the attention of her stepfather and with her stepmother and stepsister for the attention of her father, Mary felt doomed to lose in both competitions. She explained this to herself in terms of her body defect and the associated fantasies of defectiveness, or badness.

Mary's mother brought her for psychiatric consultation when Mary stopped complaining about the split-custody child-care arrangement. The mother interpreted Mary's change as a sign that something was interfering with the usually good communication between mother and daughter. Indeed, as the evaluation proceeded, Mary grew openly antagonistic toward her mother. At the same time, Mary had lost what her mother called her good self-esteem.

Mary's parents had been divorced when she was two years old. Since then she had lived half the week with her father and half with her mother, who had become depressed during the separation and divorce. At the same age Mary had had a door slammed on her finger, causing an avulsion of the tip. Surgery to reimplant the tip had been unsuccessful. Both parents remarried within three years of the divorce, and at the time of the consultation, the mother and her husband were buying a house and were considering having a child of their own, although this was not openly discussed.

In the first hour Mary drew a picture of her family, separating her mother and stepfather in one compartment of the page from her father, stepmother, and stepsister in another. When asked where she belonged in the family, she became anxious and stopped drawing. At the end of the session, Mary made a monster steal a little girl doll out of her bed (with excited giggles), after which the girl doll went to bed with the mother doll. Thus, in the first hour Mary let the therapist know that the move by her mother and stepfather to establish their own family jeopardized Mary's sense of her position in the family and put a heavier burden on Mary's oedipal conflict with her mother. Mary retreated from the oedipal to a regressive position.

In the second hour Mary drew a "beautiful princess" with a multicolored dress and sparkles. Giggling, Mary referred to the King: "That's her father, and You Know Who's husband . . . the Queen's!" Reacting to an unspoken fantasy, Mary suddenly became anxious and scribbled over the princess's dress with black crayon. She made "dirt marks" on her face and scribbled her hair, saying, "This isn't a princess. It's really only a maid. . . . It's a 'step-maid.' " With sadness, Mary removed the princess from the competition by rendering her the lowest of the low, a "step-maid."

In subsequent hours Mary developed the theme of babies who had "something wrong" with them. Mary, playing the doctor, performed operations in which various objects were removed from the dolls' stomachs—a penny, a pearl, a doll. Mary was confused about whether the search was to find and remove a pathogenic object, or to find and replace a lost object. In the fourth hour an associated theme of something having been stolen from *her* was introduced, and Mary complained of a pain in her own stomach. The therapist, who was in the early stages of pregnancy, had not mentioned her condition to Mary. After Mary's comment about her stomach ache, the therapist asked Mary if she had thoughts about the therapist's stomach, to which Mary replied, "Well, you told me you were going to have a baby!" This, of course, was not the case.

Mary had made a connection between her own "bad" oedipal wishes and impulses and something bad and defective about herself, which she in turn related to her missing fingertip. Mary's oedipal conflict, however, was played out against a background of unresolved conflicts from earlier stages of development. Her conflicts about her injury had become mixed up with the conflicts she had had with her mother when she was a two-year-old, when the injury occurred. Her struggles for autonomy were associated with the anal fantasies of having something precious inside which the mother might take away from her; she also had fantasies of being full of destructive anger, capable of killing her mother if it got out of control.

Mary's oedipal conflict had been further complicated by her having a stepfather, stepmother, and stepsister. When her mother and her husband talked about having a baby of their own, Mary saw her mother winning the competition and also displacing her from the family. In the negative oedipal position, Mary felt that she had lost the rivalry with her stepfather for her mother's love. Mary's sensitivity to the therapist's pregnancy showed the intensity of her "have-not" feelings of low self-esteem organized around the missing tip of her finger. For her, the finger represented not only the loss of a body part but also the loss of a fantasied penis-baby-feces.

The therapist helped Mary separate these confused conflicts by interpreting her fantasy of what might have happened during the operation she had had when she was two. The therapist clarified the reality that nothing—neither a baby nor a penis—was taken away during the operation, that the real loss was the tip of her finger in the accident. Although Mary cared about the fingertip because that was part of her, it was only the tip of her finger; Mary had all she needed to get what she wanted out of life.

Following these interpretations, Mary came in with a new attitude of self-assurance. She suggested designing a board game on a large piece of paper. Unlike the earlier play, when anxiety stopped the activity at numerous points in the hour, Mary remained engrossed in constructing and playing the game. The board game involved a journey from "Home" to another safe place, the "End." In between were many dangers, including varied and exciting monsters. Mary, bright with confidence, invented ingenious ways to avoid these pitfalls and in playing with the therapist competed successfully. This game seemed to symbolize the progress of Mary's development: The increase in her self-esteem during this final hour was striking.

DISCUSSION

It is important to note that both these children had basically good relationships with loving, "good enough" parents, and that both had impressive strengths. Each was a first child and greatly appreciated by her family, and each was unusually bright and attractive. For neither was the body defect severely disfiguring nor did it significantly impair their functioning.

For Sarah, the theme of narcissistic injury had begun at birth when her parents felt the narcissistic loss associated with a defective child (Niederland, 1965; Anthony, 1968). They defended against their painful feelings with a kind of reaction formation, calling her extra thumb "special." Their unconscious negative feelings about the defect, such as their anger and disappointment at their imperfect child, were expressed in the exaggerated sense of her specialness they communicated to her, in their overprotectiveness, and in their difficulty setting limits. Because of the strengths of both Sarah and her parents, the symptoms Sarah had in early development—her need to feel special and her difficulty in separating from her mother—were mild.

Numerous surgical consultations about her hands before the age of two must have reinforced both in her parents and in Sarah feelings of her specialness and, at the same time, her underlying vulnerability, contributing to the difficulty of each stage of separation-individuation. These circumstances were influential in the preoedipal phallic phase, a time when the child is particularly sensitive to loss of either the object or a body part, losses which are confused with each other in the child's mind. At age two, when Sarah was still struggling with these issues, two potentially traumatic events occurred: surgery on her hands and the difficult pregnancy of her mother, followed by the birth of her sister. Sarah, whose developmentally appropriate concerns about defectiveness and feelings of vulnerability were compounded by the circumstances described above, used denial as well as reaction formation to protect herself from her painful feelings. She confused her extra thumb with a fantasied penis-baby and imagined that she was special enough to have everything. She thus avoided the normal working through of the feelings associated with genital differences and carried the conflicts into her oedipal period. This complicated her oedipal competition with her mother. Sarah imagined that for anyone as special as she, anything was possible—a conviction that significantly threatened her relationship with her mother. Feelings of omnipotence led her to believe she could win the competition with her mother for her father. Yet this heightened her already exaggerated fear of losing her mother. The same conflicts stood in the way of her making a positive identification with her mother: She was too special (had everything) yet secretly suspected she was defective (had nothing). The result was symptom formation. She developed phobic symptoms and nightmares of being stolen by kidnappers, at once representing the wish to run away with exciting, dangerous men, and the fear of doing so. This led to a regressive clinging to her mother.

When her extra thumb was removed in surgery, she felt her specialness had been taken away, as indeed it had in concrete terms. Now she felt she really could not compete and felt deprived and acutely depressed. The therapist interpreted to Sarah the confusion between the conflicts about her body defect and her other fantasies. She clarified her oedipal conflicts and also the conflict experienced by children who are born with a body defect. Sarah's improvement after this treatment allowed her to get back on the course of her development and achieve the sense of mastery associated with accomplishing developmental tasks successfully. The result was improved self-esteem.

For Mary, the marital discord and unhappiness of her parents in her second year, followed by their separation and divorce, resulted in object loss during a critical stage of separation-individuation. During the same period she sustained an injury, losing part of her body. Mary experienced narcissistic injury and in the vocabulary of the preoedipal phallic period felt she was lacking fingertip-penis-baby (Niederland, 1965; Galenson and Roiphe, 1976). Conflicts about body image were thus fused with preoedipal conflicts related to separation and narcissistic issues of gender identity. These intermingled conflicts were repressed, preventing resolution. Mary, because of her strengths and those of her parents, was not symptomatic. Still, she entered the oedipal stage vulnerable to loss and feeling herself a defective "step-maid."

When her mother's second marriage was consolidated and the couple was househunting and talking about having a child, Mary felt like a "have-not" who could never compete with her mother. Her "have-not" feelings were organized around the missing tip of her finger, which also represented the fantasied penis-baby. Mary felt helplessly angry at her mother, whom she blamed for her state of defectiveness and whom she envied. Complicated in this way, Mary's oedipal conflict was inaccessible to successful resolution by identification with her mother, even with the help from her now quite available parents.

After therapy, Mary felt less in a "have-not" position and was able to improve her relationship with her mother and to begin moving on with her development. She felt a surge of optimism about herself and her future in the last hour. Mary's ability to sort out the conflict about body image from her oedipal conflict allowed her to move towards resolving both sets of conflicts and resulted in increased self-esteem.

CONCLUSION

Both the cases I have presented illustrate the confusion of conflicts about body image with stage-specific, and in these cases, oedipal, developmental conflicts. This confusion may occur at any stage of development and can interfere with good self-esteem by preventing the resolution of both the body image conflict and the stage-specific conflict. Such confusion can also occur in children without objective physical defects. In these cases the child will focus on a physical attribute as the organizing factor for feelings of defectiveness. The physical attribute may be body size, such as height or weight, or a body part. The frequent requests for plastic surgery to change a body part and the common resort to drastic diets represent attempts to improve self-esteem by making a change in the body. Although a superficial approach to feelings about a physical deformity can be disastrous, concrete changes can sometimes initiate a process of intrapsychic change. This change can be better understood if we appreciate the significance of the body image as an organizing factor for feelings of defectiveness.

REFERENCES

Anthony, E. J. (1968), The child's discovery of his body. *Physical Therapy*, 48:1103–1114.

Arnheim, R. (1966), *Toward a Psychology of Art*. Berkeley: University of California Press.
Dowling, S. (1977), Seven infants with esophageal atresia: A developmental study. *The Psychoanalytic Study of the Child*, 32:215–256. New Haven: Yale University Press.
Freud, S. (1923), The ego and the id. *Standard Edition*, 19:12–66. London: Hogarth Press, 1961.
Galenson, E., & Roiphe, H. (1976), Some suggested revisions concerning early female development. *J. Amer. Psychoanal. Assn.*, 24(Suppl.):29–59.
Kleeman, J. (1976), Freud's views on early female sexuality in the light of direct child observation. *J. Amer. Psychoanal. Assn.*, 24(Suppl.):3–29.
Kohut, H. (1971), *The Analysis of the Self*. New York: International Universities Press.
Lichtenberg, J. (1978), The testing of reality from the standpoint of the body self. *J. Amer. Psychoanal. Assn.*, 26:357–385.
Longacre, J. J. (1973), *Rehabilitation of the Facially Disfigured*. Springfield, Ill.: Charles C Thomas.
Macgregor, F. C. (1974), *Transformation and Identity: The Face and Plastic Surgery*. New York: Quadrangle/The New York Times Book Co.
Mahler, M., Pine, F., & Bergman, A. (1975), *The Psychological Birth of the Human Infant*. New York: Basic Books.
Niederland, W. (1965), Narcissistic ego impairment in patients with early physical malformation. *The Psychoanalytic Study of the Child*, 20:518–534. New York: International Universities Press.
Schilder, P. (1956), *The Image and Appearance of the Human Body*. New York: International Universities Press.
Tisza, V., Silverston, B., & Rosenblum, O. (1958), Psychiatric observations of children with cleft palate. *Amer. J. Orthospychiat.*, 28:416–423.
Viederman, M. (1979), Monica: A 25-year longitudinal study of the consequences of trauma in infancy. *J. Amer. Psychoanal. Assn.*, 27:107–126.

4

Self-Esteem as Related to Bodily Change in

Children With Craniofacial Deformity

MYRON L. BELFER, M.D.

The presence of a craniofacial deformity may have a significant adverse impact on the development of self-esteem. Craniofacial surgery now permits rapid, major change to take place in the physical appearance of children with craniofacial deformity (Murray, 1975; Converse, Wood-Smith, McCarthy et al 1974; Edgerton, Jane, Berry, et al 1975; Belfer, Harrison, and Murray 1979). The question then arises as to whether corresponding changes in body image and self-esteem take place paralleling the change in physical appearance. It is now possible to study the process of change and understand the linkage of self-esteem to alterations in actual body physiognomy and body image.

A change in body image resulting from surgical procedures is a complicated process occurring over a period of time and is influenced by the psychological development of the child, the nature of the surgical procedure, and societal and familial factors. In addition to manifest physical change, a corresponding adjustment in the child's perception of his body image, as well as an adjustment in the perceptions of parents, teachers, and peers, must occur to allow the child to internalize the physical change gradually. It is postulated here that self-esteem depends on just such an internalization of a positive alteration in body image.

The concept of body image in children (Schilder, 1950; Gellert, 1962; Anthony, 1968; Bahnson, 1969; Clifford, 1972) is intimately related to the concept of self-esteem. As Harrison notes (see Chap-

The author is indebted to Joseph E. Murray, M.D., Chief, Division of Plastic and Maxillofacial Surgery for the opportunity to work in the Craniofacial Clinic at The Children's Hospital Medical Center. Aspects of this paper have been presented elsewhere in collaboration with Alexandra M. Harrison, M.D., and Francine C. Pillemer, Ed.D.
103

ter 3), the equation between bad and ugly, good and beautiful may represent an inherent aesthetic, and may be present as early as infancy, consisting of an internalized image of the human body against which comparisons are made. Suggestive evidence for this hypothesis can be found in a study conducted by Kagan, Henker, Hen-Tov, Levine, and Lewis (1966) in which an image of a distorted human face evoked a negative response from infants. These observations have significant implications for the child with a craniofacial deformity who, from the outset, presents to the world a distortion that almost universally evokes a negative or altered response from individuals. Thus the defect in self-esteem may extend from the child's earliest interactions with his parents and may become entrenched in his developing ego. If this is the case, then what is the potential for improvement of self-esteem if physical appearance is altered in congenitally deformed children?

A MODEL OF BODY IMAGE DEVELOPMENT

A model of the process of body image development, and of its linkage to self-esteem, should address four factors: (1) cognitive functioning, (2) perception of body stimuli, (3) stimuli from the environment in the form of comparison with others, and (4) responses from others (Belfer, Harrison, and Murray, 1979).

Cognitive Growth

The level of the child's cognitive functioning influences his perception of his body and defines the limits of body image development (Goodenough, 1926; Piaget, 1929; Shapiro and Stine, 1965; Katz and Zigler, 1967). Children with low intellectual potential may be limited in their perceptions of their bodies, and younger children perceive their bodies in ways different from older children partly because of their immature cognition (Gellert, 1962).

Several studies, moreover, have demonstrated that society tends to underestimate the intelligence of physically (especially facially) disfigured people (Cook, 1939). Post (cited in Macgregor, Abel, and Bryt, 1953) showed photographs of disfigured adults to 60 normal subjects who were asked to describe the individual in the picture. The most common characteristics mentioned were mental deficiency, physical disease, and immorality. Wright (1969) notes that the phenomenon occurs with respect to self-perceptions as well. Cohen and Yasuna (1978) show that facially disfigured youngsters' fears that they were mentally retarded stemmed in part from concerns about their facial structures. It is not unlikely that children with facial disfigurement internalize a sense of impaired cognitive ability which may in fact inhibit normal cognitive development and appropriate body image development in turn. At the same time, the sense of cognitive impairment may have a direct negative impact on developing self-esteem.

Perception of Body Stimuli

Normal children gain an appreciation of their own bodies and their environment from often delicate sensory input, and a sense of mastery from an increasing sense of competence in their manipulative functions, whether of the hands, feet, tongue, or other bodily parts. Deficits in perception and functioning may lead to a sense of bodily incompetence, e.g., the child with syndactyly who fails to gain tactile satisfaction due to the absence of fine manipulative ability, or the child with a cleft palate who has impaired oral perception and difficulty with nasal secretions (Tisza, Silverstone, Rosenblum, and Hanlon, 1958). The lack of a sense of mastery and competence, and the inability to appreciate subtle nuances of stimuli, deprive the child with a congenital anomaly of the sense of bodily wholeness and satisfaction that other children obtain. This sense, and indeed mastery and competence in general, are essential components of positive self-esteem.

The negative effects of craniofacial disfigurement on social interaction, by means of which the child receives most of his sensory input, may be most strongly felt in the child's encounters with his parents. Bowlby's (1951, 1969) theory of social attachment emphasizes the importance of the mother-infant interaction as a developmental determinant. Bowlby suggests that the infant emits biologically programmed responses that "trigger" nurturant behaviors on the part of the mother. Two important elicitors of maternal behaviors are smiling and vocalization. Children with craniofacial disfigurements are not only unattractive, their disfigurement may also interfere with their ability to elicit parental nurturance. A structural abnormality around the mouth, for example, could interfere with recognizable smile responses or vocalization. Some infants have high-arched or cleft palates and experience difficulty sucking or feeding. Deformities around the eye region may inhibit visual tracking and scanning; hearing functions may be impaired. While there are no direct observational studies of parents interacting with these children, the infant's ability to interact successfully with the parent appears to be impeded by craniofacial disfigurement. And positive feedback from parents is an essential component of developing self-esteem.

Stimuli from the Environment in the Form of Comparison with Others

As the infant develops, he is influenced by factors in the environment that he gradually recognizes as being outside his own body. As he begins to compare his body with those of his parents, and eventually with those of his peers, he becomes aware of similarities and differences (Kagan et al., 1966; Katz and Zigler, 1967). The child with a congenital deformity will confront this growing sense of difference as his cognition develops and his sense of awareness increases. How the child responds to this confrontation will depend not only on the objective qualities of the deformity but also on the interaction of the child with the people in his environment (Goffman, 1963).

Responses from Others

Parental appreciation of a child as having positive bodily attributes allows the child to appreciate himself and his body, and thus serves as a basis for self-esteem. Failure of this process may lead to the development of pathological psychological defenses. Very early in the disfigured child's development, his parents' attitudes and feelings about his deformity will influence his ability to cope with it.

Parental response to the birth of a defective child is of particular importance for the facially disfigured infant. Clifford (1974, 1979) compared mothers of normal and/or other disabled children on a measure designed to elicit recall of reaction to their children's births. Mothers of craniofacially disfigured children reported significantly greater negative emotions than other groups, including less parental pride in their children and more negative attitudes toward caretaking responsibilities. It is important to note that these mothers were interviewed prior to plastic surgery, a time when one would expect them to have heightened expectations for the child. These responses may indicate the lasting impact of the child's birth on the parent. The degree to which the parent's perception of the facially deformed child is fixed may limit the degree of positive change the child experiences, no matter how successful the surgery.

Other investigators have discussed parental reactions to the general category of "birth defective" children. Solnit and Stark (1961) report that parents actually experience a period of mourning following the birth of an "imperfect" child. Not having the child that was expected or wished for, the mother is faced with the overwhelming task of adapting to the demands of the defective child while working through the loss. How this grief is handled partially determines subsequent parental (particularly maternal) investment in the child. Again, investment in the child is essential for the development of self-esteem.

Greenberg (1979) views early parental reactions in the context of the negative narcissistic symbiosis (originally described by Lax [1971]) in which the disfigured infant represents in the mother's unconscious her impaired sense of self. Of particular importance for the population under discussion is that the mothers who experienced the most severe sense of narcissistic injury were those whose children had defects which interfered with feeding, eye contact, or smiling.

Richardson, Goodman, Hastorf, and Dornbusch (1961) investigated children's reactions to the presence of a physical disability in handicapped and non-handicapped children. Both the disabled and non-disabled children consistently preferred the non-disabled child. The child with a slight facial disfigurement was ranked as the next to least preferred. The results suggest that facial involvement is critical in the appraisal of another individual and that increased liking is shown for the child whose disability is more distant from the face.

Dion (1973) found that pre-schoolers three and a half years of age reliably discriminated facial photographs of unfamiliar peers based on attractiveness. Further, when asked about friendship choice on the photographs, these children showed a significant preference for better-looking children and a dislike for unattractive children; their stereotypes were consistent with adult attitudes. Attractive children were judged to behave more prosocially while unattractive children were judged to exhibit more antisocial behaviors. Similar findings involving the effects of attractiveness have been demonstrated with fifth-graders (Cavior and Dokecki, 1970), adolescents (Lerner and Lerner, 1977), in camp settings (Kleck, Richardson, and Ronald, 1974), and cross-culturally (Cavior and Dokecki, 1970).

Clifford and Walster (1973) studied the effects of attractiveness on teachers' expectations of pupil performance. The same report card was distributed to a large group of teachers with varying photographs of children attached. The attractive child was rated significantly higher on intelligence, educational attainment, educational potential, and social potential. Barocas and Black (1974), reviewing referrals for "remedial" versus "control" problems, speculate that attractive children were more likely to receive teachers' attention and help. Similarly, a number of other studies demonstrate that attractiveness influences the frequency of interaction between teacher and student (Adams and Cohen, 1974), teachers' judgments of students' intellectual and social competence (Lerner and Lerner, 1977), and teachers' willingness to incorporate children of marginal intelligence into their classrooms (Ross and Salvia, 1975). Teachers' negative expectations for unattractive children may have important consequences. The effects of teacher expectations on student performance is well documented (Rosenthal and Jacobson, 1968). It may be that teachers' negative expectations for these children actually help to "produce" the expected intellectual and social deficits.

Concern about physical attractiveness begins early in the life of a child. Dion and Berscheid's (1974) research demonstrates that unattractive children have less peer involvement than attractive children. Other studies (Waldorp and Halverson, 1971; Quinn and Rapoport, 1974; Rapoport and Quinn, 1975) indicate that the more minor physical differences young children have, the more aggressive, impulsive, or withdrawn behaviors they display, the less peer interaction they show, and the more negatively they are judged by their peers.

The physically disabled child is confronted with a number of adverse effects of his deformity, including body image distortion and lowered self-esteem, and negative perceptions by parents, peers, and teachers. Such adverse effects suggest that the child born with physical disfigurement, particularly with craniofacial deformity, is likely to suffer from cumulative assaults on his psychosocial development.

EVOLUTION OF BODY IMAGE FOLLOWING
RECONSTRUCTIVE SURGERY

Study Population

Research on children seen through the Craniofacial and Plastic Surgery Clinics at The Children's Hospital Medical Center in Boston suggests that congenitally deformed children undergoing major reconstructive surgery experience modification of their body images only gradually, in a process associated with four distinct phases: (1) the decision to undergo surgery, (2) the experience of the surgery, (3) the immediate postoperative period, and (4) a reintegration phase (Belfer, Harrison, and Murray, 1979).

The study population consisted of children with major congenital facial deformities such as Apert's, Crouzon's, Treacher Collins, and hemifacial microsomia and children with lesser lesions such as hemangiomas, nevi, and lop ears. The children were seen pre- and postoperatively and ranged in age from infancy through 25 years. Patients seen initially by the author have been followed for periods as long as seven years. Patients seen initially by others have been followed for as long as 12 years postoperatively.

Results

Adjustment to the Deformity Preoperatively

Those children with more severe deformities tended preoperatively to use massive denial to defend themselves against the painful influence of the deformity. Children with less severe objective deformities still used denial, but revealed a more pronounced unconscious sense of "badness" (as reflected in fears of their own willfulness or anger) or neediness (i.e., defectiveness equated with emptiness) (Tisza, et al., 1958; Lussier, 1960). An objectively slight deformity can thus have a psychological importance equal to that of a more obviously disfiguring deformity.

Children with lower cognitive functioning appeared to focus more on the functional limitations associated with their deformities and tended to deny or neglect their cosmetic importance. In these children, too, the child's equation of "badness" with the deformity was a matter of concern.

Psychological Development of the Child with a Deformity
Reconstructive surgery in children with physical deformities may alter three of the four factors involved in developing and maintaining body image: perception of body stimuli, stimuli from the environment in the form of comparison with others, and responses from others. As knowledge of the factors influencing bone growth are better understood (Tessier, 1971; Murray, Swanson, Strand, and Hricko, 1975), surgical correction is being considered at earlier ages than in the past. In our experience at The Children's Hospital Medical Center, earlier surgical intervention has been supported by our observation that the continuing deformity interferes with normal psychological maturation and causes primitive and maladaptive psychological defense structures to persist. Some children cling to more or less symbiotic relationships. Other children's defenses become rigid at an early age in an attempt to ward off painful affects. There is also evidence of the effects of the deformity on other ego functions, manifested in distant peer relationships and diminished school performance (Lauer, 1953; Goffman, 1963; Knorr, Hoopes, and Edgerton, 1968; Jabaley, Hoopes, Knorr, and Edgerton, 1970; Longacre, 1973). Poor school performance had been noted previously, but was attributed to retardation rather than to psychological withdrawal or maladaptation.

Evolution of Body Image Change
Although surgical intervention may produce substantial objective change in the physical characteristics of the congenitally deformed child, there is not a correspondingly rapid change in body

image. Body image is a relatively stable psychological entity with an associated defensive system that can only be modified slowly. As mentioned previously, we hypothesize a four-phase modification of body image.

In the first stage, the psychologically complex decision to undergo surgery involves a degree of acknowledgment by the patient of his problem, although the extent of this acknowledgment is often disguised. The motivation for treatment may be projected onto the parents or the doctor, and in a similar way, the parents may project the decision onto a relative or the referring physician, or feel they are surrendering themselves to some "greater good" for the child. But however the decision is made, it represents the absolutely essential start of the dissolution of what for many parents and children is a pathological denial process. The timing of the decision is the product of social awareness, self-recognition, parental and peer pressure, emotional state, and the surgeon's assessment of the potential degree of correction. The treater should urge the patient and his family to confront the decision carefully and systematically. Too ready a willingness to accept surgery may represent inadequate acknowledgment or denial of the presence of the deformity, may hide parental conflicts about the decision which might subsequently surface in a potentially destructive fashion, or may represent too strong an idealized transference to the surgeon or hospital, a transference which will subsequently be unable to sustain the family or the patient in the face of postoperative complications or disappointment. Parents and others may worry that the decision to have the surgery is a kind of negative commitment to an assault on their child. Still, we find that the child on a less conscious level derives from the decision a sense of positive investment in his well-being, with significant implications for his self-esteem.

The second stage, the operative experience, serves as a potent stimulus for the parents to penetrate their most massive defenses, if only for an instant. Their observation of the child in the recovery room or intensive care unit reinforces the fact that there was a deformity that required correction, that a decision for change was made, and that they were willing to accept the risk. This last represents a subtle manifestation of the parents' more or less unconscious negative view of their child's deformity. At this point the child and his family must finally acknowledge the reality of the surgical intervention. The acceptance of this reality sets the stage for subsequent psychological integration of the experience of physical change.

The third stage, the immediate postoperative period, involves physical pain, increased rather than decreased distortion of physical appearance, and the first grappling with expectations. While the previous psychological defenses are still substantially present in this stage, it is also a time of psychological crisis with the chance to lay the groundwork for subsequent integration of a modified body image. This crisis eventually results in the disruption of the prior psychological defenses which leads, in turn, to critical introspection and full acknowledgement of the previous existence of the deformity. The alteration of the inhibiting stimulus of the facial deformity calls into question, as it were, the defenses of the past and brings to the surface long-repressed feelings and conflicts, as illustrated by the following case example.

David underwent reconstructive surgery for Crouzon's disease at the age of 17. Before surgery he had led a circumscribed life with few friends and had held a cynical view of his world. He had difficulties in school stemming from ostracism. At the time of surgery, he was ambivalent, having difficulty elaborating possible benefits from the surgery, and was unable to convey meaningful affects of pleasure, anger, or sadness. Approximately one year postoperatively, when his facial appearance was essentially that of a normal young man, his behavior changed markedly. His "acting out," his shift to modish dress, his use of alcohol, and his engagement in minor physical altercations all suggested that it had taken him nearly a year to acknowledge the deeper feelings that he had previously denied. He was then able to express the pent-up aggression, anger, and sadness of years. Many characteristics of his rebellion can be equated with a delayed adolescent reaction. Further scrutiny revealed that in the latter stages of the postoperative period, the patient was able for the first time to talk of longstanding fears of injury to his eyes, his sense of "dumbness" as a result of the reactions of others, and his paranoia. He had been unable initially to come to grips with the radical change in his facial appearance that had made him a stranger to his friends and to himself. After achieving this enhanced ability to acknowledge and cope with psychological conflicts, David began to feel comfortable with his new image.

Many patients with improved facial appearance after surgery exhibit an upsurge of feelings with a distinct increase in anger, happiness, or sadness. David "acted out" in his behavior the psychological conflicts associated with the integration of his body change. This behavioral component or "identity crisis" should be accepted as part of the process. It is significant that only in the postoperative period was David able to acknowledge openly his longstanding sense of low self-esteem, reflecting his craniofacial deformity. The subsequent improvement in his peer relationships reflected not only the more obvious change in his facial appearance, but also his sense of enhanced esteem.

In the fourth or reintegration stage, the patient's appreciation of the modification of his body is manifested in a reorganization of defenses, a sense of psychological and, at times, intellectual freedom, a reordering of social priorities, and an increased engagement in interpersonal relationships. This last stage usually occurs six weeks to six months postoperatively and is often dependent on the postoperative course and the expectations of the patient about the degree of physical improvement. Children with lower cognitive functioning tend to focus on positive functional change such as improved mastication or ocular changes. They derive enhanced self-esteem from the sense of improved bodily competence. This enhanced esteem may then be generalized in the social and academic spheres of the child's life.

Parental responses during this stage remain largely unpredictable, despite our efforts at parental assessment and support during the pre- and postoperative periods. There is an unstudied vulnerability in the parents that leads to upsurges of intense anger and depression. Longstanding marital conflicts frequently surface as a response to stress, but also as a result of the perceived loss of the "defective" child whose presence had held the conflicts at bay. The inability of parents to invest themselves emotionally in their children can undermine the potential for enhanced self-esteem made possible by the surgical outcome.

Paul, a child with Crouzon's disease, underwent craniofacial surgery at the age of 10. Following an initial positive response to surgery with an improvement in peer interaction, school per-

formance, and family integration, there appeared a leveling in
response, and over a two-year period, a regression to the style of
pre-operative adjustment. Psychiatric diagnostic assessment over
a prolonged time revealed that, preoperatively, the father had
rejected Paul, and only in the immediate postoperative period had
he invested himself emotionally in his son. When Paul began to
adjust in the postoperative period and go through normal ad-
aptational processes, the father had difficulty coping with the
adjustment and withdrew, leving Paul with an objectively improved appearance, but a clear deficit in self-esteem and body
image based on lack of improved parental response.

An important part of the psychological assessment of these children involves the use of the Draw-A-Person test. It is now well
documented in a large series of cases that children integrate a
distorted body image at an early age and can show a positive
change in body image through their drawings. Draw-A-Person
figures are more expansive, complete, and symmetrical in the
postoperative period, with changes frequently noted as early as
the third week. Further, children can demonstrate through pictures an understanding of the process of change as it relates to
their deformity (see Figures 1–4).

The degree to which Draw-A-Person reflects an internalized
shift in self-concept remains unclear, however. The stability of the
alteration is called into question by the tendency of patients with
apparent positive alterations in self-concept in the postoperative
period to regress when faced with later life stresses. Some patients
regress when they face increased demands from enhanced social
interaction or face the normal vicissitudes of adapting to social
and vocational disappointments. The regression involves a return
to a focus on bodily deformity as causative and undermines self-
esteem gained over the period following the surgery.

CONCLUSION

Self-esteem in craniofacially deformed children is influenced
by body image development and can be enhanced by surgical
intervention. While body image is a stable and complex psychological entity, it is not immutable. The positive change in body
image that can result from a shift in self-perception and percep-

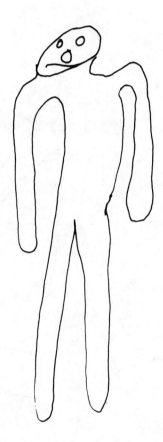

Patient D.L. - Pre-op : Hemi-facial Microsomia

Figure 1

Patient D.L. - Post-op : Hemi-facial Microsomia

Figure 2

PATIENT J.C. - PRE-OP : HEMI-FACIAL MICROSOMIA

Figure 3

PATIENT J.C. - POST-OP : HEMI-FACIAL MICROSOMIA

Figure 4

tion by others can significantly enhance self-esteem. This enhancement may be fragile, however, if there is withdrawal of support by others or a subsequent inability to negotiate stressful experiences.

REFERENCES

Adams, G. R., & Cohen, A. S. (1974), A naturalistic investigation of children's physical and interpersonal characteristics as input cues that effect teacher-student interactions: Some suggestive findings. *J. Experiment. Ed.*, 43:1–5.
Anthony, E. J. (1968), The child's discovery of his body. *Physical Therapy*, 48:1103–1114.
Bahnson, C. B. (1969), Body and self-images associated with audiovisual self-confrontation. *J. Nerv. Ment. Dis.*, 148:262–280.
Barocas, R., & Black, H. (1974), Referral rate and physical attractiveness in third-grade children. *Percept. & Mot. Skills*, 39:731–734.
Belfer, M. L., Harrison, A. M., & Murray, J. E. (1979), Body image and the process of reconstructive surgery. *Amer. J. Diseases of Child.*, 133:532–535.
Bowlby, J. (1951), Maternal care and mental health. Geneva, World Health Organization.
——— (1969), *Attachment*. New York: Basic Books.
Cavior, N., & Dokecki, R. R. (1970), Physical attractiveness and interpersonal attraction among fifth-grade boys: A replication with Mexican children. Presented at a meeting of the Southeastern Psychological Association, St. Louis, Mo.
Clifford, E. (1972), *Psychological Aspects of Orofacial Anomalies: Speculations in Search of Data*, Report 8. Wash., D.C.: American Speech and Hearing Association.
——— (1974), Insights and speculations: Psychological explorations of the craniofacial experience. Presented at the Conference on Evaluation of Recent Advances in Craniofacial Surgery, Chicago.
——— (1979), Craniofacial surgery: Psychological evaluations and impressions. Presented at a meeting of the American Cleft Palate Association, San Diego, Cal.
——— & Walster, E. (1973), The effect of physical attractiveness on teacher expectations. *Sociol. Ed.*, 46:248–258.
Cohen, F., & Yasuna, A. (1978), Cognitive and psychological assessment of the child with craniofacial abnormalities. Presented at Symposium on a Comprehensive Approach to Craniofacial Deformity, Boston, Mass.
Converse, J. M., Wood-Smith, D., McCarthy, J. G., et al (1974), Craniofacial surgery. *Clin. Plast. Surg.*, 1:499–557.
Cook, S. W. (1939), The judgment of intelligence from photographs. *J. Abnorm. Soc. Psychol.*, 34:384–389.
Dion, K. (1973), Young children's stereotyping and facial attractiveness. *Devel. Psychol.*, 9:183–188.
——— & Berscheid, E. (1974), Physical attractiveness and peer perception among children. *Sociometry*, 37:1–2.

Edgerton, M. T., Jane, J. A., Berry, F. A., et al (1975), New surgical concepts resulting from cranio-orbito-facial surgery. *Ann. Surg.* 182:228–239.
Gellert, E. (1962), Children's conceptions of the content and functions of the human body. *Genetic Psychol. Monogr.*, 65:293–405.
Goffman, E. (1963), *Stigma.* Englewood Cliffs, N.J.: Prentice-Hall.
Goodenough, F. (1926), *Measurement of Intelligence by Drawings.* Yonkers, N.Y.: World Book Co.
Greenberg, D. M. (1979), Parental reactions to an infant with a birth defect: A study of five families. Presented at the Biennial Meeting of the Society of Research in Child Development, San Francisco, Cal.
Jabaley, M. D., Hoopes, J. E., Knorr, N. J., & Edgerton, M. T., (1970), The burned child. In: *The Chronically Ill Child and His Family*, ed. M. Debuskey. Springfield, Ill.: Charles C Thomas, pp. 103–129.
Kagan, J., Henker, B.A., Hen-Tov, A., et al. (1966), Infants' differential reactions to familiar and distorted faces. *Child Devel.*, 37:519–532.
Katz, P., & Zigler, E. (1967), Self-image disparity: A developmental approach. *J. Personal. & Soc. Psychol.*, 5:186–195.
Kleck, R. E., Richardson, S. A., & Ronald, L. (1974), Physical appearance cues and interpersonal attraction in children. *Child Devel.*, 45:305–310.
Knorr, J. N., Hoopes, J. E., & Edgerton, M. T. (1968), Psychiatric-surgical approach to adolescent disturbances in self-image. *Plast. Reconst. Surg.*, 41:348–353.
Lauer, E. (1953), The family. In: *Facial Deformities and Plastic Surgery: A Psychosocial Study*, ed. F. E. Macgregor, T. M. Abel, & A. Bryt. Springfield, Ill.: Charles C Thomas, pp. 103–129.
Lax, R. (1971), Some aspects of the interaction between mother and impaired child: Mother's narcissistic trauma. *Internat. J. Psycho-Anal.*, 53:339–344.
Lerner, R. M., & Lerner, J. (1977), Effects of age, sex, and physical attractiveness on a child-peer relative, academic performance, and elementary school adjustment. *Devel. Psychol.*, 13:585–590.
Longacre, J. J. (1973), *Rehabilitation of the Facially Disfigured.* Springfield, Ill.: Charles C Thomas.
Lussier, A. (1960), A boy with a congenital deformity. *The Psychoanalytic Study of the Child*, 15:430–453. New York: International Universities Press.
Macgregor, F. E., Abel, T. M., & Bryt, A., Eds. (1953), *Facial Deformities and Plastic Surgery: A Psychosocial Study.* Springfield, Ill.: Charles C Thomas.
Murray, J. E., Swanson, L.T., Strand, R. D., et al. (1975), Evaluation of craniofacial surgery in the treatment of facial deformities. *Ann. Surg.*, 182:240–264.
Piaget, J. (1929), *The Child's Conception of the World.* New York: Harcourt, Brace, Jovanovich.
Quinn, P. O., & Rapoport, J. L. (1974), Minor physical anomalies and neurologic status in hyperactive boys. *Pediatrics*, 53:742–747.
Rapoport, J. L., & Quinn, P. O. (1975), Minor physical anomalies (stigmata) and early developmental deviation: A major biologic subgroup of "hyper-active children." *Internat. J. Ment. Health*, 4:29–44.
Richardson, S. A., Goodman, N., Hastorf, A. H., & Dornbusch, S. M. (1961),

Cultural uniformity in reaction to physical disabilities. *Amer. Sociol. Rev.*, 26:241–247.

Rosenthal, R., & Jacobson, L. (1968), *Pygmalion in the Classroom*. New York: Holt, Rinehart & Winston.

Ross, M., & Salvia, J. (1975), Attractiveness as a biasing factor in teacher judgments. *Amer. J. Ment. Def.*, 80:96–98.

Schilder, P. (1950), *The Image and Appearance of the Human Body*. New York: International Universities Press.

Shapiro, T., & Stine, J. (1965), The figure drawings of 3-year-old children. *The Psychoanalytic Study of the Child*, 20:298–309.

Solnit, A. J., & Stark, M. H. (1961), Mourning and the birth of a defective child. *The Psychoanalytic Study of the Child*, 16:523–537. New York: International Universities Press.

Tessier, P. L. (1971), The definitive plastic surgical treatment of severe facial deformities of craniofacial dysostosis: Crouzon's and Apert's diseases. *Plast. Reconstr. Surg.*, 48:419–442.

Tisza, V. B., Silverstone, B., Rosenblum, O., and Hanlon, N. (1958), Psychiatric observations of children with cleft palate. *Amer. J. Orthopsychiat.*, 23:416–423.

Waldrop, M. F., & Halverson, C. F. (1971), Minor physical anomalies and hyperactive behavior in young children. In: *Exceptional Infant: Studies in Abnormalities*, Vol 2, ed. J. Hellmuth. New York: Brunner/Mazel.

Wright, B. A. (1969), Spread in adjustment to disability. *Bull. Menn. Clin.*, 28:198–208.

5

The Development of Self-Esteem and Self-Esteem Regulation

NANCY S. COTTON, Ph.D.

The vast interdisciplinary literature on self-esteem is marked by widely disparate vocabularies, theoretical constructs, research paradigms, and kinds of data discussed. The literature is further confused by the tendency to mix intrapsychic and interpersonal levels of understanding (Ornstein, 1981), or to ignore one of these levels entirely. The current task of any model of self-esteem is thus to establish conceptual bridges which can connect the different kinds of data referred to in psychoanalysis, psychiatry, social psychology, child development, education, and sociology.

While a review of the self-esteem literature is beyond the scope of this paper,[1] I would like to propose that a "developmental perspective" provides a synthesizing and integrating principle. Attention to the development of a child reveals the significance of multiple sources of self-esteem which have a differential influence on both the origin and sustenance of self-esteem at different points in the life cycle.

This paper will construct a developmental line for self-esteem from infancy through adolescence. According to Anna Freud (1965), there are normal, consecutive phases which characterize points along a progressive path moving from a state of immaturity

I am grateful to the members of the study group from which this volume arose for their support and helpful ideas, many of which are woven into this paper. My thanks also to Paul Cotton and Shelley Ehrlich for their editorial assistance, and to Nick Browning and Virginia Demos for their useful critiques.

[1] Reviews of the major clinical theories of self-esteem can be found in White (1965, pp. 125–150), Coopersmith (1967, pp. 25–44), and Rosenberg (1979, pp. 54–57). Wylie (1961, Chapter 13) reviews the social psychological literature on self-esteem as a dimension of the self-concept.

(i.e., more dependent) to a state of greater maturity (i.e., greater independence). In assessing children, a developmental line describes the "historical reality" for a particular child. The line conveys the mixture of that child's personal achievements or failures in a particular area of development (Freud, 1965, p. 64). The developmental line of self-esteem should highlight the progression from simple, more isolated structures and functions to more complex, integrated regulatory processes for the maintenance of self-esteem.

The literature on self-esteem refers to three main sources of self-esteem: (1) the esteem of others; (2) competence; and (3) the "self" viewed as a selective filter of the first two functions. Each influence operates during every developmental phase, although its significance shifts during the life cycle. Initially separate, these influences become increasingly intertwined as development proceeds. Thus, positive self-esteem and smooth self-esteem regulation depend on the healthy development of each strand and a certain degree of working harmony between them. Conversely, pathological self-esteem regulation and low self-esteem will result from the failure to develop or defective development of any one strand and/or conflict in the organization of the strands. Regulation refers to the process of organizing the multiple sources of self-esteem, i.e., the selection of information, the assignment of value to different sources, and the synthesis of contradictory information from the sources.

For heuristic value, I will discuss each strand separately in this paper, though, of course, they are rarely isolated in one's experience or in clinical observation. For each phase in the developmental line I will suggest the new ways in which the strands of self-esteem operate during a phase to sustain high self-esteem, remedy previous levels of low self-esteem, or in less optimal outcomes produce low self-esteem and defective self-esteem regulation. The developmental line of self-esteem regulation from infancy through adolescence will be described in five phases.

PHASE I

The rudiments of positive self-esteem are laid down in infancy in relationships with empathic others, in the unfolding of autonomous ego functioning, and in the emerging differentiation and cathexis of the self.

Almost all theories of self-esteem discuss the significance of the opinion of others upon developing self-esteem and self-esteem regulation (James, 1890; Cooley, 1912; Adler, 1927; Stern, 1914; Mead, 1934; Rogers, 1951; Sullivan, 1953; A. Freud, 1965; Rosenberg, 1965; White, 1965; Coopersmith, 1967; Gardner, 1971; Kohut, 1971). The esteem of others creates the positive emotional milieu in which self-love develops, and provides specific information about what is worthwhile and lovable about the person. Finally, the opinions, attitudes, and feelings of others become a part of the intrapsychic structure of the self.

The infant experiences positive feelings of well-being from birth if the parent-child relationship is empathically responsive to the infant's individual temperament, needs, and wishes. "Mothering" confirms an infant's experience when it is in "harmony" with (Sander, 1962) or "mirrors" (Kohut, 1971) the infant's actions. The parent-infant fit creates a basic affective experience which will be associated later with feelings of positive self-esteem. A cycle of interpersonal interactions begins in which basic trust develops. Erikson (1959) refers to the infant's trusting in the "reality of 'good' powers, outside and within" him or herself (p. 140). The affective side of positive self-esteem is what provides the vigor, vitality, and pleasure of "being" oneself and "doing" for oneself.

A child's beginning mastery of skills and achievements is the "basis in reality" for self-esteem (Coopersmith, 1967, p. 37; also Adler, 1927; Hartmann, 1939; Murphy, 1962; A. Freud, 1965; White, 1965; Seligman, 1975). Just as approval and love from accepting parents leads to pleasure and pride in "being" someone, the real successes a child has had will foster his or her pleasure in "doing."

Competence develops out of the basic experience of effectance: the motivation to act on the environment to gain a predictable consequence. White (1965) describes effectance as "the inherent energies of the ego apparatus [which] prompt the child to keep trying out the effectiveness of his ripening capacities" (p. 33). From birth the infant acts on the environment, and his or her successful interactions contribute to the first feelings of well-being. Through effectance, the infant gains the experience of causing something to occur, disappear, or change in some way.

Piaget's theory of cognitive development in infancy confirms the central role of the infant's actions (Piaget, 1937). Self-initiated and self-rewarding activities occur as the infant perceives, manipulates objects, moves, and develops cognitive and language skills. Babies look at mobiles for the sake of looking, listen to music boxes for the pleasurable sound, and soon roll over, sit up, and walk for the sheer pleasure of doing. Effectant behavior occurs apart from instinctual-need-fulfilling behavior and "requires no social reward or ratification by others" (White, 1971, p. 273).

Murphy's (1962) descriptions of normal children abound with vignettes illustrating the association between basic "I can do it" feelings ("triumph") and a "sense of well-being" (pp. 372–373). Effectance leads through a logical progression to a sense of efficacy, to competence, and to a sense of competence (White, 1965). A sense of efficacy is the infant's feeling of "personal power" (White, 1971). The opposite of personal power is, of course, a sense of helplessness, which leads to self-judgments of low self-esteem and feelings of depression (Seligman, 1975, p. 139).

The first two strands entwine early. While competence originates in the arena of autonomous ego functions, a child's pleasure in acting is enhanced by the recognition and approval of his or her interpersonal world. Harmony between the strands enhances the development of each and the relationship between them. Competence becomes connected with the esteem of others when the mother first delights in her baby's play with a toy or in his or her persistent attempts to sit up. If such approval is absent, the development of ego functions may be retarded, and in extreme cases, as with institutionalized babies, these functions can atrophy (Provence and Lipton, 1962).

The empirical literature on child development supports the position that healthy self-esteem regulation depends upon a competent child developing within a supportive, praising world of loving adults. Sroufe (1979) and his colleagues, for example, have shown that the support of an empathic parent has a "transactional effect" on the development of mastery and competence.[2]

---

[2] A transactional effect occurs when the presence of one factor increases the likelihood of occurrence of other factors. Thus, children from deprived homes are twice as likely to have recurrent admissions to a hospital than children from higher socioeconomic brackets (Quinton and Rutter, 1976).

. . . early adaptations in turn influence the quality of autonomous functioning in the toddler period. . . . The child who I as
developed mastery skills, the capacity for affective involvement,
and a sense of confidence within the caregiver-infant relationship will be more enthusiastic, persistent and effective in facing
environmental challenges on its own. Later, given continued
support by the caregiver, this child will be confident, skilled,
and positive in dealing with peers and other tasks of the preschool period [Sroufe, 1979, p. 837].

The self acts like a "selective filter"regulating the "flow" (White's
term, 1965) of sources of self-esteem via the interpretation and
mediation of these sources. The structure of the self imparts personal meaning to all life experiences, interpersonal relationships,
and individual growth and development. Clinical study or empathic observation of children vividly shows that they experience
their present realities in terms of their own pasts. For the infant
the selective filter is relatively simple.

The first self-representation is that of a body-centered or "sensorimotor" self which develops out of the infant's preconceptual
experience of his or her internal and external worlds (Piaget,
1937). The earliest self perceptions are of bodily pleasure and
pain and the "coordination of sensations and actions from different body areas" (Breger, 1974, p. 54). The body-self schema
becomes the foundation for all later conceptions of the self. Psychosexual development as described by Freud also contributes to
the early body self through the differentiation and channeling of
drives. The oral and anal body zones become "two major highways
on the child's journey . . . toward a basic connection to the real
object world and the gradual organization and internalization of
the inner self and object schemata" (Roiphe, 1979, p. 121). The
sensorimotor self "filters" external and internal sources of well-
being through the constitution, temperament, neurological intactness, activity-type, and drive level of the child.

Starting at birth, the infant begins to construct a self from his
interaction with innately given sequences of maturation and environmental events. Parental empathy is the key to early confirm-
ing and validating interactions for the development of the self:

Therein lies the essence of parental empathy: that the parent
does not respond out of his/her own needs, not in keeping with

prescriptions as to how to be a good parent but that his/her responses are determined by the needs of the particular child at a particular time in the child's life [Ornstein, 1981, p. 448].

Kohut (1971) has described how parental behavior, such as echoing, soothing, guiding; parental personality, including peculiarities, attitudes, and temperament; and the emotional milieu created by the entire family serve as "transitional structures" which are incorporated into the initial representation of the self.

The self structure continues to form in infancy through the process of differentiation. The child begins to distinguish him or herself from the human and nonhuman environment. And the sensorimotor self differentiates within itself, i.e., the inside from the outside, particular organs from one another, and the various affects and motives.

PHASE II

For the toddler, self-esteem regulation continues to depend upon parental attitudes, opinions, and behavior. These are a child's "earliest guidelines" (Gardner, 1971, p. 516). The development of self-esteem in children requires both positive (acceptance and praise) and negative (limit-setting) guidelines. Coopersmith (1967) identifies parental acceptance and firm limit-setting as two major conditions present in the lives of children with high self-esteem.

During this stage of development the child learns to walk, explore, play, talk, put things in things, push, pull, throw, reach, pretend, kiss, hug, reject food, and say "no." With each accomplishment, the child looks to the parents for their emotional reaction. Stern (1914), referring to the second and third years of life, states that a child

feels a craving not only for sympathy, but for applause for his little accomplishments from those around him. No child really flourishes without the sunshine of this praise, with the encouragement it gives to ever-renewed effort [p. 503].

Self-esteem is also enhanced when parents provide clear limits and rules; when they enforce these rules with tolerance for the child's appropriate dissent within the limits; and when they provide realistic expectations for the toddler's behavior. Limits, rules, and appropriate expectations provide structure for the child's burgeoning assertiveness and aggression (Erikson, 1959; Murphy, 1962; Coopersmith, 1967; Gardner, 1971; Kohut, 1971). The effective copers in Murphy's study were also the children with high self-esteem, the capacity to assert themselves, and good control over their aggression. The battle of wills, characteristic of parent-toddler relationships, attests to the emergence of a separate self. A toddler's negativism "protect[s] self-esteem" (Allport, 1961, p. 119; also Ausubel, 1950). Psychosexual development contributes to the regulation of self-esteem as children first value their stools as part of themselves and then learn to value their control over the stools. Erikson (1959) describes how parental handling of the "battle for autonomy" during the toddler period affects a child's budding self-esteem:

> From a sense of self-control without loss of self-esteem comes a lasting sense of autonomy and pride; from a sense of muscular and anal impotence, a loss of self-control, and of parental overcontrol comes a lasting sense of doubt and shame [p. 68].

Gradually the child comes to value the esteem of particular individuals and groups of individuals over the esteem of others. Praise and respect from another person or acceptance into a group do not necessarily enhance self-esteem; the child must value the person or group as a potential source of information about his own worth.

Children develop a hierarchy of persons and groups needed to validate their self-esteem. For the toddler, the radius of emotionally significant people has grown to include not only parents but siblings and peers as well. Group membership begins to influence self-esteem. The toddler begins to form a gender identity and to identify himself as part of a family. If the gender and family are valued, then the toddler's self-esteem is enhanced.

Almost all descriptions of toddlers and preschoolers refer to their pride in new areas of proficiency. The toddler's development of competence is enhanced by the "elation" which accompanies the experience of newfound motor, cognitive, and language skills (in Mahler's "practicing subphase" of the separation-individuation process [Mahler, Pine, and Bergman, 1975]). When one observes the toddler's joy as he learns to walk, run, jump, and name objects, it appears that self-esteem is being born. The toddler's characteristic exuberance and delight are clearly related to a "sense of competence" (White, 1965) or "pleasure in achievement" (A. Freud, 1965, p. 81).

Competence "describes a person's existing capacity to interact effectively with his environment. . . . [it is] a cumulative result of the whole history of transactions with the environment . . ." (White, 1965, p. 39). High self-esteem in the absence of a minimal level of proficiency in some area may only be possible in a psychotic state.

Self-esteem regulation becomes more dependent on intrapsychic structure as the child creatively constructs a self from his or her life experiences: an intrapsychic organization of experience that is felt as continuous over time and space, stable and cohesive (Kohut, 1971, 1972, 1977). In Mahler's story of separation-individuation (Mahler, Pine, and Bergman, 1975) the child becomes increasingly separate (in an intrapsychic sense) from the people in his life. This sense of separateness leads to clear intrapsychic representations of the self, the external world, emotionally significant people, and loving relationships. Object permanence and object constancy help to stabilize these internal structures. Self-representations are built with preoperational thought in which mental images can be sustained over time (object permanence). Object constancy allows internal representations of self and others to endure through intense and conflicting affects.

During the second year of life the child begins to refer to him or herself as "I," attesting to the formation of a self-concept. Various investigators (e.g., Mahler, Pine, and Bergman, 1975, p. 269) have observed that by the second year of life the child's behavior is more integrated and increasingly more expressive of certain central themes, (providing evidence of a cohesive self. The "rapprochment subphase" described by Mahler coincides with the child's initial identifications. During this time (approximately 15 to 24 months of age) the child's need to define the self through movement away from significant people is modified by active efforts to integrate attachment and separation:

> . . . as awareness of separateness grows—stimulated by his maturationally acquired ability to move away physically from his

mother and by his cognitive growth—he seems to have an increased need, a wish for mother to share with him every one of his new skills and experiences, as well as a great need for the object's love [Mahler, Pine, and Bergman, 1975, p. 76].

Mahler describes this phase as the "fulcrum" of psychological development; it is also a milestone in self-esteem regulation. At this age the child observes the self and begins to make realistic self-evaluations (Blanck and Blanck, 1979, p. 62). In the sense that "self-esteem presupposes self-judgment and the involvement of a self-critical institution that must not only observe, but also evaluate the self" (Jacobson, 1975, pp. 171–172; also White, 1965),[3] real self-esteem does not exist before this capacity appears.

The child's capacity to form identifications is becoming apparent in the copying of parental behavior, posture, attitudes, facial expressions, and language expressions. The self will be increasingly shaped by imitation of, and identification with, parents, siblings, and other adults and children. The internalization of the characteristics of meaningful people and groups expands the self even further.

With the growth of preoperational thought the child confronts the reality of his or her relative smallness and helplessness. Ausubel (1950) compares the early childhood shifts in the child's self-image to the pre- and post-Copernican views of the solar system. Children move from seeing themselves as the center of the universe to seeing themselves as satellites attached to more powerful and competent parents. Through imitation and identification the child begins to incorporate parental qualities, roles, and power into the developing self, thereby maintaining self-esteem in a time when it is particularly vulnerable to the child's new awareness of his or her relative incompetence and impotence. Thus, the experience of devaluation as a direct result of cognitive development is partially responsible for the taking in of parental standards and roles.

---

[3] Several theorists define the general human propensity to assess and evaluate as a basic process in self-esteem regulation (James, 1890; Osgood, Suci, and Tannenbaum, 1957). In Rosenberg's (1979) words:

Almost invariably, to see ourselves in whole or in part is to assess, evaluate and pass judgment on what we see. We seem scarcely capable of even looking at any of our physical characteristics, dispositions, or social identity elements without immediately deploring or applauding what we observe. This obvious fact . . . has profound implications for self-esteem [p. 26].

By the third year, the child's personality has become more cohesive and integrated. To the self of the early toddler years is added the capacity for self-awareness (two-and-a-half to three-and-a-half years old) and the capacity of the child to report about him or herself. Language has progressed beyond naming into expressing simple ideas and the use of "I" to describe personal wants and preferences. More sophisticated language skills add to the broadening self-concept of the child. The "self-definition" game becomes a favorite—Anna's cup, Anna's seat, versus Mommy's shoes, Daddy's keys. The toddler then values or devalues the multiple self-representations he is constructing. Mahler and her colleagues describe the last phase of early childhood as the "consolidation of individuality." The self is firmly established as a separate, constant structure differentiated from the clearly perceived, separate mother and the internal representation of the mother. There are also definite signs of internalizations of parental demands indicating formation of superego precursors.

Because of the fragility of the toddler's inner representations, the strength of drives relatively unmediated by an ego structure, and the realistic incompetence of the toddler, self-esteem regulation depends heavily on parental acceptance and approval of the child's emerging identity and self-evaluations. With parental support, "what is me" is also endowed with feelings of "me is good."

PHASE III

The radius of people significant to the child continues to expand as the child develops friends, relationships with teachers, and more intimate relationships with siblings, extended family members, baby sitters, and neighbors. But, to repeat, while the young child interacts with increasingly larger numbers of people, not all relationships influence self-esteem in the same way. The impact of the opinions, attitudes, and behavior of people who are valued and trusted by the child gradually becomes more emotionally significant than the responses of strangers or people peripheral in the life of a child. A toddler may collapse in despair at the reprimand of his parent or teacher. Development intensifies the significance of a few people. Rosenberg's (1979) empirical studies of children through adolescence show that "children who trust the judgment and insight of the significant other are more likely to be affected by what they perceive the other thinks of them than those who do not" (p. 93).

Now the child is acquiring competence in particular areas of functioning—motor skills, language, and social skills among them. And the child needs to master new or stressful situations—meeting new friends, doctor's appointments, sleeping in the dark, going to school. In a study of normal children coping with the stresses of everyday life, Murphy (1962) observes:

> over and over again, we saw how the impact of a new challenge intensified the child's awareness of himself; his capacity to meet such a challenge enhances his pleasure, his sense of adequacy, and his pride [p. 374].

The successful mastery of development itself is a third arena of competence. Erikson (1959) proposes that "self-esteem is confirmed at the end of each major [developmental] crisis" (p. 89).

Competence needs to develop in multiple areas and levels of the personality for the child to sustain consistently high self-esteem. Children who feel good about themselves usually have a general level of competence in the major areas of the personality (e.g., physical, social, emotional, and psychological development) with relative strengths and weaknesses in specific areas, though a child may also sustain positive self-esteem based on talents in one particular area. The areas of competence are arranged in the order of their significance to the child. A child must value his talent or skill if self-esteem is to be enhanced by competence in that arena. The valuing of particular areas is determined by the self structure.

The formation of a more complex self structure is the milestone of self-esteem regulation in this phase. A series of imitations, identifications, and internalizations, and the negotiation of psychosexual stages of development, lead to the development of a self concept, a superego, an ego ideal, and an inner world enriched by object representations of emotionally significant people. But while initial internal structures develop during this phase, they do not mature until late adolescence.

The self concept is comprehensively and precisely defined in Rosenberg's (1979) theoretical and experimental work as a child's image or picture of what he or she is ("extant self"), what he or she would like to be ("desired self" made up of the ego ideals and superego), and what he or she wants others to think he or she is ("presenting self"). Children gain broader, richer images of themselves as they expand the boundaries of the self to include the groups, statuses, and categories to which they belong; the qualities which describe them (attitudes, abilities, preferences, personality traits); and their physical characteristics (weight, body parts, body image). These are the contents of the extant self that are evaluated during self-esteem regulation (Rosenberg, 1979, pp. 9–17). The fate of anything experienced as "me" by the child can thus influence self-esteem regulation. The self-concept "filters" the evaluations by what it includes and excludes and by how it organizes its parts. The breadth and depth of the self concept explain why self-esteem is influenced by experiences in diverse areas. If a person is "identified with" or considers his hometown to be a part of the self, then such seemingly remote events as a baseball team's winning or losing can influence the individual's level of self-esteem.

Self-esteem is not influenced equally by all parts of the self-image. The self concept is a subjectively organized structure in which some aspects of the self are central, others more peripheral. Rosenberg's (1979) "principle of psychological centrality" describes how the self organizes its parts into a hierarchy of what is important.

> . . . to know that someone considers himself deficient with regard to a particular quality is plainly an inadequate indication of what he thinks of himself. We must also know how much he values this quality. If a particular component is vital to one's feeling of worth, then negative attitudes concerning it may be personally devastating, but if the component is trivial or insignificant, then the individual may blithely acknowledge inadequacy in that regard with scarcely a twinge of discomfort [p. 74].

The preschool child's hierarchy of valuable parts of the self is based on his mode of self-conceptualization, competencies, identifications with parental qualities, roles, and values, and the developing superego and ego ideal. In that preoperational thinking is concrete, egocentric, and lacks abstraction and introspection, children define themselves by overt aspects of themselves and by the intense feelings about good and bad that develop during this period. Magical thinking, blurred concepts òf fantasy and reality, and egocentric thinking cause the young child's self-worth to be extremely vulnerable to everyday experiences. Rosenberg's work on the self concept describes how a child's "mode of self-concep-tualization" changes throughout development (1979, p. 22) with cognitive development and the development of ego functions such as reality testing, object constancy, and object permanence.

In addition to the self concept, the formation of the superego and ego ideal in early childhood are milestones in the develop-mental line of self-esteem regulation (Jacobson, 1975). The child constructs "internal criteria for ascertaining self-worth" (Gardner, 1971, p. 517), determined by the ethical and moral standards (superego) or worldly goals and ambitions (ego ideal) the child adopts. Self-worth is increasingly determined by the result of cal-culations involving what "I am" (extant self), what "I should be" (superego), and what "I wish to be" (ego ideal). Among theorists who have described the role of subjective calculations in the reg-ulation of self-esteem (White, 1965; Gardner, 1971; Jacobson, 1975), Coopersmith (1967) emphasizes how a child's values and aspirations influence the "regulation" of the flow of external sources of self-esteem and the "interpretation of external sources and successes" (p. 37).

Needless to say, positive self-esteem is enhanced only if the child's behavior and self-image meet internal standards, so that he or she must develop *attainable* moral standards and a *realistic* ego ideal. Self-esteem will thus suffer in a child who has average intelligence when the child cannot achieve the goal of a straight A report card in a highly competitive school in which his or her father had been first in his class.

Healthy self-esteem regulation depends upon the quality and intensity of the child's reactions to the inevitable discrepancies between the actual and ideal self. Children need to be able to tolerate discrepancies in goals and performance, to try again when they fail initially, and to return to a state of positive self-esteem in a reasonable time without dwelling on failure, disappointment, and rejection. Parental mediation of the preschool child's initially intense reactions to failure and rejection help shape more emo-tionally tolerable reactions.

The quality of self-esteem regulation is influenced not only by the content of the child's identifications, but also by the affects which motivate them: the desire to be like the loved person; the desire to be like the more competent and powerful person; the need to be like the person who has been lost; or the desire to be like the hated and frustrating person (identification with the aggressor [Breger, 1974, p. 144]). Breger describes this process in the following way:

> Since identification involves an internalization of an external relationship (a change in self by incorporation of a new role), it follows that the child will feel the same way toward the new part of himself as he did toward the parent he is identifying with. When he adds the role of a parent out of love or the wish to be powerful, he comes to love or be proud of this new part of himself. But when he adds new roles out of anxiety or anger he will experience these emotions in regard to parts of himself. Identifications of this sort lead to an inner ambivalence [1974, p. 145].

Psychosexual development continues to have a direct impact on self-esteem regulation as oral, anal, and oedipal issues affect the stability of the child's internalizations—the child's negotiation of dependency versus independence, aggression and its control, pleasure and its renunciation. Self-esteem regulation will thus be vulnerable in excessively dependent, aggressive, or sexually inhibited children.

PHASE IV

By the time the child enters school, the three sources of self-esteem have become integrated in such a way that it hardly becomes possible to discuss them separately. The self as it serves as a selective filter for development in the other two areas becomes the major tool for the regulation of self-esteem. Thus, the impact of praise on self-esteem is highly dependent on whether the child values the praising person and the area of the self which is being praised. Many children have developed self structures by this age which render them relatively invulnerable to minor slights. But intense negative patterns are also in place by this time. Children may appear to be incapable of feeling good about themselves regardless of the nature or extent of environmental support for developing competence or identification with positive models. The self has become a filter which selectively values new experiences because they validate a negative self-image which has been formed out of past experiences.

The latency-age child continues to believe that "the ultimate truth about the self is to be found in some external source" (Rosenberg, 1979). Thus, the latency-age child and early adolescent seek out information from others because they believe valued adults have a more accurate view of themselves than they have (pp. 241–255). Parents continue to influence self-esteem in major ways. Emotional relationships with parents are the affective context in which approval is most meaningful to the child. The absence of approval and praise from parents is often the cause of low self-esteem even in the presence of competence, acceptance among peers, and teacher approval. Evaluation reveals an impaired mother- or father-child relationship with excessive criticism, unreasonable expectations, or marked neglect of the child's psychological needs.

In latency, the boundaries of the self increase widely as the child's radius of significant people broadens from parents and families to teachers, peers, and membership in racial, religious, and national groups. Just as parts of "me" can be valued or devalued, children come to value or devalue the social categories by which they define themselves. Rosenberg's (1979) work shows that self-esteem may be lowered when a child compares himself to others in a dissonant social context, e.g., a black child in a primarily white school, a Catholic child raised in a non-Catholic neighborhood, or middle-class children attending lower-class schools (pp. 99–127). In a "consonant context" a child can use similarity with other children to validate his self concept. A person's perceptions and interpretations of group membership continue throughout the life cycle to sustain or inhibit positive self-esteem.

Latency is the period of skill-building and learning. Realistic capabilities gain heightened significance for the self concept. Erikson (1959) calls it the time when the self is defined as "I am what I learn" (p. 82). The capacity to make things well (industry) and success in school lead to positive feelings of self-esteem. Children with learning disabilities, developmental delays, or physical handicaps find it difficult to maintain positive self-esteem during these years when academic competence is so central.

School-age children have constructed both specific images and general images of themselves. Self-esteem levels are correspondingly specific and global, as children make multiple self-evaluations in separate areas of the personality (e.g., good reader, good athlete) and overall self-evaluations which reflect their general images of themselves. It is usually not possible to generalize from one level to the other (Rosenberg, 1979, p. 22). Thus, a child may be smart or popular but still have a low level of self-esteem based on his or her inability to satisfy ego-ideal or superego standards.

Latency-age children think of themselves in behavioral, moral, and specific terms (Rosenberg, 1979). They focus on abilities and achievements and describe themselves in terms of physical characteristics or elements of their social identity (sex, age, race, class, etc.). Self-esteem regulation appears to be particularly vulnerable during latency to failure, rejection, or defects in the overt "social exterior." When younger children were asked the question, "What about yourself makes you most proud or ashamed?", their responses focused on the most visible aspects of the self (Rosenberg, 1979, p. 207).

At the onset of latency, the child has already formed the rudiments of an ego ideal and superego. The self of latency is also formed by the initial resolution of the Oedipus complex, with the development of feelings about oneself as a good or bad person, a wanted or unwanted person, and an attractive or unattractive boy or girl. Gender identity is elaborated further by the identification with the parent of the same sex as the child gradually develops the ability to gratify indirectly his Oedipal strivings.

During latency the superego is refined by the development of concrete operational thinking and the further structuralization of the ego (Sarnoff, 1976). Defense mechanisms appear in sharper focus, such as repression, fragmentation, displacement, symbol formation, synthesis, secondary elaboration, and fantasy formation (Sarnoff, 1976, p. 31). Piaget (1932) and Kohlberg (1963a, b) describe the "moral reasoning" used by the latency-age child to arrive at decisions. Whether a child can live up to his moral decisions has a major impact on self-esteem regulation in latency, which is a time when moral behavior is of central concern to parents, teachers, and other cultural "guides."

PHASE V

During adolescence the structures of self-esteem regulation are radically transformed by rapid and dramatic physical, cognitive, and social changes (e.g., Blos, 1962, pp. 52–157; GAP, 1968, pp. 59–93). The self is reorganized and consolidated during the process of integrating the changes in these areas.

The physiological upheaval of puberty brings about a refocusing on the body, threatening the self-image of childhood. The adolescent attempts to construct a new body image which connects the body image of childhood with that of adolescence. Self-esteem can plummet during this process as the adolescent questions whether he is still a boy, whether he can control his voice ever again, or whether his skin will clear. The body image is as central to the adolescent as the sensorimotor self was to the infant and toddler (e.g., Sommer, 1978, pp. 47–49). Researchers have shown that on the average early maturers have more favorable self-concepts than late maturers (particularly true for boys). But the crucial factor appears not to be chronological age, but psychological maturity, which includes how the adolescent perceives his body changes and how prepared he is for them (Sommer, 1978, p. 48).

Cognitive development leads to formal operational thinking. Abstract thought and introspection alter the mode of conceptualizing the self and the focus of self-evaluations. Introspection turns the adolescent's attention from the concrete social exterior to the "psychological interior": "the private world of emotions, attitudes, wishes and secrets" (Rosenberg, 1979, p. 22). How the adolescent defines him or herself partly determines the impact of events on self-esteem. Thus, a physical defect or the inability to drive an expensive car may be more devastating to early adolescents who see themselves according to their "social exteriors"; whereas sadistic fantasies, unacceptable feelings, or incestuous wishes may have a similar effect on older adolescents who define themselves more by the "psychological interior."

Rosenberg's research confirms that self-esteem is regulated differently as a result of this new mode of conceptualizing the self. When older children were asked to describe their "points of pride" ("what was best about them") and their "weakest points" ("things not as good about them"), they answered in terms of conceptualized traits, i.e., desired emotional facets, emotional control, qualities of character, and abilities to engage in interpersonal relations (1979, p. 209). When asked what the person who knows him or her best knows that others do not know, the adolescent was most likely to answer in terms of general thoughts, feelings, and wishes or personal desires, aspirations, and secrets.

Studies of self-esteem in adolescence reflect this process, showing that younger adolescents generally have poorer self-images than do older adolescents (Offer and Howard, 1972). Apparently, introspection leads to heightened self-consciousness and preoccupation with the self, which leads in turn to self-criticism and concomitant lowerings of self-esteem.

Abstract thinking allows the adolescent to concern himself with the past and the future as well as the present. The self concept is no longer limited to concrete images. The capacity to construct and test hypotheses expands the scope of the self concept. The adolescent can generate options and explore them systematically. The adolescent can imagine possible selves which are more future-oriented, idealistic, and related to worlds less personal and reality-bound. The self concept is time-oriented rather than merely present-oriented. Of course, self-esteem regulation still depends on current perceptions as well as anticipated worth. In the same way, self-esteem regulation is influenced by qualitative differences in the contents of the superego and ego ideal. Hypothetical idealized selves are evaluated alongside the adolescent's current self.

A "sense of ego identity" (Erikson, 1950, 1959) emerges in the later stages of adolescence through the consolidation of childhood identifications. Erikson (1959) and Blos (1962) refer to late adolescence as the "phase of consolidation." The self results from the creative synthesis of childhood identifications and roles. Erikson (1959) defines the sense of ego identity as

> . . . the inner capital accrued from all those experiences of each successive stage, when meaningful identification led to a successful alignment of an individual's basic drives with his endowment and his opportunities [p. 94].

With the closer and more stable alignment of drives, assets, and environmental opportunities and stresses, the adolescent evaluates him or herself against a more mature and realistic ego ideal. Blos (1979) considers the "adult ego ideal" formed during adolescence as the unique self structure of adolescence. The ego ideal now becomes an "agency of aspiration" (Blos, 1979, p. 328) toward realistic occupational pursuits and interpersonal relationships. Self-esteem is enhanced by the more stable and realistic basis upon which self-evaluations are made.

The influence of the opinions of others on self-esteem changes in significance during adolescence. Cognitive development causes the adolescent's "locus of knowledge" to shift from the belief that the truth about him or herself comes from without to the belief that it comes from within (Rosenberg, 1979). Still, the esteem of others plays a major role in self-esteem regulation. The hierarchy of significant persons expands and shifts. There is an increasing dependence on extrafamilial figures, such as peers and teachers. The shifting of alliance from parents to peers allows the adolescent to use peers to maintain self-esteem. Peers may be more appropriate sources of positive self-esteem than parents who "lose touch with, and may even feel alienated from, the younger generation" (Wolf, 1980, p. 127). Thus, an adolescent girl may bolster her self-esteem by following the ethical code of her peer group rather than by using her parents' more rigid and outdated standards.

We continue to negotiate the issues of self-esteem and to a less extent the regulatory mechanisms of self-esteem throughout the life cycle. Each developmental period presents unique challenges to the organization of self-esteem and self-esteem regulation. Mature self-esteem regulation occurs when a person can sustain a relatively high level of self-esteem by means of the realistic valuing of skills and accomplishments; can rely on internal standards of achievement and moral virtue that are flexible and appropriate to the person's life situation; and can be appropriately concerned with the approval of valued others and groups. A developmental line that summarizes the milestones of each phase is given at the end of this chapter.

DEVELOPMENTAL TRENDS IN THE FORMATION OF SELF-ESTEEM REGULATION

Six developmental trends can be said to characterize the development of self-esteem regulation in general: (1) Self-esteem is lowered as a person moves from one stage to another; (2) self-esteem is enhanced as each developmental period is successfully negotiated; (3) the period of formation of the self is a sensitive period for positive self-esteem; (4) during the course of development, the individual shifts from relying exclusively on external sources of self-esteem to greater dependence on internal structures; (5) self-esteem will always depend to some extent on recognition, validation and praise from external sources; and (6) during periods of "new learning" there is a return to external sources of self-esteem with a telescoped recapitulation of the shift from external to internal sources of self-esteem.

The initial lowering of self-esteem which occurs during the period of transition from one developmental stage to another is usually accompanied by anxiety (Breger, 1974; also Kohut, 1972). This anxiety "threatens the security of an established way of being, of a known identity" (Breger, 1974, p. 257). The empirical literature on self-esteem reports a significant correlation between high levels of anxiety and low self-esteem (e.g., Bledsoe, 1964; Lipsitt, 1958). For example, global self-esteem was lower in children entering adolescence (12–14 year olds) as compared to 8 to 11 year-old children (Simmons, Rosenberg, and Rosenberg, 1973). This anxiety can be growth-enhancing if it leads to a more adaptive, flexible reorganization of the self; but the old organizations must be challenged first and found wanting. Self-esteem will be lower during the period of reorganization.

Self-esteem is enhanced at the end of a developmental period if the child successfully completes the developmental challenge of that stage (Erikson, 1959, p. 89). Earlier experiences of positive self-esteem prime the child for later experiences of positive self-esteem creating benign cycles of development: "The very experience of adequacy, that is, optimal fulfillment of the developmental purpose, adds to the sense of self-evaluation" (Blanck and Blanck, 1979, p. 59). Murphy's (1962) longitudinal work on coping and adaptation frequently refers to the benign cycles of development which occur when positive self-esteem is established early. She writes: "Each experience of mastery is not only a momentary conquest, but a promise of more to come, a reassurance of the capacity to grow" (p. 373). Self-esteem is never finally settled; it is renegotiated at each developmental crisis. But earlier success begets the anticipation of success in the next phase of development and equips one with more competence to meet future developmental challenges.

Kohut (1972) formulated the third developmental trend—that there is a "sensitive period" for the development of healthy self-esteem regulation. The vicissitudes of the early formation of the self prime the child for healthy or pathological self-esteem regulation later on. Kohut refers to this period as:

> . . . the prototype of the specific forms of later vulnerability and security in the narcissistic realm; *of the ups and downs in our self-esteem*; of our lesser or greater need for praise, for merger into idealized figures, and for other forms of narcissistic sustenance; and of the greater or lesser cohesion of our self during periods of transition whether in the transition to latency, in early or late adolescence, in maturity, or in old age [p. 369].

The structure of the "filter" is set down during the initial period of intrapsychic development. If the initial prototypical experience of the self is faulty, subsequent periods of reorganization of the self are more likely to suffer. Thus, if the child brings a negative self-image to an experience in the present, even when the experience provides positive social feedback or demonstrates marked competence, the child will reject the experience because it contradicts his or her self-image. Clinical practice abounds with patients who actively select (and in some cases elicit) negative experiences to confirm their negative self-images and chronic low self-esteem. Early conflictual experiences with emotionally significant people are recreated in current relationships (Littner, 1960). Thus, abused children elicit further abuse in new placements, which perpetuate negative cycles of relationships and a further negative impact on self-esteem regulation (Martin and Beezley, 1977).

Early experience of healthy self-esteem regulation can also protect against traumatic assaults on the core self. Positive self-esteem is sustained by the reactivation of positive early experiences. A dramatic illustration of the significance of core identity is given in Rabinowitz's (1976) account of Jewish survivors of Nazi concentration camps. She contrasts the early life histories of the Jews and the SS guards who were their captors. The former generally experienced well-to-do, educated, intact childhoods. The guards were frequently from psychologically, economically, and culturally deprived, broken families. In reference to the former prisoners, she writes:

They had been brought up to think well of themselves. . . . The time came that they were abased and degraded. They had survived it, and though they had lost everything, though their experience had left them innocent of no evil, they did not lose the core of their early lives, which had taught them that they were worthy [p. 133].

The term "sensitive period" is used instead of "critical period" to reflect a dynamic approach to development. For while structuralization usually occurs during this stage, failures of structural development can be corrected or modified during later developmental periods.

The fourth developmental trend describes a general shift in childhood and adolescence from reliance on the esteem of others to reliance on internal criteria for self-esteem regulation (Gardner, 1971; Spruiell, 1975; Blanck and Blanck, 1979; Rosenberg, 1979). The child internalizes the qualities, roles, attitudes, standards, and expectations of others into the self, particularly significant others. Self-esteem regulation relies increasingly throughout development on the work of such internal structures as the self concept, object representations, the superego, and ego ideal. Mature self-esteem regulation depends upon the capacity of the individual to construct and rely on his or her own internal resources and standards. Riesman's (1950) "inner-directed person" relies less on the esteem of others for direction than the "outer-directed person." The literature on Rotter's scale of internal as opposed to external locus of control supports this hypothesis (Lefcourt, 1966; Rotter, 1966). Self-esteem is higher in those people who see themselves as able to control what happens to them in life as opposed to people who see the source of change as located outside themselves. Pathological self-esteem regulation occurs when this shift in ways of regulating self-esteem does not occur. Thus, in the narcissistic disorders, patients suffer from an almost exclusive dependence on external sources to supply the experience of self-worth (e.g., Kohut, 1971, 1972, 1977).

The fifth trend suggests that the shift to a reliance on internal sources for self-esteem regulation is never complete. One will always depend to varying degrees on recognition, validation, and praise from external sources. The notion that maturity involves utter independence from the opinions and attitudes of others is another pathological form of self-esteem regulation. As Erikson eloquently describes in his writings, men are psycho*social* beings in continual need of recognition from their fellow men for their sense of self-worth. Throughout the life cycle, personality development is a process of constant, complex interdigitation with family members, peers, social institutions, and ethnic groups. Erikson uses the word identity (as opposed to self) because identity implies a mutual relationship between the self and its interpersonally significant environment. Cultures vary markedly in the extent to which an individual self is encouraged to develop independently of the cultural self. Thus, cultural encouragement and support will shape the extent to which self-esteem regulation will require validation by significant others and the group. As Wolf (1980) states, "self-object needs and relations do not disappear with maturation and development; they become more diffuse and less intense" (p. 127). Wolf compares the need for the continuous presence of a psychologically nourishing self-object milieu with the continuing physiological need for an environment containing oxygen. "It is a relatively silent need until it is not met" (p. 128).

The sixth trend refers to the process which occurs when a person approaches a new learning situation or attempts to cope with traumatic stress. In these cases the child (and later the adult) returns temporarily to a greater dependence on external sources for information, support, and approval. Specific feedback on what one is doing correctly or incorrectly is essential when learning a new skill, whether it be learning how to ski or to care for a first baby. And the "moral support" of others validates the person's basic self-worth and competence during the temporary period of awkwardness, ignorance, and self-doubt which characterizes any new learning. Thus, a person recapitulates the general trend from reliance on external to internal criteria for self-esteem regulation. In this way, new learning situations are experienced in much the same way as are the transitional periods between developmental stages.

CONCLUSION

The multidimensional developmental model presented in this paper can provide a conceptual tool with which to integrate the complex, fragmented, and seemingly unrelated information accumulating in the fields of psychoanalysis, psychiatry, social psychology, child development, education, and sociology.

Self-esteem and self-esteem regulation can now be defined in the following way: Self-esteem regulation is a complex ego function which synthesizes and organizes self-evaluations made from all areas and on all levels of the self. The self-esteem structure is the evaluative dimension (based on the judging function of the ego) of the concurrently evolving "cohesive stable self" (Kohut, 1971; Ornstein, 1981). Self-esteem is a conscious experience accessible to introspection and description. It is also an unconscious process, reflecting a person's inner psychic structure. Unique and intense feelings are complexly related to self-judgments. A person with good self-esteem feels proud, worthy, enthusiastic, and effective. A person with poor self-esteem feels shameful, unworthy, and helpless.

Finally, it should be noted that the developmental line of self-esteem and self-esteem regulation referred to in this paper is a general one. It needs to be made more specific for girls as opposed to boys, and for children from different cultures.

THE DEVELOPMENTAL LINE FOR SELF-ESTEEM REGULATION

I. During Phase I, the infant experiences positive feelings of well-being

(1) from the mother-infant relationship if the care-giving is empatheticaly responsive to the infant's individual temperament, activity level, needs, and wishes;

(2) in and from his own body when he experiences his own capacity to affect change in the environment; manage anxiety, and develop autonomous ego functions;

(3) through the incorporation of primarily positive "transitional structures" (such as parental behavior, personality, emotional milieu of the family) into the sensori-motor self;

(4) through the positive cathexis of the gradually emerging inner world.

Feelings of well being are further enhanced at this stage by the mutually supportive interaction of all three strands.

II. Phase II is marked by

(1) parental positive (acceptance, praise) and negative guide-lines (limits, rules, realistic expectations) to bolster positive self-esteem. Due to the fragility of the inner representations, external validation is particularly important.

(2) the toddler's elation at learning to walk, run, jump and name objects.

(3) advanced differentiation of self from non-self through neg-ativism, increased mastery of motor, cognitive, and language skills and integration of the approval for the developing self from sig-nificant others.

(4) observation and evaluation of the self. Realistic self-evalu-ations are possible. Language conveys this process through the use of "I."

(5) expansion of the self through negotiation of the oral and anal stages of development and identification with competent, loving models.

(6) development of gender identity.

III. Phase III: further "structuralization" of the child's inner world occurs through identification and incorporation and negotiation of the oedipal period.

(1) Parental praise and approval for the older toddler's per-formance continues to bolster positive self-esteem. The child is gradually incorporating these standards and affects (formation of the superego and ego ideal).

(2) Mastery of specific skills and abilities enhances self-esteem and determines in part what areas of the self are valued. Peer interaction assists the development of social skills with people out-side of the family.

(3) Identification with parental qualities, roles, and power adds breadth and self-confidence to the self-image.

IV. The onset of Latency marks Phase IV in which the self acts as a developed "selective filter" regulating self-esteem:

(1) The number of valued people expands from the home (parents and siblings) to school (peers and teachers).

(2) Mastery of the psycho-social conflict of industry versus inferiority leads to investment in skill-building and learning in school. Real mastery of skills is valued as opposed to fantasized accomplishments.

(3) Self-esteem is enhanced if the ability praised is central to the self-concept and the praise comes from a valued person.

(4) Concrete operational thinking shapes the nature of the self. The child defines himself according to the "social exterior"; focusing on abilities, achievements, physical characteristics, and social identity elements. Positive self-esteem is vulnerable if rejection, failure or defects occur in these areas.

(5) The regulation of self-esteem is shifting from a focus on meeting the standards of others to meeting internal standards of the superego and the ego ideal.

(6) Gender identity is elaborated by increased identifications with the same-sex parent, resulting from negotiation of the oedipal conflict.

(7) The structure of latency provides new defense mechanisms to achieve greater impulse control leading to enhanced self-esteem.

V. During Phase V, the structures of self-esteem regulation are radically transformed, initiated by the rapid, dramatic physical and cognitive changes of adolescence.

(1) The esteem-of-others strand shifts from a primary reliance on parents to peers. Self-esteem regulation relies heavily on peer acceptance, support, and praise.

(2) Pubertal changes lead to a refocusing on the body and leading to assessment of whether the body is sufficiently attractive, strong female or male-like.

(3) Formal operational thinking leads to a new basis for self-evaluation. The adolescent focuses on abstract qualities and thoughts; evaluates comparisons of past, present and future possibilities; and uses introspection to redefine the self in terms of the "psychological interior." Self-esteem regulation evaluates the private, invisible world of emotions, attitudes, wishes and secrets.

(4) Consolidation of the self into a sense of ego identity creates a more stable level of self-esteem.

(5) Realistic ego ideal becomes the inner guide for self-esteem judgments. Combined with the new appreciation of the future, this structure leads the adolescent to set appropriate goals for himself which enhances the possibility of maintaining self-esteem in the future.
(6) The development of a personal, attainable, ethical system and the defenses and adaptive skills to maintain adequate impulse control further enhances positive self-esteem.

REFERENCES

Adler (1927), *The Practice and Theory of Individual Psychology*. New York: Harcourt, Brace Jovanovich.
Allport, G. W. (1961), *Pattern and Growth in Personality*. New York: Holt, Rinehart and Winston.
Ausubel, D. P. (1950), Negativism as a phase of ego development. *Amer. J. Orthopsychiat.*, 20:796–895.
Blanck, J., & Blanck, R. (1979), *Ego Psychology. II. Psychoanalytic Developmental Psychology*. New York: Columbia University Press.
Bledsoe, J. C. (1964), Self concepts of children and their intelligence, achievement, interests, and anxiety. *J. Individ. Psychol.*, 20:55–58.
Blos, P. (1962), *On Adolescence: A Psychoanalytic Interpretation*. New York: Free Press.
———— (1979), *The Adolescent Passage*. New York: International Universities Press.
Breger, L. (1974), *From Instinct to Identity*. Englewood Cliffs, N.J.: Prentice-Hall.
Cooley, C. H. (1912), *Human Nature and the Social Order*. New York: Scribner's.
Coopersmith, S. (1967), *The Antecedents of Self Esteem*. San Francisco: Freeman.
Erikson, E. (1950), *Childhood and Society*. New York: Norton.
———— (1959), *Identity and the Life Cycle*. New York: International Universities Press.
Freud, A. (1965), *Normality and Pathology in Childhood: Assessments of Development*. New York: International Universities Press.
Gardner, R. (1971), *Therapeutic Communication with Children: The Mutual Storytelling Technique*. New York: Aronson.
Group for the Advancement of Psychiatry (GAP) Committee on Adolescence (1968), *Normal Adolescence*. New York: Scribner's.
Hartmann, H. (1939), *Ego Psychology and the Problem of Adaptation*. New York: International Universities Press.
Jacobson, E. (1975), The regulation of self-esteem. In: *Depression and Human Existence*, ed. E. J. Anthony & T. Benedek. Boston: Little, Brown, pp. 169–181.
James, W. (1890), *The Principles of Psychology*. New York: Dover, 1950.
Kohlberg, L. (1963a), The development of children's orientations toward a moral order: I. Sequence in the development of moral thought. *Vita Humana*, 6:11-33.

—— (1963b), Moral development and identification. In: *Child Psychology, 62nd Yearbook of The National Society for the Study of Education*, ed. H. Stevenson. Chicago: University of Chicago Press, pp. 277–332.

Kohut, H. (1971), *The Analysis of the Self*. New York: International Universities Press.

—— (1972), Thoughts on narcissism and narcissistic rage. *The Psychoanalytic Study of the Child*, 27:360–400. New Haven: Yale University Press.

—— (1977), *The Restoration of the Self*. New York: International Universities Press.

Lefcourt, H. M. (1966), Internal versus external control of reinforcement: A review. *Psychol. Bull.*, 65:206–220.

Lipsitt, L. P. (1958), A self-concept scale for children and its relationship to the children's form of the Manifest Anxiety Scale. *Child Devel.*, 29:463–472.

Littner, N. (1960), The child's need to repeat his past; some implications for placement. *Soc. Serv. Rev.*, 34:128–148.

Mahler, M. S., Pine, F., & Bergman, A. (1975), *The Psychological Birth of the Human Infant*. New York: Basic Books.

Martin, H. P., & Beezley, P. (1977), Behavioral observations of abused children. *Develop. Med. Clin. Neurol.*, 19:373–387.

Mead, G. H. (1934), *Mind, Self and Society*. Chicago: University of Chicago Press.

Murphy, L. B. (1962), *The Widening World of Childhood*. New York: Basic Books.

Offer, D., & Howard, K. I. (1972), An empirical analysis of the Offer Self-Image Questionnaire for Adolescents. *Arch. Gen. Psychiat.*, 27:529–537.

Ornstein, A. (1981), Self-pathology in childhood: developmental and clinical considerations. *Psychiat. Clin. of N. Amer.*, 4:435–453.

Osgood, C. E., Suci, G. J., & Tannenbaum, P. H. (1957), *The Measurement of Meaning*. Urbana: University of Illinois Press.

Piaget, J. (1932), *The Moral Judgment of the Child*. New York: Free Press, 1948.

—— (1937), *The Construction of Reality in Childhood*. New York: Norton, 1951.

Provence, S., & Lipton, R. (1962), *Infants in Institutions*. New York: International Universities Press.

Quinton, D., & Rutter, M. (1976), Early hospital admissions and later disturbances of behavior: An attempted replication of Douglas' findings. *Devel. Med. & Child Neurol.*, 18:447–459.

Rabinowitz, D. (1976), *New Lives*. New York: Knopf.

Riesman, D. (1950), *The Lonely Crowd: A Study of the Changing American Character*. New Haven: Yale University Press.

Rogers, C. R. (1951), *Client-Centered Therapy: Its Current Practice, Implications, and Theory*. Boston: Houghton Mifflin.

Roiphe, H. (1979), A theoretical overview of preoedipal development during the first four years of life. In: *Basic Handbook of Child Psychiatry*, Vol. 1, ed. J. D. Call, J. D. Noshpitz, R. L. Cohen, & I. N. Berlin. New York: Basic Books, pp. 118–127.

Rosenberg, M. (1965), *Society and the Adolescent Self-Image*. Princeton: Princeton University Press.

—— (1979), *Conceiving the Self*. New York: Basic Books.

Rotter, J. B. (1966), Generalized expectancies for internal versus external control of reinforcement. *Psychological Monographs: General and Applied*, 80:1–28.

Sander, L. W. (1962), Issues in early mother-child interaction. *J. Amer. Acad. Child Psychiat.*, 1:141–166.

Sarnoff, C. (1976), *Latency*. New York: Aronson.

Seligman, M. E. P. (1975), *Helplessness: On Depression, Development, and Death*. San Francisco: Freeman.

Simmons, R. G., Rosenberg, F., & Rosenberg, M. (1973), Disturbance in the self-image at adolescence. *Amer. Sociol. Rev.*, 38:553–568.

Sommer, B. B. (1978), *Puberty and Adolescence*. New York: Oxford University Press.

Spruiell, V. (1975), Narcissistic transformations in adolescence. *Internat. J. Psychoanal. Psychother.*, 4:518–536.

Sroufe, L. A. (1979), The coherence of individual development, early care, attachment, and subsequent developmental issues. *Amer. Psychol.*, 34:834–841.

Stern, W. (1914), *Psychology of Early Childhood*. New York: Holt, 1930.

Sullivan, H. D. (1953), *The Interpersonal Theory of Psychiatry*. New York: Norton.

White, R. W. (1965), *Ego and Reality in Psychoanalytic Theory*. [*Psychological Issues*, Monogr. 11.] New York: International Universities Press.

——— (1971), Urge towards competence. *Amer. J. Occupational Ther.*, 25:271–274.

Wolf, E. S. (1980), On the developmental line of selfobject relations. In: *Advances in Self Psychology*, ed. A. Goldberg. New York: International Universities Press.

Wylie, R. (1961), *The Self-Concept: A Critical Survey of Pertinent Research Literature*. Lincoln: University of Nebraska Press.

6

The Relationship of Self-Esteem and

Narcissism

Judith N. Huizenga, M.D.

Self-esteem results from the transformation of narcissism into an autonomous ego function by means of which we value our accomplishments and regulate our well-being. The purpose of this paper is to trace the relationship of self-esteem to narcissism from infancy through the oedipal period.

Spruiell (1975) describes three developmental lines that arise from narcissism: self-love, omnipotence, and self-esteem—all being modified by maturation, internalized object relationships, and interaction with the environment. In his view, these developmental lines are separate but related. Thus, self-love, as it originates from the mother's loving responses to her child and to his growing competence and mastery, serves as the basis for the internalized approving function central to self-esteem; while omnipotence, in turn, serves as the basis for the child's developing competence. At first the infant experiences the gratification of his needs by his mother as magical expressions of his own power and action. Only gradually does he surrender his omnipotent feelings in favor of a more realistic appreciation of the limits of his efficacy. With this more realistic appreciation comes a greater understanding of his own competence and, concurrently, the good feelings about mastery that were originally associated with omnipotence. Thus the mother's approval of her child's accomplishments represents a transitional link between these developmental lines. The third developmental line, which Spruiell traces to a primary precursor of self-esteem—the regulation of one's well-being—is intimately related to the other two. For at this stage of development the child's needs primarily involve the maintenance of stable levels

151

of stimulation. The mother's assistance in this regard becomes the basis for the child's eventual ability to regulate his moods and his general sense of well-being. Finally, all three lines issue in the development, during the oedipal period, of the ego ideal, an internalized structure that serves to transform early narcissism into the autonomous regulatory functions of self-esteem.

Before I consider each of these developmental lines in detail, I should like briefly to comment on the evolution of our conceptions of narcissism and self-esteem. While self-esteem derives from and is supported by narcissism, it is obviously not synonymous with it. It is rather a complex ego state (Pulver, 1970) that requires not only the capacity to make judgments and establish values but also the capacity to form images of oneself and compare these images with external others. In recent thinking, these images are seen to form a cohesive psychic structure, generally termed the "self." The maintenance of this structure involves a continuing process of conceptualization that integrates past experience with present, and the internal psychological world of narcissism with the external world of important others. The evolution of this conception of the "self" can be traced, in an important sense, to the development of psychoanalytic thinking about narcissism.

In this regard, it is important to recall that narcissism is a term used primarily to designate a form of libidinal psychic energy (Schafer, 1968). Freud (1914) originally defined narcissistic pathology as a withdrawal of cathexis from external objects onto one's own ego. In his view of child development, Freud saw the newborn child as existing in a state of primary narcissism, in which the child's own body was the object of his libidinal investment. Gradually, the infant developed a capacity for object love and cathected important external others. But this cathexis could be withdrawn from the object and turned back on the ego in the form of secondary narcissism. In its extreme version, secondary narcissism led to the severely pathological behavior of narcissistically disordered patients; in its more normal form, it resulted in the formation—by way of identification with valued objects—of the ego ideal.

Freud's theory of the inverse ratio between self-directed libido and object-directed libido has by now been rejected. Reflecting the contemporary emphasis on healthy development, Kohut

(1971) defines narcissistic libido as a form of psychic energy that supports the cohesiveness and continuity of the "self." In the modern view, the capacity to form attachments with others and the capacity to love one's self are directly connected and indeed mutually supportive. Rather than the either/or situation described by Freud, narcissism is seen as a necessary condition for the full emergence of object love.

With this brief theoretical orientation, I should now like to turn to the three developmental lines described by Spruiell. The developmental line of self-love suggests just how the early preoedipal narcissistic object fosters the child's developing sense of self. In the symbiotic phase, the mother supports the primary narcissism of the infant by providing comfort, appropriate stimulation, and protection against inappropriate stimuli (Nagera, 1973). Unable to separate himself from his mother, the infant experiences the dyad as a unit. The mother's empathic responses reinforce the experience of oneness and, what is more important, the experience of wholeness. The infant's experience of the symbiotic unit is thus the earliest precursor of his sense of the self as cohesive and continuous. A disturbance in the early mother-child relationship may grossly distort the child's sense of himself (Nagera, 1973; Mahler, Pine, and Bergman, 1975).

With the onset of the separation-individuation phase, the boundaries between mother and child begin to be established. As the child takes his first tentative steps toward separation, the empathic parent mirrors back his feelings, acknowledging his separate existence. When the mother approves of the child's assertiveness and mastery, she expresses her understanding of his need for autonomy. The child internalizes these experiences of mirroring and approval as self-love. This aspect of narcissism is dealt with clinically in Kohut's "mirror transference."

The sense of well-being, a primary precursor of self-esteem, grows out of the parent's reliable caretaking. The child learns to anticipate that his needs will be met and he trusts that his mother will eventually take care of him. He gradually develops his own ability to soothe himself and to generalize from his mother to others who can help him (Spruiell, 1975). His feeling of well-being becomes less dependent on the presence of his mother for immediate gratification. The child's ability to regulate his moods and his self-esteem provides him with the stability he needs not to be overwhelmed by anger and disappointment. Thus the sense of well-being derives not only from parental responses, but from the child's ability to influence these responses. The child's capacity to act and produce a desirable result decreases his sense of help-lessness and adds to his feeling of stability and self-cohesion.

During the second half of the first year, the infant has illusions of omnipotence, the third developmental line arising from nar-cissism. The infant cognitively experiences his actions as magi-cal—he kicks and a light illuminates a room (Wolff, 1976). He anticipates that kicking will turn on a light until further testing proves otherwise. He recognizes that his actions have an effect, but does not yet understand causality. He does not realistically appreciate his mother's role in gratifying his wishes; he feels that he controls the world.

When his mother is unable or unwilling to meet his demands, the child's sense of omnipotence is challenged. So too is his sense of his mother as an omnipotent provider. His sense of importance (gradiosity) and power (omnipotence) must be modified, an aspect of narcissism expressed clinically in Kohut's idealizing transfer-ence. Actual disappointing experiences correct the child's view of his omnipotent mother; he gradually confronts his parent's lim-itations. The surrender of the illusion of both his own and his mother's omnipotence must be supported by an increase in com-petence and mastery to avoid overwhelming disappointment. He must develop abilities to control his environment so as to expe-rience only tolerable amounts of helplessness. He must be more able to regulate his own sense of well-being (Kohut, 1971; Mahler, Pine, and Bergman, 1975; Spruiell, 1975). The following case illustration suggests the importance of the stepwise replacement of omnipotence by a sense of mastery.

John was a four-year-old boy, elf-like, intelligent, and highly verbal (WISC 145). He had been referred to therapy by his nurs-ery school teacher for tantrums, inability to accept limitations, difficulty playing with children, and poor toilet control. John had become angry after the birth of his brother when he was three. He had had a very close relationship with his mother, who had turned to him as a friend because of marital difficulties. His mother said that she did not want to spoil his creativity. She did not set limits for him, and exaggerated his considerable accomplishments, not noticing that he had great difficulty with fine motor coordination. He was, for example, unable to draw or hold a pencil correctly. When frustrated by not being able to do the same quality of drawing as his friends, his self-esteem suffered. Rageful, he tore up the papers of his classmates, unable to understand why his peers did not recognize him to be as great as he wished to be. Disappointed in himself and angry at his mother, he retreated into fantasy. During the first therapy interview, he threw a paper rocket, saying he would like to return to the moon. He played out stories of leaving the moon and returning to an earth full of robbers. His cars refused to obey traffic rules in play, and crashed into other cars. In psychotherapy he worked on his feelings of being small and helpless, and having a baby brother. His mother began to regard him more realistically, and the therapist encouraged her to control John's behavior. His teacher gave him writing and drawing tasks that were not quite so frustrating. Giving up his omnipotent illusions, John sadly began to see himself as a little boy who went to nursery school. Later, he took pride in reading well and in his vocabulary. Slowly, he began to talk of being a businessman like his father. His omnipotent illusions had been replaced by a realistic conception of his own competence; he saw himself as someone who could cope with angry feelings, play with friends, and succeed in school.

The joy of efficacy and approval, both external and internal, is a source of positive affect toward one's self that modifies and connects the three developmental lines of narcissism. The infant discovers that a contingency exists between his activity and a desired effect (White, 1963). The result of cumulative experiences of efficacy is an internal sense of competence. Thus, Mahler and Kaplan (1977) note that the elation of children aged six to 18 months when they accomplish a task comes from within them and is autonomous. They label this the "primitive evaluation of their accomplishments." Anna Freud (1965) comments that pleasure in achievement is linked only secondarily with object relationships. Broucek (1979) describes an experiment by Papoucek demonstrating the presence of "effectant's pleasure" at a very young age. When the subjects, aged four to five months, rotated their heads 30 degrees, multicolored lights appeared for five seconds. The infants expressed their joy and pleasure at being able to affect their environment in gestures and vocalizations. The experiment was then modified so that the infants were no longer able to affect the environment; lights did not appear when they rotated their heads. The infants became withdrawn and showed signs of distress in uncoordinated movements and vocalizations.

The mother supports the infant's pleasure in efficacy in two ways: first, by setting up an environment responsive to the child's initiative; second, by her own joy in the child's autonomous actions. With regard to the former, Sander (1962) notes the importance of reciprocal interactions between the mother and child as early as three months, and later the importance of the child's ability to initiate interactions. Thus, a child's smile usually causes a smile to appear on the mother's face; a cry from a child may get him lifted from his crib; an angry parent can become playful or loving when the infant smiles or kisses her. To repeat, the child then feels that his sense of well-being derives not only from his parent's response, but from his own ability to influence that response. He can then surrender his omnipotent illusions of himself and his parents in favor of a sense of competence and environmental mastery. Continuing adaptive behavior reinforces this sense of competence.

The case of Sandy illustrates the kind of problem that arises when a mother does not encourage a child's initiative.

Sandy was a quiet, complacent infant who seemed content to stay in his crib. Between six and 18 months he remained quietly in his room; depressed, his mother would leave him with his toys. He tried very few tasks. His mother fed him in a highchair with no table, so that he did not practice feeding himself. Fearful of her own anger, the mother became emotionally unavailable to him. During the early part of the second year, she confined Sandy to a playroom on the second floor. A gate at the top of the stairs kept him from coming down to see her. He then became angry and aggressive, throwing his toys down the stairs and hitting the door with them. He began biting and destroying books. The mother recognized his distress and consulted her pediatrician. She noted that she was not giving her son the attention he needed and responded by increasing her interaction with him, especially by reading stories, teaching him colors, and having him name items. Between the ages of two and two and a half, Sandy made startling progress. Now he loved to show what he knew, running happily around the room. He was affectionate and full of energy. As the mother became more flexible and more responsive to Sandy's overtures, the child began to initiate independent actions, physical affection, and play with his mother. He had begun to exert some control over his environment and had begun to contribute to his own sense of well-being. He appeared to have developed an adequate sense of his own importance. He was interested in mastery, loved to practice reading, coloring, and playing. His ability to influence his environment will apparently allow for the development of increased self esteem.

The corollary to the encouragement of the child's initiative is the approval of his efficacy, given first by the mother and later internalized by the child. This approval must be for real accomplishments. Erikson (1959) points out that children cannot be fooled by empty praise and condescending encouragement. They may have to accept the artificial bolstering of their self-esteem in lieu of anything better, but their ego identity gains real strength only from wholehearted and consistent recognition of their actual accomplishments.

When parents approve of the child's competence and autonomy, they provide a connection between the child's desire for increasing autonomy and his reliance on them for his sense of well-being and self-love. The child identifies with his parents' method of doing tasks and their standards of competence. These identifications are aided by his view of his parents as powerful and loving people. The child's maturation increases his ability, which, in turn, delights his parents. The child then internalizes his parents' approval and delight. This internalized approval supports his pleasure in efficacy and generates good self-esteem.

The need to be separate and to function autonomously and the desire to be with the mother become sources of conflict during the second and third years of life. During Mahler's rapprochement subphase (Mahler, Pine, and Bergman, 1975), the child becomes aware of his separateness from his parents in that he no longer needs his parents in order to accomplish a particular task. The parents' approval of his mastery makes his awareness of separateness more bearable. Still, the child often acts out the conflict between his desire for independence and his wish for closeness in ways with no easy resolution. Thus, he may want to go outdoors but may not want to put on proper clothing. He may *want* to tie his shoes but be unable to do it. The mother helps the child tolerate frustration and the fear of independence by staying nearby, encouraging autonomy but not at too great a distance. She can play, teach, be physically close with her child, and approve of what he learns, preventing the child's feeling of aloneness.

When the child does not receive parental approval, his anger at not being understood and his fear of independence increase his ambivalence. This ambivalence threatens the maintenance of his newly acquired but still unstable inner image of himself. Mastery may also feel to the child like competition with his parents. The withholding of parental approval may then be experienced as discouragement of his competitive wishes. The conflict between mastery and competition reaches its height, of course, during the oedipal years.

The following case illustrates some of the difficulties that may arise when a parent's failure to approve of her child's autonomy exacerbates the conflict between separation and mastery.

Sally was a three-and-a-half-year-old girl who entered psychotherapy with encopresis and constipation that had begun following the birth of her brother when she was two and a half. In her first two years of life she had had a solid feeling about herself and a good understanding of and identification with her mother. She was a charming, petite, extraordinarily neat child who ate a crumbling cake over a napkin, rather than spill it in the therapist's office. Precocious in her ability to feed and dress herself, she had been asked by her mother to look after her younger brother. Her mother did not permit her to express competitive and angry feelings toward her brother, nor was she allowed to run around the house and be messy; there was no joy in Sally's physical actions and she felt unable to initiate certain play activities. The mother, trying very hard to control her anger at her husband's lack of interest in the household after the birth of the boy, tried to control Sally's aggressive, assertive behavior by giving her love only when she did what she was asked, and by withholding love when she did not. During the first therapy interview, Sally told a story about a timid little monster who wanted to stay in the house, but was ignored by everyone there. During the second and third interviews, this monster became more aggressive and wanted to eat up the baby boy. Sally then became more actively aggressive toward her brother, and during one interview hit him with a glove.

The mother was helped to understand that this might be a normal reaction to Sally's feelings about her brother. She then admitted that she too was sometimes unhappy with the demanding little boy. Later, she was able to talk about how displeased she was with her husband's unwillingness to do housework.

Subsequently, Sally became free of constipation, but insisted that her mother "catch her" when she was about to have a bowel movement and lift her onto the toilet. In the therapist's view, this reflected Sally's desire to have her mother acknowledge and approve her successful accomplishment of a developmental task.

In the fifth session, Sally made the monster bigger, noisier, and more active. The monster entrapped the mother and slept in the bed with the father. Sally became interested in her father, particularly in his physical activities. Both parents became more approving of her assertiveness and autonomy and more accepting of her aggression toward her brother and her fighting with her mother. She became less jealous toward her brother, more demanding, more typical of a three-year-old, and had no more soiling problems. In the last interview, the monster became a superwoman who could fly and the superwoman took her mother flying too. Sally began to run all over the office and to take delight in the pleasures of being active, expressing elation in appropriate phallic behavior.

In the latter part of the oedipal years, the child develops an ego ideal, an internalized structure that serves to transform early narcissism into the autonomous regulatory functions of self-esteem. Freud (1914) called the ego ideal "the heir of narcissism." Reflecting the internalization of the child's wishes to be as competent and as powerful as the idealized parent, the ego ideal allows the child to provide for himself the approval his parents had given him before. The idealized representations of the parents and others, now internalized, are guides to adaptive behavior. The ego thus has both internal and external points of comparison with which to assess self-representations. The level of self-esteem then reflects the result of this assessment of self-representations against ego ideal, of self-representations against external others (Teicholz, 1978). Jacobson (1964) defines the level of self-esteem as expressing the harmony or discrepancy between one's own self-representations and one's wishful concept of the self. If a parent has been overidealized, or overcritical, excessively high parental standards may be internalized as unrealistic ego-ideal expectations, and the child's ability to value himself may be compromised. For this reason, some inhibited or depressed patients may not be able emotionally to differentiate aggression from mastery and may be unable therefore to acknowledge their assertive wishes and actions with approval. The following case illustrates such a problem.

Evelyn was a 30-year-old single woman who worked as an administrator. Complaining that she was "hooked" on the love and approval of others, and that her efforts to give to others so as to get this approval in return were draining, Evelyn was markedly inhibited in doing things for her own pleasure, particularly in her sexual relationships with men. Excellent at her work, she needed immediate satisfaction and approval from both her boss and her assistants. During psychotherapy, the same problems were repeated. Breakthroughs, particularly with regard to sex and competition, were not experienced with a sense of joy. She regressed to earlier issues of separation, of being abandoned by the therapist, with expectations of criticism from the therapist rather than approval.

At the age of two she had been expected to take care of her new brother, with not much attention being paid to her needs. Her autonomous actions had not been supported and she had been unable to internalize approval from her parents for independent behavior. She felt loved, but also unable adequately to control her environment. She pictured herself in dreams as a very small car, the size of a suitcase, or a Volkswagen with flat tires, or an engine with a pin missing. She felt comfortable when her friends and colleagues agreed with her and mirrored her feelings. She felt least comfortable when she tried to do something for herself that would increase her sense of competence and mastery. Thus, she had been unable to complete her application for graduate school and had become entangled in an ambivalent, dependent sexual relationship, reminiscent of the child-parent relationship in the rapprochement subphase. One dream in particular illustrates her conflict: In it, she looked out the window at the joys of the world; when she turned around, her bed was missing. Her association to this dream was that if she left her house, she would be unable to return to her idealized mother.

This patient lacked an internalized capacity to take pleasure in her own autonomous actions. What pleasure and sense of well-being she experienced was connected entirely to feelings of being mirrored and approved by others. Her omnipotence had not been replaced by her own recognition, appreciation, and approval of her competence. Rather, it had given way to a desire to be taken care of by an idealized, powerful person. Thus she desired her male companions to be bigger and more important than she was. She wanted their love to make up for her own feelings of lack of accomplishment. Preoccupied with the social status of her male friends, she could not make judgments about their reliability or commitment to her. She was unable to maintain attachments to men based on realistic expectations of affection and support.

Evelyn's case is hardly an isolated one. Many patients rely heavily on the love and approval of others for narcissistic support and regulation of self-esteem. Their loved ones then become valued for the contributions they make to self-image rather than for their own attributes. This external reliance on other people leads to unstable self-esteem as well as an inability to love outside of the narcissistic orbit (Eisnitz, 1969).

SUMMARY

The developmental relationship of self-esteem to narcissism provides a connection between the new psychology of narcissism and the older, more traditional psychoanalytic structural psychology. Narcissism is modified by internalized object relationships and by the developing ego. Self-love, the regulation of well-being, and omnipotence are three developmental lines of narcissism that can be traced. Continuing mastery and adaptiveness, supported by approval, first external and then internalized, substitute for the narcissistic illusion of omnipotence and become the basis for good self-esteem. As Freud stated in 1914: "Self-regard does have a very intimate dependence on narcissistic libido." We would add now: when narcissism is transformed.

162   *Judith N. Huizenga*

REFERENCES

Broucek, F. (1979), Efficacy in infancy: A review of some experimental studies and their possible implications for clinical theory. *Internat. J. Psycho-Anal.*, 60:311–316.
Eisnitz, H. F. (1969), Narcissistic object choice, self-representation. *Internat. J. Psycho-Anal.*, 50:15–25.
Erikson, E. H. (1959), *Identity and the Life Cycle.* New York: Norton.
Freud, A. (1965), *Normality and Pathology in Childhood.* New York: International Universities Press.
Freud, S. (1914), On narcissism: An introduction. *Standard Edition*, 14:73–102. London: Hogarth Press, 1957.
Jacobson, E. (1964), The self and the object world. In: *Essays on Ego Psychology.* New York: International Universities Press, pp. 113–141.
Kohut, H. (1971), *The Analysis of the Self.* New York: International Universities Press.
Mahler, M, Pine, F., & Bergman, A. (1975), *The Psychological Birth of the Human Infant.* New York: Basic Books.
———— & Kaplan, L. (1977), Developmental aspects in the assessment of narcissistic and so-called borderline patients. In: *Borderline Personality Disorders*, ed. P. Hartocollis. New York: International Universities Press, pp. 71–85.
Nagera, H. (1973), Additions to Anna Freud's developmental profile. Unpublished paper.
Pulver, S. E. (1970), Narcissism: The term and the concept. *J. Amer. Psychoanal. Assn.*, 18:319–341.
Sander, L. W. (1962), Issues in early mother-child interaction. *J. Amer. Acad. Child Psychiat.*, 1:141–166.
Schafer, R. (1968), *Aspects of Internalization.* New York: International Universities Press.
Spruiell, V. (1975), Three strands of narcissism. *Psychoanal. Quart.*, 4:577–593.
Teicholz, J. G. (1978), A selective review of the psychoanalytic literature on theoretical conceptualizations of narcissism. *J. Amer. Psychoanal. Assn.*, 26:831–860.
White, R. (1963), *Ego and Reality in Psychoanalytic Theory.* New York: International Universities Press.
Wolff, P. H. (1976), Developmental and motivational concepts in Piaget's sensorimotor theory of intelligence. In: *Infant Psychiatry*, ed. E. Rexford, L. Sander, & T. Shapiro. New Haven: Yale University Press, pp. 172–186.

7

The Parent-Child Relationship and the

Development of Self-Esteem

FRANCES GIVELBER, ACSW, LICSW

Rexford, Sander, and Shapiro (1976) conceptualize the parent-child relationship as "an open, interactive, regulative system, each component member participating in exchanges which mutually influence and regulate the behavior of the other" (p. xvii). This conceptualization is consistent with Winnicott's idea that "the infant and the maternal care together form a unit" (1976, p. 39). Indeed, Winnicott was so insistent on this point that he stated somewhat facetiously that the infant as an entity does not exist at all (1976, p. 39). From the earliest moments, the parent-infant relationship is shaped by reciprocity[1]; the qualities of both partners determine how they influence and change each other and their shared experience.

My emphasis in the paper is on the early parent-child relationship. I will not attempt to delineate the discrete tasks of mother and father.[2] Rather, I intend to focus on the *commonality* of parenting functions. In my view, five parenting tasks are crucial to the evolution of self-esteem:

Winnicott's term, *"good enough" mothering* (1976, p. 145), describes a quality of parenting that responds to the basic physiological and emotional needs of the infant. These essential features

---

[1] Sander defines " 'reciprocal' interaction" between mother and infant "as that showing the quality of stimulus-response alternation," typified by smiling interchanges between mother and infant (1976, p. 136). He believes that the success of later development depends on the dyad's ability to find new areas for reciprocity, such as vocalizing or play (1976, p. 138).

[2] It is beyond the scope of the paper to discuss the specific functions of the father in early child development. A number of authors have written in this area. See Abelin (1971, 1975), Burlingham (1973), Herzog (1977, 1980), and Stoller (1979).

of mothering include acceptance, responsiveness, sensitivity, and tolerance of the infant and his particular needs.

Separateness describes the parent's ability to differentiate a child's needs and feelings from his own and to acknowledge and support the child as a separate person.

Anxiety mastery refers to the parent's capacity to teach the child that anxiety can be tolerated. A parent, given his own ability to handle anxiety, empathically encourages the child to meet and triumph over new and frightening experiences.

Mirroring of affect and achievement reflects the parent's understanding of the child's feelings and pleasurable responsiveness to his achievements. Kohut defines mirroring as an empathic response to "a child's demands for attention, approval, and for the confirmatory echoing of its presence" (1971, p. 124).

Promotion of growth and maturation refers to the parent's effort to guide the child toward an increasingly realistic sense of himself and the world. Optimal frustration is understood as necessary for development.

These five parenting tasks are essential to the development of self-esteem regulation. Healthy self-esteem regulation is a highly sophisticated evaluative function that develops in the context of a successful reciprocity between parent and child. It is an ego function that "expresses . . . approval or disapproval and indicates the extent to which an individual believes himself to be capable, significant and worthy . . . a personal judgement of worthiness" (Coopersmith, 1967, pp. 4–5). Conscious and unconscious components of the inner psychic structures of ego, superego, and ego ideal contribute to the evaluation, which is essentially a measure of the gap between what one is and what one wants to be.

The ability to provide the experiences of "good enough" mothering, separateness, anxiety mastery, mirroring, and support for growth and maturation does not derive solely from the qualities of the parents; the ability to parent evolves in part from parenting itself. Mutuality leads each partner in the parent-infant dyad to influence the other so that the very nature of the experience is affected. The quality of the parent-child reciprocity affects the parents' own sense of themselves, their feelings of competence and self-esteem as parents.

To be successful the reciprocity must allow for growth and adaptation to changing developmental needs and reality. Two essential paradoxes are contained here. The parent needs to accept the child's *being*, his current level of functioning, while encouraging the child's *becoming* more mature. The parent must also empathically and momentarily feel *what the child feels* while maintaining an ongoing psychological *separateness*. Good self-esteem evolves from the parental ability to maintain these seemingly paradoxical positions.

Many factors shape a mother or father's self-esteem in the parenting role. Conditions predating the birth of the child contribute, including the economic and social well-being of the family, the meaning of the new baby to the family, the parents' relationship or lack of it, as in single-parent families, the emotional health and maturity of the parents, especially their own histories of being valued and loved as children. The reciprocity between husband and wife bears directly on the parenting experience. The husband supports and nurtures his wife so that she can care for the infant without becoming depleted (see Herzog, 1977, p. 15; Stoller, 1979, p. 839).

Becoming a parent reactivates identifications with one's own parents and with one's self as infant and child. If these identifications are based on positive self- and object representations, parenting is more easily pleasurable and enhances self-esteem. The parent will be relatively free to perceive and respond to the child's needs in creative and adaptive ways. If the identifications are based on negative self- and object-representations, parenting will be burdened by efforts to overcome the dreaded identifications—by perfectionism, for example, with rage breaking through at inevitable failures. Identification with the aggressor, the parent's own unempathic parent, may lead the new parent to repeat with his child his own parent's painful attitudes toward himself. Preoccupied with their own internal struggles, parents can be distracted from being optimally attuned to the needs of the child. This lack of competence in parenting may further depress the self-esteem of the parents.

The self-esteem of the parent is influenced by the mother-child fit, the coming together of the mother's particular rhythms, character, and skills with the individual features of her baby. The

infant arrives with his unique characteristics: the maturity of his
neurostructure, temperament, tolerance for stress, patterns of
engaging his parent, and ability to be soothed. Tolpin (1971) uses
the concept "good-enough infant-mother unit" to stress the baby's
innate qualities as they affect the mother (p. 334). The concept
of fit refers not to sameness, but a harmonious adaptation that
reflects back to the mother evidence of her worth. The parent can
feel competent in his or her role only to the extent that such a fit
is achieved—to the extent that each partner in the dyad can make
the necessary adaptations. Some mothers can adapt only to a baby
with predictable rhythms; others can be relatively comfortable
with more erratic behavior. In either case, the mother must feel
that she knows her baby and that he is flourishing and responsive
to her interventions. In this process of mutual adaptation, the
mother is the leader; Sander (1976) believes that the mutuality
achieved depends on how a mother balances empathy and objectivity. Empathy helps her to *feel* her child's needs; objectivity allows
her to assess her baby's particular cues. Parents vary widely in this
balance which determines how appropriately the mother responds
to her individual baby (p. 132).

Parents see in their child's well-being a measure of their own
worth, which, in turn, affects their ability to respond to their
children. Unresponsive or fretful infants can deprive their parents
of this kind of measure. There is a reciprocal relationship between
a child's sending ability and a mother's capacity to mother. The
baby whose responses are muted can subtly rebuff a mother who
may then pull back in a rejected, helpless mood. In writing about
the circular nature of mother-child relationships, Erikson (1950)
draws our attention to the interdependence of positive feeling
states: "The relationship [is] an emotional pooling which may
multiply well-being in both, but which will endanger both partners
when the communication becomes jammed or weakened" (p. 181).
Any developmental difficulty in the child can stimulate feelings
of failure in the parents. A defective child can lower the parent's
self-esteem; but parental self-esteem can also suffer with the less
seriously abnormal child, or with a normal baby in a bad fit. Lax
(1972) describes "the narcissistic trauma" to the mother who bears
an impaired child; to the extent that she experiences her child as
an extension of her defective self, the mother will be depressed

(pp. 339–340). (These issues are also applicable to fathers.) The child's responses play a part here too; an impaired child may be less able to engage and respond.

Early development offers a chance to study the five parental tasks crucial for the growth of a child's self-esteem. Although I am focusing on parental behavior, I am also assuming that the outcome of each developmental stage depends upon the mutual adaptation of parent and child; the innate attributes of the baby are as significant as the attributes of the parent.

To clarify, let me discuss these five tasks in a developmental sequence, thereby to indicate the critical stage or stages for each parental function. This is not to say that once it appears, a task ever totally disappears; it remains an important factor in the parent's continuing responses to the child. The tasks do not emerge and disappear at discrete moments, but interweave in the harmonious complexity of parental relating. But the relative importance of each task shifts as the child internalizes the parental function.

In the first year of life, the parent must respond empathically to the baby's emotional and physiological needs. The mutual regulation and adaptation of the first developmental period grow directly out of this ability. The baby who experiences "good-enough" mothering develops the important feeling of omnipotence and also feels a confidence (as distinguished from a delusional omnipotence) based on his real competence in the relationship; for example, in cuing and engaging his mother. This confidence is a precursor of later feelings of internal capability, in time connected to actual abilities and skills. If successful, these early interactions give the infant a deep sense of worthiness, of what Erikson calls "inner goodness" (1950, p. 219).

The process of separation-individuation climaxes in the second half of the second year of life. Yet the parent must encourage separation-individuation even as the infant is still totally dependent, by recognizing the infant's increasing ability to signal the mother to express needs (Winnicott, 1976, p. 50). Winnicott emphasizes that the parent must shift from an empathic interpreting of the infant's needs to recognizing the infant's signal. He places this change in the context of beginning separation—perhaps at five months—but even from the earliest moment infants cue their parents to their preferred ways of nursing, being held, soothed, etc. As the baby matures and the initial symbiosis gives way to differentiation, a more complex empathy is required of the parent; he or she must move from empathy that is an intuitive leap to empathy that is an intricate response to the baby's signals. The parent affirms and validates the baby's separateness and uniqueness by respecting his signals.

Parental attitudes towards the child's assertiveness are crucial. Can the parents show pleasure in the toddler's steps *away* from them? Can they acknowledge and support (or at least not crush) their child's early initiative—favored and hated foods, insistence on holding his own spoon? The parent must accept and contain within flexible limits the child's unavoidable rages and tantrums. This acceptance allows the child to sustain his feelings of inner goodness and omnipotence, now modified by awareness of his separateness from the mother and his own relative helplessness. The child learns to keep this feeling of goodness even when his parents are absent; he also learns that his parents' acceptance of him is not based on his passive compliance, but includes his active assertion of individuality.

The parent must foster the tolerance and mastery of anxiety. This task begins early in infancy as the sensitive mother or father responds to the infant's physiological stress early and adequately enough so that the infant does not too often experience overpowering anxiety. Winnicott's concept of "holding" describes this parental function (1976, p. 47). Thus the process of separation-individuation must occur in a gradual way that does not overwhelm the child with anxiety. Mahler (1980) has delineated the specific subphases of this process and the quality of maternal accessibility that the child requires to avoid traumatic anxiety. The practicing subphase (7–10 through 15–16 months) and the rapprochement subphase (15 months through 22 months or longer) are of particular importance in this process (pp. 3–19). Tolpin (1971) introduces the idea of phase appropriate or "just right" anxiety with implications for the development of self-esteem. If the parent can regulate the level of anxiety, the child internalizes the mother's soothing function and develops signal anxiety. If the expected pattern for the dyad is then stress, signal anxiety, pleasurable maternal intervention, and relief, then signal anxiety can be associated with mastery (pp. 339–345). This experience of mild stress as a welcome challenge is an early component of self-esteem. The child learns to bear anxiety and separateness; this sense of mastery is then integrated into the child's self-concept. To tolerate anxiety furthers the child's ability to deal with new situations, learn, bear uncertainty, and move ahead.

A number of writers use the concept of mirroring to describe a particular parental responsiveness necessary to a child's identity and positive sense of himself.[3] For Kohut mirroring implies an empathic relatedness, including understanding, approval, and delight, all of which the child needs throughout his development (1971, p. 117). At first, when the parents respond to the infant's random movements, gestures, and moods, their mirroring organizes the infant's experience, giving it affective meaning. The baby's developing sense of self is formed through this interaction.

During the toddler period of grandiosity, the parent's admiration nurtures the child's self-love (Mahler, 1974, p. 99). As the child gradually surrenders his omnipotence, the parent's mirroring allows the child to emerge with self-esteem intact, able to invest in learning new skills. Even in latency the mirroring function supports the child's unsteady ability to praise himself for his own achievements.

Although over time mirroring occurs with actual achievements, it is essential that the parents first accept the child as a person, including his assertiveness, drive expression, exhibitionism, and grandiosity. The mother and father's acceptance and joy in the child become incorporated into the child's sense of himself.

The fifth parenting task is to support the child's developmental thrust towards growth and maturation, encouraging such ego capacities as verbalization, frustration tolerance, sublimation, and object relations. These ego capacities enable a child to find diverse and realistic sources of self-esteem in the world apart from his family. The task begins in the second year of life. The standards set by the parents must not be too far ahead of the child's ability; a toddler needs his mother's help to control his aggression and possessiveness, to verbalize his wishes and his feelings, and to learn

[3] See Winnicott's discussion of the "mirror-role of mother and family in child development" (1971, p. 131) and Mahler's description of the function of the mother's "mirroring admiration" of the toddler (1974, p. 99).

object-related behavior. When the parents expect competent behavior, they support the child's ability to learn this behavior. The
parent must respond to regressive behavior with understanding
and empathy for the anxiety the child is experiencing and with
an expectation of eventual resumption of age-appropriate behavior.

Small failures in parental empathy are unavoidable and, in fact,
help the child mature. As these failures occur, throughout the
preoedipal and oedipal period, the child's resulting frustration
leads to self-object differentiation; his aggression toward the parent aids in separation. If these failures are not excessive, a child
learns to accept these inevitable disappointments in his idealized
parents. He separates psychologically, becomes increasingly real-
ity-oriented with respect to them and himself, and internalizes the
parent's soothing function (Kohut, 1971, p. 64). These inevitable
failures are growth-promoting for the child; they further the development of internal psychic structures which make independent
functioning possible.

Parental approval must shift in response to the changing developmental needs of the child. The original grandiosity is slowly
transformed into attainable goals through the identifications of
the oedipal and latency period; impulses are mastered and adaptive energies are nurtured. In this way a child develops a realistic
self-image based on healthy identifications and actual skills. This
complex, evolving process is important during the second half of
latency when the parent encourages the gaining of skills in learning, athletics, sublimations, and peer relationships.

In the final section of this paper I will look at three clinical
examples of mother-child relationships to illustrate how the major
parental tasks aid in the development of self-esteem in the child.
These tasks combine the parent's attitudes and behavior, expressing to the child the parent's idea of who the child is and who he
can become—the parent's belief in the child's basic goodness and
badness, capability or inadequacy. The parent's belief becomes
part of the child's own sense of his worth. The specific behavior
of the parent influences ego development, making mastery possible.

Ruthie, a well-adjusted and independent three-year-old who
had experienced previous separations from her working mother,

began to exhibit separation anxiety when dropped off at her day care center. Efforts to ease the child's tearful distress by prolonging the "goodby" were unsuccessful. Finally, the mother offered her daughter an unusual transitional object—a hastily drawn sketch of a dog mother and father wheeling their dog baby in a pram. The child grasped the picture with delight, and morning partings became manageable with the aid of this new ritual. The device worked well for both mother and child: It bound the mother's anxiety and guilt about leaving her daughter and gave her a sense of active mastery as a parent. Ruthie was soothed in a way that allowed her to feel that her "baby" wishes were recognized and accepted, but that her "schoolgirl" abilities were also encouraged.

This simple interchange contains in distilled form all the parental tasks important in the development of self-esteem, but it especially illustrates the mother's role as teacher in mastering anxiety. In discussing this issue, Weigert (1970) uses the evocative expression "mother as stable leader." The mother must not fully identify with the child's anxiety, but with his "growing potentialities" (p. 169). She must respond to the signal of fear with both empathy and the expectation that eventually the child can master the fear.

With Ruthie the successful outcome depended on well-functioning reciprocity—the child's signal of stress and the mother's multidimensional response of empathy, expectation of mastery, and a specific aid to enable mastery. The qualities of both partners contributed to the resolution—resourcefulness and creativity in the mother and a corresponding flexibility and capacity for symbolic representation in the child. Another mother might have responded with more abruptness, anxiety, or less play. Another child might have been unable to accept the drawing as restitution and might have continued to protest unconsolably.

The second illustration comes from the treatment of a professional man in his forties, Mr. E. Although functioning in a highly competent manner, validated by career advancements, he retained an unreliable sense of self-worth and felt that his outward achievements were a sham and only hid his inner repulsiveness.

His developmental history pointed to a bad mother-infant fit. He was a colicky baby who cried constantly. As a toddler he had clung and screamed when his mother tried to leave the room. Mother and son were never able to establish a mutually enhancing reciprocity. Conveying her own sense of failure and rejection, his mother had told him, "You were miserable from the day you were born." At the age of six, Mr. E functioned as a third parent, helping in the physical care of his two younger brothers. The complicated role gave him a special, valued position in the family and in his eyes, but he was mortified by his awareness of his secret jealousy and anger toward his brothers and parents. He developed a public sense of himself as a good boy and a secret sense as a bad, angry boy. The good boy was a responsible helper at home, first in his classes at school, called "Einstein" by his father. The bad boy told lies, stole toys from other children, scribbled on the walls, and let a younger brother take the blame and beating. He remembered worrying that God would punish him for his evil ways.

His parents had been able to praise him for his academic achievements, but had been unable to respond to his emotional needs. When he was seven, he was sent on a week's vacation to unfamiliar grandparents. Acutely lonely and frightened, he felt unable to tell his parents; they could not sense his unhappiness from the phone calls and extended the separation an extra week. His parents did not know how to help him acknowledge, understand, and bear his feelings of neediness, anger, and jealousy. When upset, he would scream and hide in his closet, listening for footsteps, but his parents usually let him "cry it out." His mother told him that he had "tyrannized" the whole family. Mr. E. remembered being convinced that he was a "potential murderer" and that his parents had kept away from him during his tantrums because they were frightened of him.

Here is an example of reciprocity gone awry, of the cost when a parent emphasizes and reinforces hypermature functioning without accepting and responding to the whole child. Self-worth suffers because the child feels that his achievements are an exterior pretense, a "false self" constructed to comply with his parents' wishes (Winnicott, 1976, pp. 140–152). The child also feels that the parents' mirroring is based on a false identity and that the true, hidden self is evil, inadequate, or unlovable. Such a development does not provide for true mastery of affects, but leads to an unstable solution based on walling off parts of the self.

Because of their own problems with impulse control and modulation of affect (the father identified his son's outbursts with his own father's violent psychosis; the mother had explosive rages), neither parent could help their son control his tantrums and communicate his underlying depressed or helpless feelings. His choice of a closet for the temper tantrums seemed to reflect an effort to substitute physical structure both for absent emotional holding and for his corresponding lack of inner controls. Self-esteem regulation remained an ongoing problem.

An eight-year-old boy, Billy, and his mother were referred to a psychiatric inpatient children's unit after unsuccessful outpatient treatment. Billy, intelligent and engaging, was a highly anxious child, unable to modulate his impulses or affect either at home or in school. He was provocative, had tantrums, and hit children. Clinical assessment and projective testing revealed an angry, impulsive child with low self-esteem. He felt vulnerable, deprived, and bad. While his teacher was writing a psychosocial evaluation, Billy commented, "Write down that I said I wanted to die."

From the beginning a series of stresses had jeopardized the mother-child relationship. His mother, unstable emotionally and alcoholic until Billy was two, had never wanted the pregnancy. The ensuing marriage to Billy's father soon ended, and when the father disappeared when Billy was five months old, the mother was overwhelmed by motherhood. Her parents criticized her parenting and competed with her over Billy's care. Her self-esteem as a mother was low; as she said to her social worker, "I wouldn't pass a test for motherhood." Both her family and the negative feedback from the school confirmed her view.

By the first grade, Billy's behavioral symptoms were severe. His mother treated him as "the man of the house," was seductive with him, and could not nurture him as a little boy. Before one of the diagnostic interviews, Billy fixed himself a drink in the staff room, implying that he had been "helping himself" for a long time.

Although the mother was upset by Billy's behavior, especially by the school's pressure and criticism, she seemed unaware of his suffering and anxiety and could not help Billy learn to control his anger. He ordered her around like a bossy husband or father and she complied or tried to distract him, alternating between appeasement and sudden angry punishments. She felt as helpless as Billy and had no more flexibility than he did in modulating anger. She would ask, "Should I ignore him or hit him?"

The unit staff viewed their relationship as a "closed system" that did not easily permit outside influence. The mother told the staff, "I've always felt that it was me and Billy against the world." Although frustrated by his behavior, she revealed that she "admired his strength and his fight." She sabotaged treatment efforts to help Billy with his behavior.

Billy's aggressive behavior reflected an immature ego overwhelmed by anxiety and unneutralized rage. His primitive omnipotence had not been successfully modified by the reality-based experience of turning to his mother in distress and having her respond to his feelings and needs. His animal choice, "Godzilla, a fire-shooting giant," indicated his counterphobic way of handling situations that made him feel inadequate or helpless. His statement that he did not want to be "an ant . . . I'd get stepped on" revealed his conviction that he was worthless, powerless, and in danger. Billy's aggressive behavior may have originally been a desperate attempt to signal his mother and attract her attention. Depressed or in an alcoholic haze, she had not responded, causing him to increase his efforts to engage her, or had responded angrily, leading to the same result. A pathological reciprocity had begun early, maintaining a maladaptive relationship between mother and son and, for Billy, a self-defeating style of meeting the world. He preserved a false sense of control and power to cover up an inner feeling of being little and helpless.

A child's capacity for self-regulation and mastery depends on the parents' ability to set appropriate limits. Limits on a child's demands and drives set expectations for mature functioning. Coopersmith (1967) found that clear and enforced limits correlate positively with high self-esteem in the child. Limits help the child differentiate between himself and the environment. The clarity of parental expectations allows him to assess his own behavior without reliance on others (pp. 238–239).

In not enforcing limits, Billy's mother unconsciously joined his protest, his feelings of deprivation, and his rage. She seemed to be reworking earlier struggles with her own parents, who had controlled her tightly as a child. She planned, for example, to drive Billy to her father's house for a spanking. This identification with her son prevented Billy from resolving his painful conflicts and resulting feelings of loss, deprivation, and rage. Billy, not free to use his adaptive energies in the pursuit of realistic achievements and satisfying relationships, continued to elicit only negative responses from his world. He internalized these criticisms and felt an inner sense of badness. There was no area in his life in which he felt successful, competent, and valued.

CONCLUSION

If the parent successfully accomplishes the tasks necessary for self-esteem, the child feels that his unique self is worthy and capable; he is free to develop skills and to evaluate himself and his life in an increasingly independent and realistic way. This implies a true psychological separation from one's parents with the conviction that one's pleasure in self-initiated activity is possible, safe, and does not risk the loss of the parent's love. The process of maintaining positive self-esteem continues throughout development; the issue of one's self-worth is never settled permanently, but meets new challenges at each stage of growth.

The developmental movement of self-esteem is toward independent, internally regulated functioning so that the particular kind of parent-child reciprocity of the early years is not needed by the older child, the adolescent, or the adult. But the independence of one's self-esteem from external input remains a relative matter so that even healthy adults need some positive affirmation from their environment. Schafer (1968) takes issue with aspects of classical analytic theory that pose an ideal of a completely internalized regulation of self-esteem: *"To some extent and within limits* people with highly developed moral standards continuously redefine what is moral and estimable about themselves in terms of what the environment appears to recognize, accept and reward" (p. 157). The maintenance of self-esteem for the individual is only possible within the context of ongoing object relations and the wider social situation.

REFERENCES

Abelin, E. (1971), The role of the father in the separation-individuation process. In: *Separation-Individuation: Essays in Honor of Margaret S. Mahler*, ed, J. B.

McDevitt & C. F. Settlage. New York: International Universities Press, pp. 229–252.
——— (1975), Some further observations and comments on the earliest role of the father. *Internat. J. Psycho-Anal.*, 56:293–302.
Burlingham, D. (1973), The preoedipal infant-father relationship. *The Psychoanalytic Study of the Child*, 28:23–47.
Coopersmith, S. (1967), *The Antecedents of Self-Esteem*. San Francisco: W. H. Freeman.
Erikson, E. H. (1950), *Childhood and Society*. New York: Norton.
Herzog, J. (1977), Patterns of parenting. Presented to the American Academy of Child Psychiatry, Houston.
——— (1980), Sleep disturbance and father hunger in 18- to 28-month-old boys. The Erlkönig Syndrome. *The Psychoanalytic Study of the Child*, 35:219–233. New Haven: Yale University Press.
Kohut, H. (1971), *The Analysis of the Self*. New York: International Universities Press.
Lax, R. (1972), Some aspects of the interaction between mother and impaired child: Mother's narcissistic trauma. *Internat. J. Psycho-Anal.*, 53:339–344.
Mahler, M. S. (1974), Symbiosis and individuation. *The Psychoanalytic Study of the Child*, 29:89–106. New Haven: Yale University Press.
——— (1980), Rapprochement subphase of the separation-individuation process. In: *Rapprochement: The Critical Subphase of Separation-Individuation*, ed. R. F. Lax, S. Bach, & J. A. Burland. New York: Jason Aronson, pp. 3–19.
Rexford, E. N., Sander, L. W., & Shapiro, T. (1976), Introduction. In: *Infant Psychiatry: A New Synthesis*, ed. E. N. Rexford, L. W. Sander, & T. Shapiro. New Haven: Yale University Press, pp. xv–xix.
Sander, L. W. (1976), Issues in early mother-child interaction. In: *Infant Psychiatry: A New Synthesis*, ed. E. N. Rexford, L. W. Sander, & T. Shapiro. New Haven: Yale University Press, pp. 127–147.
Schafer, R. (1968), *Aspects of Internalization*. New York: International Universities Press.
Stoller, R. J. (1979), Fathers of transsexual children. *J. Amer. Psychoanal. Assn.*, 27:837–866.
Tolpin, M. (1971), On the beginnings of a cohesive self: An application of the concept of transmuting internalization to the study of the transitional object and signal anxiety. *The Psychoanalytic Study of the Child*, 26:316–352. New York: Quadrangle.
Weigert, E. (1970), *The Courage to Love*. New Haven: Yale University Press.
Winnicot, D. W. (1971), *Playing and Reality*. London: Penguin Books.
——— (1976), *The Maturational Processes and the Facilitating Environment*. New York: International Universities Press.

8

Clinical Illustrations of the Regulation of

Self-Esteem

DAVID VAN BUSKIRK, M.D.

The work of the individual psychotherapist with a child or adolescent centers upon the discovery of themes that fit conceptual frameworks of the developing mind. In this paper I shall use two case abstracts to illustrate a conceptual framework for self-esteem relevant to the clinical situation. In each, the reader will be aware of several possible alternative formulations, based on object loss, depression, or narcissism. My purpose here is to take self-esteem as a primary focus so as to advance our understanding of its clinical significance.

CASE 1

Veronica was a seven-year-old child whose adoptive parents had become upset by her angry outbursts and black moods. So unmanageable had her behavior become toward the end of the first grade that the school principal had resorted to suspending her for days at a time to provide her teacher and classmates relief from her kicking, namecalling, and scratching assaults. At home, there were days at a time when she was scowling, sullen, and destructive of her own dolls and toys.

Veronica had been adopted when her foster brother was four years old. His own delivery had been such a life-threatening experience for his mother that her obstetrician had warned her not to risk another conception. When they decided to adopt, the parents were living in the Far East and were sent to talk with a

I am grateful to Elizabeth Van Buskirk for her help in editing this paper.

pregnant teenager about the possibility of adopting her child. Veronica's natural mother was described as healthy, intelligent, and well-mannered. At home, the two-week-old infant was found to be fussy and demanding. According to mother, Veronica mastered the milestones of development during that first year, but never accommodated herself to a household schedule that included four regular feedings a day, bedtime at seven o'clock, and a three-hour nap each afternoon. Once she had begun to walk at 11 months, there was an endless series of struggles. She refused to accept limits—not to touch the dishes on the table or to open kitchen cabinets. Her mother revealed the intensity of her wish "to break her stubbornness" in a succession of measures: spanking, closeting Veronica in her room, tying her into a chair. When she defiantly grabbed some cake, her mother slapped her hand; when she did so again, she was locked in her room without dinner. The parents pursued order and demanded control while Veronica fought incessantly against them.

At nursery school her need to dominate other children emerged. She would loudly demand certain dolls and snatch them away from others. With babysitters she became stubbornly negative, hit and kicked when it was time to go to bed, and drove several sitters away from her care. The "black moods" had been noticed for almost three years and Veronica's parents were puzzled by their inexplicable recurrence. During this time she called herself "shitty" and "stupid." She savagely hit her treasured stuffed animals and pulled arms and legs from a favorite Barbie doll. Again and again she provoked her parents into sending her away from the dinner table by poking her older brother with her shoe or by spitting in her food. As abruptly as they had appeared, the moods lifted and there were weeks when Veronica's helpfulness and imagination charmed those around her.

When she played in her suburban neighborhood, Veronica sought younger children whom she could easily dominate. She had long sessions with them of housekeeping, encouraging a four-year-old child to curl up in her lap while kissing and fondling and talking baby talk, and imaginatively creating meals of playdough cakes and cookies. But occasionally Veronica's peaceful play ended in wild rages. She chased one five-year-old with a baseball bat and beat him with it on the legs. Without the intervention of an adult, it appeared that she would have continued her assault on the child.

After a few good weeks in the first grade, where she mastered reading skills quite well and interested the other children by telling exciting stories, Veronica's initial school adjustment deteriorated. She furiously scratched a boy who stood ahead of her in a lunch line and kicked him repeatedly when he tried to push her away. She spat at her teacher when her back was turned and called her "the ugly witch lady." The teacher found that her performance continued to slip and wrote movingly of her own personal dilemma:

> I have been attempting to be positive but realistic. We often—in fact, each day we start out—being affectionate and friendly. Usually by the end of the day, there have been so many incidents that it has been difficult to keep up a good mood. Lately I have been depressed about the fact that I seem to be scolding her so often. The needs of other children must also be met. It is difficult to avoid noticing or to overlook too many of her difficulties. She is being harmed by having so much negative attention brought on her.

The teacher tried to help Veronica gain self-control by sending her out of class, having her stay in the principal's office for at least an hour each day. But her behavior became more provocative during the spring months, and the principal told her parents to keep Veronica home until they obtained psychiatric help.

When Veronica first came to my office, she was prettily dressed in a skirt with embroidered butterflies and flowers. Her features were delicate and her hair carefully braided in tight pigtails. Although she entered my office enthusiastically, she was cautious in exploring it. She looked into each bin of toys, picked up a puppet and then a game, but gingerly replaced each as she had found it. She seemed to be awaiting words from me as to what would be permitted. As she crayoned a picture of a house, she told me of a mother who lived there with two babies. The mother took them to see the doctor, but they were afraid of needles and ran away. She then drew a picture of a girl and meticulously copied a butterfly from her skirt for the girl's dress. However, she found that she had made one arm shorter than the other, tried to lengthen it, and, becoming upset, crumpled the picture and threw it out. The next drawing seemed better proportioned, but part way through the detailing of the skirt she proclaimed, "It's awful, awful, awful!" and threw it out. When I commented on the embroidered butterflies on her skirt, Veronica said, "She makes me wear this. I like to go barefoot and wear jeans. She says I'll get athlete's foot like my brother has." She then told a story of a two-year-old girl who got mad at her mother and ran away.

At the conclusion of my evaluation, I explained my findings to Veronica's parents and recommended that both mother and daughter be seen in individual treatment by separate therapists. Her mother complained about the lack of understanding in the school and told me that they had suggested that Veronica repeat the first grade with a new teacher the following year. Although they agreed to the recommendation that Veronica begin therapy in the fall, they rejected the referral of the mother to treatment. As a compromise, it was arranged that they would meet monthly with me to discuss Veronica's current behavior.

During six months of weekly play therapy, Veronica expressed themes charged with self-loathing, fury, and magical solutions. She played house, telling of the mother whose efforts to tend her children were interrupted by a witch who forced the mother to drink poisonous lemonade: The mother narrowly escaped death. The little girl who lived there was "bad because she talked too much," and wanted to feed her mother and her baby sister. Since her mother wouldn't let her, she fed the squirrels instead. Veronica brought in numerous stuffed animals during the early months of therapy, and told me how her panda and her kitten were going on trips around the world. Her play in the doll house with a mother doll, crabbing at the baby girl because she wouldn't sweep the floor, would be interrupted as she took her stuffed panda on another Asian or Florida adventure. And to save the animals from the tornados or attacking eagles or spiders in trees, she developed a series of magical medicines and flying helpers who hid out inside caverns deep under the mountains. One day she spoke of how she was born far away and that her real mother was still there. She knew that she had left before her mother had even taught her how to speak, and that her new mother and father had now forgotten the seven words of her native language which they had once known. Efforts to help her go on with this led to her drawing tight designs and refusing to comment even upon the colors she chose. Her preoccupation with mothering also came out with a family of stuffed squirrels which she often brought with her to therapy. Once, a little squirrel had gone across the street to the big park and caught "tree pox." She made him a pillow from cotton, a blanket from paper, and covered him with a "quilt" made from a piece of cloth she had taken from home. She asked me to make some pills so that she could doctor her sick squirrel. In a later session, the girl squirrel had a broken tail. One day, Veronica told me that the baby squirrel had swallowed "black gum from the tree" and that it ran right out to the tip of the baby's nails. "Anyone can see that's why he's sick and bad," she stated.

Although Veronica's behavior and achievement had seemed to improve during the fall and winter months, after six months of treatment her principal called to tell me that she had stolen money from her teacher's desk, had lied about bringing a book from home, and had falsely accused a classmate of stealing a Barbie doll and burning its hair off. Nothing in the parents' prior reports accounted for this. Her therapy had seemed to be progressing. Veronica's parents blamed the school and therapy for failing to prevent her stealing. They turned aside my explanations about the need for continued treatment and despite all my efforts to convince them that Veronica needed time to work on these issues, they terminated her visits.

CASE 2

Annette was 18 when her mother brought her to see me for an evaluation after she had dropped out of college. During her first months away, she had cut classes, used street drugs, and avoided papers and tests. When she found herself on academic probation, she decided that she would return home. Going away to a university in a distant city had been especially difficult for her, causing the breakup of a love affair which had become the major focus of her emotional life.

Annette had two younger sisters. Her father, a promising young professional, had died from a heart attack when Annette was five. His relationship with her mother had been tumultuous, with bitter arguments terminating in months of separation. He had been irregular about weekend visits to his children, but Annette remembered looking forward to seeing him and feeling that she was his favorite child. Before his death he had particularly encouraged her physical activities, urging her to try to climb ever higher on a rope ladder, to do acrobatics, and even to learn to dance the Irish jig. Physical skills, which Annette mastered so readily, especially delighted her father because he had been in an automobile accident not long before her birth and had suffered residual handicaps. Annette's mother was also enthusiastic about her daughter's coordination and agility and found a ballet class for three-year-old girls. Both the dancing teacher and her nursery school teacher encouraged her motoric achievements, enjoying her talent and enthusiasm.

After Annette's father died, her mother sought to orient herself to the future by focusing on her three small children and on her own career. In her need to develop a tightly knit family she emphasized the values of coping and keeping expressions of grief to a minimum. She quickly enlisted Annette in helping with the care of the younger girls, but shielded the children not only from their father's memorial service, but later from the airing of their loss.

In elementary school, Annette's charm and politeness led others to perceive her as a happy child. She learned readily, and always found friends in the neighborhood. But her enthusiasm for dancing flagged, and she was rarely singled out by her teacher thereafter. It was not until adolescence that social and developmental stresses began to prove her adjustment to be fragile; she resorted to smoking marijuana to mask her fear and anxiety. Unsure of herself around boys, she did little socializing, but had intense sexual fantasies about older men including neighbors and teachers. Her desires were realized when she became involved with a man twice her age during the summer before starting college. She described that time with him as a paradise which had come to an abrupt end when she left home.

When Annette initially came to see me, she appeared barely able to control her feelings. Her clenched fists and halting speech signalled some great distress. I had to question her actively and clarify her comments to enlist her participation. She told me that she was not sad, was sleeping well, and that she had a good appetite, but that she rarely ventured away from home and her younger sisters. My inquiries about current drug use were first turned aside, but as some alliance developed, she did admit that she was continuing to use marijuana each morning and evening. With firm support over the short span of a few weeks, she gave up that dependence almost entirely.

In the third month of our intensive therapy, Annette began to giggle and flirt with me. She alluded to her lonely life and watched my every movement. She also began to mail me cryptic notes, one of which stated, "I understand the thoughts you are sending." She found my given name on a billboard and believed that this signaled a rendezvous with me. With continuing support, Annette could share her delusion that I had installed a transmitter in her eardrum to keep in touch with her. Similarly, she believed that the radio in her kitchen contained a special receiver from which, at night, she heard her father's voice praising her and saying, "You have a terrific body." She attempted to work as a salesclerk, but felt that the supervisor was sending her vibrations. She left feeling overwhelmed. When she learned that I would be going away for a week, leaving her only with a substitute psychiatrist to call in case of emergency, she was crushed. Her fragmentation became worse, she could scarcely sleep, her thoughts raced, and she was admitted to a hospital with a developing psychosis.

During these tumultuous months of treatment, several fixations on her body emerged when she came to see me from the hospital. One of these concerned her hair, which she had dyed blond in the belief that "blonds have more fun." It seemed that one teacher about whom she had daydreamed had paid more attention to a blond cheerleader than to Annette. She had believed that her "mousey brown hair" had made her sexless, but now she began to believe that the peroxide had turned her hair to straw. Other "defects" included "stubby fingers" and her "shiny big forehead." When feeling very low, she became self-conscious about her legs and ankles. Once she sat on the floor, tucking her legs beneath her skirt and smiling as if she felt that she had transformed herself. At such moments she pleaded for approval from me. These incidents led us to a discussion of her father and of his physical handicaps and she began to describe his legs as "withered and bent." She remembered him as stooped over and walking with his cane. Annette began to grasp the link between these memories and her own need to flex and to crane her "too squashed neck." It also became clear that she came to each therapy hour expecting a judgment from me as to whether she was "ugly and deformed" or "sexy and lovable."

As we continued to explore and to clarify her need to seek praise, Annette came to see how profoundly she missed her father. She became less anguished in her intensive therapy. Her need for phenothiazines and for the structure of the hospital waned and she could once more take college courses. But the intense sexual desires were still predominant and not long after discharge she was so frustrated by my unavailability that she impulsively went off for the weekend with a man she had briefly met in the hospital.

After two years of treatment, a better compensated Annette moved into a college dormitory. Her preoccupations shifted from fantasies about me and her professors to extended relationships with boyfriends. As part of her greater equilibrium, she could demonstrate her intelligence in papers and examinations and could develop her skill in modern dance. She began to feel more worthwhile on the basis of these evolving activities.

A CONCEPT OF SELF-ESTEEM REGULATION

Self-esteem permeates all of the structures and functions of the mind. It is observed by clinically abstracting from the words, body language, play, or life stories of our patients. Low self-esteem resembles sadness, but persists far longer, for days or weeks. The ability to regulate self-esteem depends upon processes within the ego and superego which follow a pathway of development consistent with more familiar developmental lines.

The earliest precursors of self-esteem are found in the mutual states shared by mother and infant. So intertwined are feeding, caring, and warmth—or tension, distress, and fear—that we speak of merging in connection with this early period (Stechler and Kaplan, 1980). Self-esteem depends upon a judgment concerning one's value compared to some standard of worth. Thus the first source of self-esteem (the mother, father or surrogate) is external and such early emotional responses from the outside are what become incorporated into the feeling state of the infant.

The openness of the mind to external judgments remains a major aspect of the regulatory mechanism of self-esteem, but, over time, cathected internal representations of parental figures provide a stable alternative to the reliance upon others for praise to counteract low self-esteem. For protection against the negative judgments of others, the young child relies upon the defenses of denial and avoidance as his capacity for self-judgment increases.

The ego of the infant develops a kind of membrane, as it were, between the self and the outside world. At the start of life this membrane is entirely open to the passage of external affects such as love or shame. These are experienced by the infant as a raising or lowering of the level of self-esteem. In the earliest stage of development the membrane gradually becomes thicker and can shield the child from the intensity of such outside responses. The child begins to regulate his level of self-esteem, and the membrane becomes semi-permeable: that is, it begins to select what may pass into the self. Once this "semi-permeable" structure is achieved, the child may begin the active process of recruiting praise from parents or surrogate figures through behaviors known to evoke their praise. These parental attitudes are then internalized as object representations. Protected by the semi-permeable membrane, the child may proceed to master tasks which are known to induce internal judgments of worthiness. Finally, the adult's regulatory apparatus will be uniquely individual and dependent upon the relative impact of such factors as genetic endowment, life events, familial values, and cultural emphases. These factors will have affected the permeability of the membrane to praise or criticism, influenced the characterological reliance upon others for recruitment of their praise, and determined the availability of mastered activities to bring good feelings from internal sources.

The case of Veronica highlights the early stages of this developmental sequence. The initial rejection by her natural mother and the inability of her adoptive mother to provide her with repeated experiences of positive esteem left her without the continuity of acceptance from which stable internal representations might have developed. In other words, what passed through the membrane was negative rather than positive.

In her next stage, because her needs as an infant had been thwarted, Veronica was not able to develop the thickened membrane which might have protected her from harsh responses, and failed to establish the internal resources for stable self-judgment. Her aggressive identifications pressured her to search for outside interactions to neutralize her sense of internal badness, but in so doing she merely repeated her earliest experiences and became overwhelmed by negative responses from current peers and teachers. Her membrane lacked the protection which semi-permeability would provide in the face of rejections.

Only if the child develops an increasingly protective membrane can affirming internal judgments concerning behavior and relationships grow in importance. With that development, the individual decreases dependence upon unsolicited external sources to maintain self-esteem and becomes more skilled at actively recruiting the desired positive responses of other important persons. It is as if the ego finds a method of actively transporting praise from others across the membrane to satisfy its own needs for enhancing self-esteem. In contrast to Veronica, Annette would appear to have successfully accomplished the development of the semi-permeable membrane in early childhood. She was the first born, the favorite of her father, and despite the friction in their marital relationship, both her parents had given Annette love and approval in their own ways. Her enthusiasm for activities calling for physical coordination suggests how she had begun to experience the mastery of skills which led her to feel good about herself. Her father's death, however, deprived her of a primary source of esteem at a time when oedipal interest made active transport of his praise of paramount importance. As discussed by Wolfenstein (1976), a five-year-old child lacks the essential superego structures necessary to mourn the death of a parent, which leads, in turn, to deficiencies in ego development. For Annette the development of the apparatus for self-esteem regulation was arrested by the loss of her father.

At first Annette appeared to maintain her early strengths; her elementary school years were viewed as successful by others. But her dependence on drug use in early adolescence was a significant indication of the inherent fragility of her ego functioning.

The reopening of oedipal desire in these years heightened Annette's need for a restitutive object. This led first to daydreams and later to a lover almost twice her age as she sought to restore the assistance she had lost in the regulation of her self-esteem. The tenuous equilibrium provided by the adoration of her lover was disrupted when she departed for college. It was as if her view of herself as worthwhile had become so dependent upon the active recruitment of praise that the loss of the source of that praise left her with only unbearable sadness and loneliness. Overwhelmed by these feelings, she retreated into psychosis.

During that regression, Annette had a need for constant assurance that her body was lovable and that I was not deserting her. Her reality testing had faltered under the weight of her frustration, while the immensity of her need to find a source of self-esteem appeared in the delusion that there were transmitters bringing her messages from me. Although active transport across the metaphorical semi-permeable membrane was continuing to occur (in the sense that she still sought external praise), the distortions of psychosis temporarily transformed the source of that praise into an installation in her ear. During Annette's recovery the regulation of self-esteem shifted in stages from the delusional love emanating from the transmitter (active transport become psychotic), to attempts to seek esteem from me by trying to elicit praise of parts of her body, to an increasing focus in the transference upon her activities and how they might please me. The regulatory functions of her self-esteem apparatus had matured in a way such that she could rely on increasingly sublimated areas of behavior (her college successes) as she shifted from a depressive position. Her appreciation of her own mastery could replace her exaggerated reliance upon the praise of others.

CONCLUSION

I have suggested that a focus on the regulation of self-esteem is valuable in understanding some of the failures of child development. To return to my metaphor, the successful development of a semi-permeable membrane will so protect the level of esteem in the self that ego activities may develop. Specifically, active recruitment of praise by pleasing others and mastery of skills for the renewal of the child's sense of self-worth serve to assist the ego in the regulation of self-esteem. Assessment of the degree to which an individual possesses these capabilities informs the clinician of that individual's capacity to achieve and stabilize an adequate level of self-esteem. In the first example, early rejection so impaired the development of an effective membrane that the child manifested severe behavioral problems, and stable self-esteem was unattainable. In the second, a girl's loss of her father at the height of her oedipal needs arrested the development of her capacity for internal self-judgments and led to a pathological reliance upon love from his replacements.

REFERENCES

Stechler, G., & Kaplan, S. (1980), The development of the self: A psychoanalytic perspective. *The Psychoanalytic Study of the Child*, 35:85–105. New Haven: Yale University Press.
Wolfenstein, M. (1976), Effects of object loss in the first five years. *J. Amer. Psychoanal. Assn.*, 24:659–668.

9

The Functioning of Self-Esteem in

Childhood Depression

CARL P. MALMQUIST, M.D.

Depression in children is essentially related to a loss of self-esteem. A dysphoric mood state coexists with a loss of interest or pleasure in many of the usual childhood activities. The child is down-in-the-dumps and irritable; he has feelings of hopelessness, and his general physiognomy and facial expression convey sadness. He has vegetative symptoms such as altered sleep patterns, weight or appetite disturbance, loss of drive, apathy, agitation or hypoactivity, lasting for at least two weeks. Feelings of worthlessness or inappropriate guilt, difficulty in thinking, and some type of self-destructive mentation or behavior may be present. I should add that, in my view, the criteria of *DMS-III* have sufficient construct validity for an affective disorder of childhood that we need not enter into the continuing debate about whether depression can exist in children or not. In other words, I begin with the assumption that the criteria for a depressive episode in childhood have already been established. I should now like briefly to look at the history of earlier formulations of depression and the importance assigned to self-esteem issues. I shall then examine how narcissistic instability coexists with self-esteem dysfunction in depressed children. In all of this, the key question may be what is the most workable theoretical framework within which to view the role of self-esteem in a given psychopathological state. Many developmental and neurophysiological variables may be playing a role in the etiology of the child's illness. Our task, and the task of the theoretical framework to which I refer, is to sort these out.

If the essence of depression in children lies in a loss of self-esteem, what is the significance of earlier formulations focused on aggression? To my mind, the most striking aspect of these formulations is the emphasis they place on antecedent variables at the oral stage. The developmental deviancy might be seen as a constitutional basis of excessive oral needs with disturbances in eating, drinking, or mouthing activities. Abraham, of course, extended his thinking beyond oral manifestations, noting that problems with pride and esteem were also present in depression (1927). And Freud made a crucial distinction between mourning and melancholia, the latter assuming the dimensions of an extraordinary fall in self-esteem in which the ego was seen as "inclined to self-reproaches" (1917).

Freud was here following a line of thinking that can be traced to "On Narcissism" in 1914 and even before that, to *The Interpretation of Dreams* in 1900. The infant was viewed by Freud (1914) as existing in a state of "primary narcissism," in which the child's own body was the object of his libidinal investment. The infantile states of omnipotence and gradiosity were gradually tempered by the frustrations of a non-accommodating world; relative helplessness in dealing with states of excitement or deprivation impinged on grandiosity. Formulations such as "hallucinating pain away" (1900) were efforts to explain how narcissistic equilibrium was maintained. The child's sense of self-esteem was viewed as being contingent on something outside himself or its maintenance.

Originally such experiences were those of remedying an immediate "unpleasurable" situation; in time, they involved the avoidance of unpleasurable states in the long run. This formulation of the ontogenesis of esteem was thus based on an equation between the elimination of an unpleasurable stimulus and wellbeing. By extension, it would mean that the absence of unpleasure would lead to the absence of depression. Clinical and research investigations contradicted this simplistic formulation, revealing that esteem is not based simply on the absence of unpleasure. But the important point is that the theory provided a model in which only someone or something from the outside world could rescue the child from a state of helplessness. In effect, it was a model not dissimilar to the more contemporary model of learned helplessness related to depression (Seligman, 1975).

The oral model postulated that self-esteem was related to supplies of "psychological nourishment," these supplies being located outside the self. The formulation was: as I receive and am given to, I feel good; conversely, if I am not given to, I feel badly. To continue to feel good and avoid feeling states of emptiness, badness, neglect, etc., the child will pay a heavy price by adapting to demands made on him. Freud postulated that this was the price for civilization being transmitted. An unpleasure avoidance model was thus the basis for the oral deprivation analogy as the diathesis for depression. Self-esteem played a peripheral role, entering secondarily when there was a threatened loss of oral supplies.

Once superego functioning became subject to scrutiny, however, it became possible to view the connection between self-esteem problems, depression and loss in a much more elaborate way. The relationship between self-esteem and such functions as judging actions, critical self-observation, self-punishment, demanding expiation or contrition, and praising or loving for accomplishments suggested new vistas. And if an intrapsychic agency had the power to regulate self-esteem, it had the correlative power to regulate states of depression. But, of course, superego-induced states cannot be characterized solely in terms of feelings of loss. The theoretical problem was to avoid the mistake of viewing every withholding or critical judgement directed at the self by the superego as a loss analogous to a loss of oral supplies.

Thus, the depressive process was seen as mediated by a mechanism of incorporating the characteristics of a disappointing or lost object (Freud, 1917). The hypothesis was that the ambivalently perceived object became part of the self. Aggression directed against the self then accounted for the guilt and self-punitive aspects of depression. Self-esteem was lowered through self-accusations. Ambivalence toward the other, now incorporated as an aspect of the self, raised the fear of retaliation. The retaliatory role was taken by the superego, and the original hostility was expressed intrapsychically.

Where did this leave self-esteem as a critical variable with respect to depression? One position, perhaps best represented by Freud's thinking on melancholia, viewed it as a secondary phenomenon, with primary emphasis on the degree of ambivalence toward the object. The other position, a more sophisticated version of the oral-deprivation model, viewed the person at risk for depression as more dependent on the ongoing support and esteem of others.

Clinical observations pointed to what seemed like contradictory childhood traits: pliancy and obsequiousness to insure that the needs for affection and attachment were satisfied; low frustration tolerance with angry responses when those needs were not satisfied.

One offshoot of this latter position, with its focus on the characterological deformations of the depressive personality, was a certain instrumental bias in the view of self-esteem. The potentially depressed child was seen as portraying himself as helpless and sad so as to elicit comforting responses from others. In other words, he manipulates others to support his self-esteem (Bonime, 1976). But this position is of little explanatory value: The child's expectations for gratification are disappointed; hence he suffers a loss of self-esteem; hence he seeks gratification to bolster his self-esteem. In other words, an exclusive focus on external objects brings us no closer to an understanding of what self-esteem *is*.

The intrapsychic emphasis, on the other hand, with its focus on the ambivalently perceived object introjected as an aspect of the self toward which the superego directs its reproaches, fails in the opposite direction. For it does not sufficiently account for the role of *actual* objects in the development of self-esteem and depression proneness (Rado, 1928). When there is the possibility of *actual* disappointment or failure, there is a warring of painful affect in the child. The ego may be an agent of oral incorporation in a drive sense, but it goes beyond that in its executive and defensive functioning. What the intrapsychic view fails to account for is the *experiential* state of an impotent ego (Bibring, 1953). In a child, fears of being weak or inadequate reflect present realities.

While the primary significance of self-esteem in depressed adults was suggested by Freud, it was given a major new emphasis by the ideas of Bibring. Bibring (1953) elaborated three ways in which depression could be connected with the functioning of self-esteem. Although Bibring presented his ideas in the context of depressed adults, they also illustrate what children need in the process of development. His focus was on the narcissistic aspects of development: the need to be seen as worthy, the need not to feel inferior, and the need to be loved and appreciated. A child, threatened by the absence of these experiences, may respond with a feeling of helplessness to effect change. The result is low self-esteem and clinical depression. Bibring's view comfortably accommodates both internal and external factors. Thus, a 10-year-old child may feel loved, yet feel unworthy because of emerging ego-ideal components. Another child may feel loved, yet inferior because of physical handicaps, intellectual limitations, race, or socioeconomic position.

Children often feel weak, inferior, and insecure in their daily lives. While some of these assessments owe to neurotic conflict, with the need to depreciate themselves, there is always a partial reality to their fears. In many ways, children *are* weak and inferior in comparison to adults, older siblings, and some members of their peer group. Thus, unlike the intrapsychic view of depression, Bibring's position leaves room for the role of *actual* disappointment or failure in development.

Wishes to be loved and appreciated are contrasted in the child with that aspect of the self perceived as aggressive, hateful, or destructive. Early on, superego precursors begin to lay down expectations of more than simply being given to. While initial conditions for being good originate in the fear of punishment and of losing love from parental figures, a crucial developmental step occurs when the conditions for being good become internalized. Young children have a limited capacity to distinguish the internal from the external world. The boundaries between self and object images and their associated feelings remain vague. Such a situation permits the fluctuation between introjection and projection of goodness and badness. More realistic object- and self-representations are fostered by the maturation of ego functions involving perception. In an atmosphere that is predominantly loving and caring, with minimal hate and rage, reality testing reduces the need to develop grandiose images to counter anxiety about weakness and self-esteem failure. If hate and rage become too striking, a conviction of "badness" may develop. In any case, it is clear that Bibring's view protects against the instrumentalism of the oral-deprivation model.

Thus, depression is seen not as an intersystematic conflict between the ego, id, and superego, nor primarily a result of conflict between one of these agencies and the environment. Depression is rather seen as tension within the ego resulting from an intrasystematic conflict based on ego-ideal divergences. When the self-esteem component of the ego falters, one of the conditions necessary for depression is present. A key question with children is how the self can deal with sagging self-esteem experienced as a painful state when, at the same time, the child feels relatively powerless to alter it.

The ego state of feeling helpless is not only crucial to lowered self-esteem but also to such manifestations of depression as apathy, low energy level, and a lack of interest in things. Early in development, children experience many internal and external situations which they are helpless to change. These experiences of helplessness are the developmental antecedents for the greater feelings of helplessness the child experiences in meeting the aspirations represented by the ego ideal. An important line of thinking views these early childhood experiences of helplessness as providing the anlage for later reactivations of lowered self-esteem when aspirations cannot be met. The reaction to frustrated aspirations is to deflect the child's narcissism away from the ego onto the ego ideal. Masochistic tendencies can then develop in the ego as part of the situation of helplessness. Management of self-esteem is thus related to the role of the ego ideal and to these masochistic tendencies, which often contribute to depressive symptoms.

Without deciding whether the ego ideal is a structure separate from the superego, we can discuss the impact on self-esteem of failure to meet ideal demands. Initially, the child's goal is to gain control over such physical expressions as striking out or attacking. Through identification, a host of diverse ideals are internalized. These identifications are informed by parental norms, though the child's endowment sets some outer limits. Of course, we cannot always assume that meeting certain goals of achievement, beauty, power, success, etc., will necessarily enhance self-esteem. Such accomplishments may conflict with other values, such as kindness or compassion. To be the brightest student in the class means someone else is not; to experience power over others may not be possible through kindness and compassion (McClelland, 1975).

While some see shame as a failure to live up to ego ideals, it may also be associated with reaching goals in a manner unacceptable to the ego ideal. Self-esteem is then lowered despite accomplishments. Conversely, the attainment of certain moral goals, humility for example, may represent a negative experience for the ego which associates such a demeanor with powerlessness. The result is a lowering of self-esteem. Shame may also develop when a child's moral self-evaluation conflicts with unconscious superego components. A surprising, and puzzling state of dysphoria may follow. The child does not feel pride and gratification in what was supposedly a rewarding undertaking. In all these cases, shame results from a narcissistic conflict arising from a dissonance between idealized images reflecting narcissistic goals and an ego assessment that one is weak or deficient. While some hypothesize shame as an affect connected entirely with failure to meet the ego ideal, these examples illustrate that it is not so restrictive (Lynd, 1958).

Thus, discussing the relationship of self-esteem to depression, we need to examine disturbances in narcissistic regulation. How does narcissistic pathology enter into self-esteem problems when children are depressed?

Feelings of boredom, indifference, or inhibitions in work or play in a child alert the clinician to some type of narcissistic disturbance. While a descriptive diagnosis of depression may be made, in their dynamic sense these states signify ego depletion. They are a response to unrealistic claims of a grandiose part of the self which are not capable of being fulfilled. At times there is an intense seeking out of powerful external objects seen as the suppliers of self-esteem (Kohut, 1971). Mood swings are prominent in the child's history and in the transference. Thus, a 14-year-old girl with a history of mood swings was disappointed that her psychiatrist would not respond to her calls by meeting her at restaurants or coming to her home as a psychiatrist had done in a recent movie she had seen. Depressed adults are rarely "totally" depressed even when in a psychotic state: depressed children even less so. Their moods are much more field-dependent and based on praise or achievement. There are periods of vitality and aliveness but they are erratic and lack a sustained quality. A poor mark in school, the failure of another child to respond to an overture, a teacher who does not single the child out, lack of praise, all elicit sadness and, at times, withdrawal. Other children, reacting to the external manner of a depressed child, may see him as aloof or haughty.

If depression proneness in children is related to narcissistic vulnerability, these children are at a different developmental level than that at which conflict occurs in a cohesive and stable self. *Narcissistic* conflicts become manifest when objects are not clearly differentiated from the self. They are viewed as reflecting the greatness of the self, or the self shares in their greatness. The necessary slow alteration in the grandiose and idealized aspects of the self is lacking during the course of development. Grossly unrealistic aspects then persist and impede true object relationships. The depressive child has trouble making the transition from self-objects to object relationships. A stable self does not develop. The child without narcissistic vulnerability, in contrast, can make this transition without mood instabilities, and reacts to the imperfections of and disappointment in parental figures by gradually withdrawing his investment from them. In its place, a less perfect but more realistic aspect of his *own* inner self maintains narcissistic equilibrium.

In the context of the narcissistically vulnerable child, anxiety can be seen as arising from a threat to the self attendant upon object loss, rather than merely from a threat of punishment or of loss of love. The threat from object loss is that the self will fragment, and become dependent on some type of archaic selfobject. Anxiety thus arises from the instability of the processes which evoke the self as independent from selfobjects. The narcissistic imbalance leaves self-esteem in jeopardy. The attempted remedy of seeking excessive admiration from, or attachment to, others, to stabilize self-esteem can never be completely successful. The child lacks the confidence that he can progress and differentiate himself from others. He needs a more modulated control system to give self-assurance without the narcissistic imperatives of admiration and attachment if depression is to be avoided.

Neither parents nor child are aware of the processes which produce crippled self-esteem. Only when the child (or later, the adolescent or adult) shows symptomatic behavior is attention called to the situation. The typical process is one in which a search begins for overt trauma in childhood such as divorce, death, or other object loss or a history of overt depression in a family member to account for why a child has become depressed. In some cases, perhaps a statistically significant number, such variables can be found. Yet, even when these variables are positive, they do not sufficiently explain why such a profound disturbance in self-esteem regulation has developed.

A depressed child with self-esteem problems views himself through a prism, as it were. Quite early, he has reacted to an idealized part of himself as though it were his actual self. Given such a distortion in his self-image, he has to guard against expression of genuine feelings. A false self then develops.

While fluctuations in self-esteem reflect changes in the way the ideal self is represented, it is important that we do not see the problem as involving simply a discrepancy between the actual self versus the ideal self; nor merely as reflecting a state of tension between the ego and superego. The crucial variable, rather, is the functioning of this false self. The child's effort to appear integrated to himself and others is no more than an attempt to present a perfect outer façade. The emphasis on externals and how they are seen is reflected in the unusual degree of power those with complications in self-esteem regulation attribute to visual forms of representation (De Saussure, 1971).

The result is that the child's actual strengths are seen as unreal or illusory. Small flaws in the child's self-image—arising from failures to elicit admiration—are generalized as revealing an entirely defective product. Any imperfection is seen as crucial, since even minor flaws convey the absence or loss of an ideal state. In turn, reality testing is compromised by the distorting exaggerations. In such a situation, a depressive conviction grows of inner emptiness, accompanied by anxiety in reaction to the threat of having to see something other than the false self.

Since we often fail to confirm by objective data why a depressed child begins to have low self-esteem, we can only hypothesize that certain experiences on a behavioral and developmental level have gone awry. While evidence may be forthcoming about predisposing factors, such as genetic loadings, we are still left with the presence of a painful affective state. As elusive as the concept of a "false self" is, worse yet, it has been used differently by different people in work varying from sociological theorizing to Sullivan's ideas of a self-system (1953); it seems to me heuristically meaningful to contrast a self which, developmentally, experiences itself as relatively integrated rather than fragmented, emotionally genuine rather than relying on the emotions one is supposed to feel, and competent in dealing with other people rather than plagued by perceptions of ineffectuality. What these juxtapositions reveal is a "true" self opposed to a self that serves as a model of conformity in the effort to maintain self-esteem. The model of conformity is a response to diverse influences and a means of gaining acceptance and security. While it may be adaptive to the goal of securing attachments, it is fragile and unstable. Depression and the possibility of antisocial behavior often result.

The depressed child is as dedicated as his adult counterpart to maintaining an illusion of seeming happiness. Such depressed children, and those who know them, often point to the atmosphere of affectation we become aware of during the course of their treatment. Depressed children with defective self-esteem are attempting to repress their sense of falsity. While they had wanted to be spontaneous, to be able to play, and to be free from the compulsive organization which adults around them have used to maintain their own security, these feelings are present only sporadically.

Whatever the basic predisposition for depressive illness, there seems to be a particular catenation of factors operating in the child's relationship with his parents. One factor, oddly, is empathy. While empathy is usually an asset, in the potentially depressed child it is used as a means of adapting continuously to what the child believes adults want. The result is a paradoxical situation in which the efforts of the child are to keep the parent content and happy. Given this milieu, we should not be surprised that these children have difficulty in separating from symbiotic relationships. Early symptoms and signs of separation disturbances and problems with homesickness later, can be predicted, with their accompanying deficits in self-esteem.

Unresolved conflicts in the caretakers also serve to impair the self-esteem of the child. Studies reveal they have a higher incidence of depressive illness themselves. Yet, these studies are significant only for the baseline they provide. In other words, self-esteem deficits in children are not solely related to the presence of major depression in the parents. The diathesis is rather connected to endless exposures to adults whose narcissistic expectations of what others can and should do for them have not been resolved. The adults are often in need of relationships marked by devotion, respect, and admiration. Since these needs of the adult are rarely clarified, worked out, or conscious, the situation is one in which both adult and child become baffled and perplexed.

Both adult and child profess love and dedication, but they continue to wonder why they do not have good feelings about themselves. To make matters more complex, the adult is seeking something which can never be recaptured for his own self. Nor can it be obtained from his child. Yet the child continues to strive to satisfy the unattainable goal of providing narcissistic equilibrium for his parent, with concomitant feelings of lowered esteem (Winnicott, 1960). If other adult figures have a similar relationship with the child—grandparents, teachers, counselors, or therapists—there are increased burdens. A displacement of the conflict may occur, with rebellious and angry expressions outside the home. The child's sensitivity to parental needs can thus be maintained in an unresolved state.

The deficit in the self-esteem of the child is related not only to the need he has to please those who give him security, but also to a sense of fradulence. He senses that he is less than he might be. His self-esteem is predicated on blocking the "bad" part of himself from becoming visible. He does not attempt to be anything other than what he thinks his parents want him to be. The strength of the parental need for the child to stay the same—meeting their needs empathically without showing anger, loneliness, and frustration—makes change difficult. Hence, what is gained by avoidance of change is a false sense of self-esteem, false because it is predicated on having to eliminate those expressions of dissatisfaction and anxiety in childhood that would permit genuine self-esteem to arise out of strengths rather than weakness.

Part of the fraudulence is connected with the need to banish disquieting emotions, just as though they did not exist. Self-esteem then becomes based on denial and suppression. Emotional expressions which will discomfort the parent must be watched for. A secondary elaboration is to view the existence of one's own feelings with contempt. Here is one basis for the restless behavior seen in some depressed children who have trouble applying themselves and have learning problems. Others act out their feelings in diverse ways.

The depressed child is caught in a zero-sum situation. Because he has to guard against the expression of genuine emotions, he is left with feelings of being empty and depressed. Yet to deal with his feelings, however indirectly, means to court a different set of problems, such as repetitive patterns of acting out. To compromise one's genuineness to this degree involves a sacrifice of the self. Strivings for autonomy must be subordinated, as Erikson (1963) stressed, to shame and doubt. In its place a caricature of autonomy arises. If it extends into neurotic symptomatology, we have compulsive rituals, tics, and perverse behavior patterns.

These hypotheses make it clearer why the self-esteem system of the depressed child suffers. The self of the healthy child develops in the context of a series of separations. In time, external objects are represented internally as distinct from the self-representation. Serious disturbances are seen when difficulties arise in distinguishing whether desires or feelings are actually one's own, or those of others. To the extent that a child is confused, and cannot be sure which feelings and desires are truly his, self-esteem suffers.

The child must avoid not only those expressions of affect which threaten his parents, but those which threaten their introjects as well. Caution must always be exercised. Too direct expressions of wishes for autonomy or aggression raise fears that esteem will slip. First priority is that the narcissistic needs of the caretakers be met. They are the constant regulators of self-esteem in the depressed child to be extent that the autonomy of a self-regulatory system has been handicapped. It is a relationship in which boundaries are not made clear. To do so would create anxiety in the adult who needs reassurances that the child will not separate emotionally. The threat to the child is abandonment.

At the other end of the spectrum is confusion about the degree of closeness experienced. How appropriate are expressions of intimacy and how are they supposed to shift during different periods? A 12-year-old girl bothered by mood swings, crying spells, and "hate for my mother's past two husbands" (her father and stepfather) revealed how her mother would share details of her husbands' failures. Anger and resentment toward her mother were totally absent, and all she could emphasize was her hate for these men. Her failure to relieve her mother's depression, no matter how good she was, contributed to her self-esteem problems.

According to Miller (1981), depression is a defense against the real pain over the "loss of the self." Obviously, such a definition is broader than that offered by the model of aggression directed against the ego by the superego. But what are the manifestations of a loss of self in a child? There is, most significantly, a sense of failure. This sense of failure is without regard to what some outside and objective assessor might decree. Rather, the loss of self-esteem is related to the continuous sense of having been unable to meet a set of standards of introjected figures. These internalized appraisers convey to the child that he can never truly please, leaving him in a state of perpetual conflict. The introjects then form a basis for the feelings of victimization and inferiority characteristic of the depressive personality organization (Meissner, 1981). A 16-year-old depressed girl stated, in discussing her feelings about her mother when she was younger: "I always felt frantic around her—like I was supposed to be doing something for her—but I could never figure out what it was."

Such a predicament *could* lead the child to attempt to gain esteem by achievement, which is exactly what happens when depression is mild. Many of our myths of accomplishment are constructed around the advocacy of such efforts to bolster self-esteem.

But for a child there are fewer ways to do this. The most obvious is to strive for academic excellence or artistic achievement, thereby to gain external praise. But the success of the overachieving, overconforming child merely maintains an ego state in which self and self-object remain indistinct. And while the participation of the object in the child's success brings a temporary abatement of the sense of failure, the success cannot be long-lived; the sense of fraudulence interferes. The child's values are not his own but those imposed on him by others. Yet to acknowledge this fact would mean the collapse of his denial system, with the accompanying threat of abandonment or shame. Somehow, all his successes cannot cause the child to do what would seem natural, to love himself. Rather, he continues to pursue the unavailable self-object, a self-object which cannot give sufficient comfort or esteem. In the absence of esteem based on the child's own sense of self, depression looms.

Masochistic behavior reflects yet another aspect of the failure to regulate self-esteem. When perfectionistic standards of the ego ideal cannot be satisfied, the child not only cannot love himself but despises himself as well. Consider the situation the child is in. Since the well-being of his self depends on the object, any actual or fantasized problem in the relationship is likely to be experienced as a diminution in self-worth. The more the self-esteem of a particular child is dependent on an adult with unresolved narcissistic problems, the greater the possibility of self-depreciation.

For children with masochistic tendencies, being good may involve degrees of suffering. A state of low self-esteem may represent an exhibition of how good they can be. Self-imposed deprivations or sufferings, just like good performances in other spheres of the child's life, may gain praise from an unhappy parent. The hope is that the parents will see the child's dedication to them and the price he is paying. The danger is that these maneuvers will not be restricted to interactions with parental figures.

A rather large 10-year-old girl with minimal social skills had become the butt of masochistic teasing by her classmates. While the other girls wore tennis shoes and jeans, she wore adult-looking leather shoes and dresses. Her nickname was that of a pet elephant at a local zoo. Her peer group had extended its attack beyond name-calling to pushing her down so that smaller children could jump on her back. Her few feeble attempts to strike back were met with defeat by smaller and more agile children. After being at three different schools, she was referred for psychiatric help. The parents stated they did not know how they could contend with such a "disruptive, clumsy, and embarrassing child." The girl, who clung to stuffed animals, first began treatment with loud singing and banging; when these were not condemned, she asked whether she could suck her thumb "since mother always gets mad when I do it." An important phase of treatment dealt with her role as rejected buffoon, a role which she acted out in school and in the neighborhood. By this, she was angrily reenacting her parents' own sense of awkwardness with her. She also sensed that these were behaviors her mother wanted her to perform. As she put it, "It's easier to be that way than not to be." Such behaviors gave her continued power over her mother, whose attentions to her boorish daughter, allowed her to complain of her own suffering.

By manipulating others to hurt her verbally or physically, the child exercised a measure of control over her environment. When the school counselor terminated a behavior modification approach of awarding assertiveness, she wondered why he had taken so long before giving up. Such self-destructive behavior is reminiscent of the victory of the suicide. By her clumsy belittling of herself, she was able to "make" others tease her or "put her down." Others could do no greater damage than she could do to herself. Reich described the clown as someone who makes others laugh, but is never humiliated since he induces the laughter (1949). As the girl began to deal with her depression and revealed how she fell asleep crying and holding on to one of her stuffed animals, the parents informed her that they had found a solution. She was to be sent to a private school where strict discipline would keep other children from attacking her. The focus was thereby shifted from the girl and family to the school. But even this school could not maintain control; two years later she returned to therapy when a public school sought to transfer her into special classes for learning problems.

While the depressed child may accomplish tasks consistent with maintaining the false self, he can have difficulties in other areas. A sense of shame lurks in his calling too much attention to himself. Hence, well-earned rewards may be minimized. Sincere praise may be met with silence or renunciation. We see this when a child will counter compliments with a comment or action that diminishes his achievement. When told how well she had performed in a school play, a depressed girl immediately began to describe how she did not do well in certain subjects. To guard against the risk of compliments, the child may feel it safer not to perform well enough to merit them. Patterns of holding back begin, so as not to be too successful.

A self-deprecating adolescent of 14 intentionally held back in the tryouts for an athletic team. While the therapist's initial impression was that the boy did this to avoid risking friendship if he won a starting position over a friend, continued work revealed diverse factors which made him feel unworthy in doing well in many areas of his life.

A feeling of being wronged—that he should have been recognized as being more talented—was also present. Early on, these children place themselves in situations in which some of their peer group will reject them. We see this in the child who continues to seek acceptance by a group that senses his need to be a member, but the dominant member of which keeps the seeker out. The result is a state of sadness and exclusion which confirms the child's sense that something is wrong with him. Yet this also permits him to maintain a cognitive view of himself as virtuous. The basic perversion is the act of depreciation, seen in efforts to coerce others to accept him as he is. When they do not, moral superiority is found in forthrightness. When such a child begins to express genuine anger about the behavior of others, rather than dwelling on his goodness, progress is at hand; what remains is to act to the original sources of anger, other than outsiders in his immediate life, who have predicated his goodness as necessary for their purposes. Separating from those whom they see as their "love objects" is difficult for depressive children (Jacobson, 1975). It is much easier to continue to blame themselves, which thwarts separation. Others can then continue to be seen as good, while they are bad, and not entitled to emancipation and expression of their own wishes and needs.

In what is now an axiom of therapy, the depressed child with self-esteem problems will try to place the therapist in the same controlling and rejecting role that he or she has experienced in the past. The false self is kept intact by repeating the self-depreciating experience. When the therapist does not submit to the pressure, efforts to provoke may grow stronger in the child's daily life. Such acting out suggests that material bearing on the core conflict will eventually emerge.

In time, there will be expressions of what the child would really like to be. Such wishes are often in conflict with the false self. The course is then open to examine the relationship of falsity to low self-esteem. Of course, even to talk about these differences in a cautious manner evokes guilt, shame, and anxiety in a depressed child.

A few examples from a depressed boy of nine, living with his divorced father and younger brother, illustrate many of the points of this chapter. While it was easy to focus on his depressed state as being related to his mother's departure to pursue her career, another depressive line emerged when the boy began to talk about never being able to please his father. While the father sought to give his sons as he had never been given to by his own divorced father, his hidden agenda was that at least his older son would do top work in science and enter the father's field. His narcissistic aspirations centered upon the need for the boy to be outstanding, something that he was not. The message conveyed to the boy was that such goals were not to be questioned. Only after some time could the boy risk revealing how he often took an old album out of a cabinet to look at pictures of his mother. When he cried over the pictures, the crying was not only because he missed her, which he did, but also because he missed her acceptance of him and her minimal demands. The boy saw his mother as offering a more desirable relationship because of its nondemandingness even while she left her children to pursue her own ideals. She could accept him and gain pleasure from him, in his memories, by taking him as he was.

REFERENCES

Abraham, K. (1927), A short study of the development of the libido viewed in the light of mental disorders. In: *Selected Papers on Psychoanalysis*. New York: Basic Books, 1973, pp. 418–501.

Bibring, E. (1953), The mechanism of depression. In: *Affective Disorders*, ed. P. Greenacre. New York: International Universities Press, pp. 13–48.

Bonime, W. (1976), The psychodynamics of neurotic depression. *J. Amer. Acad. Psychoanal.*, 4:301–326.

De Saussure, J. (1971), Some complications in self-esteem regulation caused by using an archaic image of the self as an ideal. *Internat. J. Psycho-Anal.*, 52:87–97.

Erikson, E. H. (1963), *Childhood and Society*. New York: Norton.

Freud, S. (1900), *The Interpretation of Dreams. Standard Edition*, 4 & 5. London: Hogarth Press, 1953.

—— (1914), On narcissism: An introduction. *Standard Edition*, 14:73–102. London: Hogarth Press, 1957.

—— (1917), Mourning and melancholia. *Standard Edition*, 14:243–258. London: Hogarth Press, 1957.

Jacobson, E. (1975), The regulation of self-esteem. In: *Depression and Human Existence*, ed. E. J. Anthony & T. Benedek. New York: International Universities Press.

Kohut, H. (1971), *The Analysis of the Self*. New York: International Universities Press.

Lynd, H. M. (1958), *On Shame and the Search for Identity*. New York: Harcourt, Brace.

McClelland, D. C. (1975), *Power: The Inner Experience*. New York: Irvington.

206   *Carl P. Malmquist*

Meissner, W. W. (1981), *Internalization in Psychoanalysis*. New York: International
    Universities Press.
Miller, A. (1981), *Prisoners of Childhood*. New York: Basic Books.
Rado, S. (1928), The problem of melancholia. *Internat. J. Psycho-Anal.*, 9:420–438.
Reich, A. (1949), The structure of the grotesque-comic sublimation. *Bull. Menn.
    Clin.*, 13:160–171.
Seligman, M. D. (1975), *Helplessness: On Depression, Development, and Death*. San
    Francisco: W. H. Freeman.
Sullivan, H. S. (1953), *The Interpersonal Theory of Psychiatry*. New York: Norton.
Winnicott, D. W. (1960), The theory of the parent-infant relationship. *Internat.
    J. Psycho-Anal.*, 41:585–595.

SPECIAL SETTINGS AND POPULATIONS

10

Learning Problems, Self-Esteem, and

Delinquency

DANIEL H. JACOBS, M.D.

Self-esteem derives in large measure from the ego's ongoing appraisal of its own success in balancing the demands upon it from without (environmental expectations and the demands of reality) and from within (drives and their press for discharge). Lowered self-esteem reflects disturbances in the ego's capacity to maintain homeostasis, to keep in relative balance these numerous and conflicting demands.

Whether a child maintains psychic homeostasis and adequate self-esteem depends not only on biological givens, the innate characteristics with which the child is born (Fries, 1944, 1977; Bergman and Escalona, 1949; Fries and Woolf, 1953), but also initially upon the relationship with the mother (Sander, 1969). Later, family and school also contribute to the formation of regulatory stability. It is in these early relationships with mother, family, and school that the growing child learns about self and other. The child slowly learns to distinguish outer reality from inner need, to choose between immediate expression and delay in gratification. The mother's own attitude and ways of maintaining homeostasis will profoundly affect the organization of her child's psyche. What the mother and, later, the family and school consciously or unconsciously "teach" is integrated, however, only within the physiological framework of each child's own unique perceptual and motor capacities. These capacities begin developing in the first few days of life.

Deficiencies in perceptual, motor, and organizational activities, some of which also appear in the first days of life, may contribute to self-esteem problems which arise later. Thus, it is not just the

209

quality of mothering but also the response of the child to the mother's efforts which contribute to establishment of regulatory stability and later to stable self-esteem in the child.

Some neonates, for example, show a poorer capacity for integration than others. Some appear to lack self-synchronization in the rhythms of their physiological subsystems. Others seem to have difficulty in synchrony with the outer world of their mothers. The capacity to synchronize motility to the maternal voice varies markedly; some infants show significant deficits in this ability. Condon (1975) notes that some children lag in their perceptive registration of the spoken word. Such minor defects, as Weil (1978) points out, although often unnoticed in babies, may nevertheless affect not only their interaction with the mother but also, with the passage of time, "the evolving development of a coherent inner world" (p. 466) and their sense of themselves. Some of these unnoticed early deficits furthermore may surface later and affect self-esteem when certain stage-related expectations make them conspicuous.

Such neuropsychological deficits are conspicuous in male delinquents (Cozal and Ronsey, 1968; Critchley, 1968; Berman and Siegal, 1976). In a recent study of 50 delinquent boys between the ages of 14 and 18 carried out in a court clinic in Cambridge, Massachusetts, a large majority of the boys showed significant difficulties in motility, perception, speech, and cognitive functions which seemed to be of long standing. Despite normal intelligence, most of the youths had extremely poor language skills. Many also had significant problems with spatial relations. Many were so poorly coordinated as to make success at athletic activities impossible. Often, visual acuity and auditory discrimination (sound recognition, blending, and mimicry) were below average (Robbins, Pries, Jacobs, Beck, and Smith, 1983).

These developmental deficits and their effect on learning contributed to the youths' personality development in two important ways. First, the influence of these deficits on ego formation was manifest in a marked tendency toward impulsivity, action orientation, and concrete thinking. Second, the inability of these youths to place themselves in the context of time and space, and their awareness of being unable to depend upon their bodies, increased their feelings of vulnerability and lowered their self-esteem. Their continuing failure to master basic skills reduced their confidence in themselves. Parental and societal expectations never seemed within their reach; compensatory skills remained minimal. The abilities of families and schools to help these youths with their deficits were often severely compromised, diminishing further the youths' sense that adversity can be met and overcome.

Perceptual-motor or cognitive deficits, however, do not automatically lead to a lowering of self-esteem. In the course of any child's development, there is usually a period when mild deficiencies and lags may show themselves in the autonomous functions of motility, perception, speech, and cognition. Whether they persist and become involved in neurotic conflict and lowered self-esteem depends not only on inborn capacities but also on environmental responses, which may serve to minimize or exacerbate the deficiency; there is a constant interplay between neuropsychological development and environmental expectation and response.

We know that mastery increases self-esteem. As one patient put it, "You gain esteem and respect for yourself out of accomplishments." When a child, for instance, can master a developmental task or learns how to speak and later to read, his sense of himself and his abilities is expanded. Failure to accomplish developmental tasks because of an innate inability or a neurotic conflict invariably lowers self-esteem and leaves the child with the feeling which another patient described as "I can't get there from here." Such failure may begin to jeopardize other areas of functioning which have not previously been compromised. Ausubel (1954) points out that "just as maturation in one area may precipitate or facilitate maturation in other areas, the converse holds equally true: relative retardation in a slowly growing function inevitably limits the full expression and complete development of a more rapidly growing function" (p. 64). Furthermore, a competent or precocious function may be underutilized if supporting functions have not developed. Utilization may be frustrated until related maturational tasks are completed. Delayed language development, for instance, may interfere with motor ability and resulting autonomy. A child's inability to organize in language the gradually expanding boundaries of his daily life—which his competent motor ability allows him to explore—may lead to confusion and distress. In some cases motor activity is then curtailed and a temporary "lack of curiosity" may develop until better ability in language develops.

Maturational lags will have different meanings for the child and may affect self-esteem differently at each stage of development. As Weil (1978) points out, poor motor ability and clumsiness in a toddler who awkwardly drops objects, or pushes or pinches too hard, may lead to sadomasochistic struggles with an anxious, prohibiting, or compulsive mother. During a later period, clumsiness may be associated with an imagined castration at the hands of the father. Accidents and injuries can reinforce these feelings of weakness or helplessness in relation to a powerful father. During latency clumsiness in comparison to peers may interfere with forming those friendships around play activities which are essential to the youth's understanding of competition and the vicissitudes of winning and losing. The boy or girl who has not engaged in the give-and-take of physical play, of being "king of the mountain" as well as being at the bottom of the barrel, may have a harder time realistically appraising his or her own physical capacities and those of others. The inability to derive pleasure from the function of the body through play in latency may contribute in adolescence to the inability to enjoy sexual activity.

Similarly, a delay in speech in the toddler years may present difficulties in the separation-individuation stage. The distinction between me and the not me is enormously reinforced when the child can articulate concepts such as "me" and "you" (Peller, 1965). Maturational readiness to speak implies an attainment of the symbolic-representational level, the understanding of language which precedes speaking. Such attainment can only be achieved if sound discrimination and sound blending, important components of auditory capacity, are developing normally. Maternal understanding may ease many difficulties. Rejections or undue anxiety on the part of parents or teacher, or their failure to recognize a disability, may, however, increase a child's anxiety and further affect his performance. Speech, silence, and the uses of language may then become associated with fear of the loss of love or may become overly infused with aggression; these unresolved conflicts may influence subsequent development. During latency, a child who has failed to resolve these conflicts about the uses of language may fall behind in learning to read or express himself. He may look upon this educational failure as confirmation of his own unworthiness.

It is particularly in early latency that a child's self-esteem may suffer because of maturational lags or mild neurological deficits. Most children entering school immediately begin to compare their performance in the classroom and on the playground with that of their peers. Certainly the child has made observations about him or herself prior to entering school in relation to parents, siblings, or peers. In school, however, comparisons become more institutionalized and concretized, in school marks, in the attitude of teachers to bright or slow children, in the developing pecking order inherent in any social situation.

Children are quick to recognize maturational variations in language and motor skills among their peers and within themselves. A slower child's self-esteem begins to suffer. How much it will suffer depends on the extent of the difficulty and the response of the parents and teacher. Betsy, for example, was a seven-year-old girl entering her first year of a mixed first-second grade class. She found herself among a number of children who were able to read, whereas she could not. She associated the "perceived deficit" in her abilities with other conflicts which she had not yet resolved. The inability to read was associated with not being as good as her older brother, whom she admired and envied. This in turn underscored conflicts about being a girl, which she associated with the "deficiency" of not having a penis. She seemed depressed, lacking in confidence, and, at times, irritable. Refusing to wear dresses, she went to school in a baseball hat and oversized jeans. She avoided any new challenges in reading, choosing only the simplest and most familiar words to sound out. Worried about their daughter's difficulties, her parents consulted the teacher, who admitted that the girl was slower than others but felt certain that she would be reading by spring. The teacher asked the parents not to pressure the girl. This sound advice and the parents' ability to take it forestalled what might have become a more serious problem in learning or taking pleasure in learning. Had the parents been more anxious or the teacher less secure in her knowledge of Betsy's abilities and in how children vary in gaining reading skills, or had the teacher been less able to communicate to Betsy and her parents her knowledge, the outcome might have been less fortunate. As the teacher predicted, Betsy was reading by spring. With this mastery of reading, Betsy's attitude changed. She became more assertive, more outspoken; the perpetual frown of six months' duration lifted. At the same time she began to shift her attention away from boys, who had been her exclusive friends, and to associate with and enjoy the company of girls. She even varied her clothes. Betsy's slowness in reading was neither serious nor out of the ordinary.

Whether a child develops skills for coping with a maturational lag or prolonged educational deficit often depends both upon the patience of family and school and upon the compensatory skills available and how much encouragement is given for employing them. Those who can compensate may suffer little loss in self-esteem. Children like those in the delinquent study who were not so fortunate as Betsy, whether because of real neurological deficits or because of schools or parents who unwittingly exacerbated a developmental problem, invariably experienced loss of self-esteem. Both families and schools found it hard to respond patiently or appropriately to the developmental problems of the delinquent youths studied. Too often attention was paid only to the adolescent's overt antisocial behavior, while his or her inner struggle for mastery or identity in the face of real impairments went unappreciated.

These adolescents suffer in school, where their poor performance is apparent to themselves and to everyone else. Often they repress a painful awareness of any deficit and substitute pathological defenses in desperate attempts to maintain self-esteem and avoid pain. They may deny the importance of school or grades. They may externalize the problem, blaming the school or the teacher. During latency they may avoid feelings of being left behind by being the "class clown" or developing somatic symptoms which keep them out of school. At an older age some may avoid the painful situation by truancy and other antisocial behavior. During adolescence they may seek gratification they cannot find in formal learning through the more immediate experiences of alcohol and drugs. If they cannot get high grades, they will at least get high. The drugs and alcohol make more syntonic their feelings of diffusion and the inability to locate self in time and space by providing a ready explanation for these feelings. The drunk adolescent, uncoordinated and confused, can say "I did it myself." He overcomes the feelings of helplessness in the face of real difficulties in cognitive and psychic integration.

One of the important reasons for failures to provide meaningful assistance to delinquent adolescents is the inability to recognize the cognitive and perceptual-motor deficits these youths often have. Regardless of the origins of such deficits (innate or acquired), they are a formidable barrier to progression in adolescence and to completion of the "second individuation process" (Blos, 1967). Any educator, counselor, or psychotherapist working with a delinquent who exhibits maturational deficiencies or lags that affect learning should understand the cognitive and perceptual world in which the youth lives. Careful testing of each adolescent, including visual acuity, auditory acuity and discrimination, and neuromuscular coordination, may be necessary. Areas of strength as well as deficiency should be noted. Careful history taking can uncover when the deficit was first noticed by parent, youth, or school and how they dealt with it through the various stages of the child's development. At the same time one can begin to understand the vicissitudes of the child's attempt to maintain self-esteem in the light of the deficit and how ego structure was influenced by asynchronous development or maturation difficulty. To maintain self-esteem while burdened with a cognitive or perceptual-motor deficit is not an easy task. One youth described his difficulties in reading as "a hurt feeling, a discouraged feeling, an embarrassed feeling." These feelings are experienced even when the deficit is more subtle and not fully recognized by parent, child, or school. They may express themselves in feelings of being different from others or in a chronic depression and lowered self-esteem. Without a full appreciation of what the youth is up against cognitively and perceptually, the therapist may fail in empathy and understanding, and misinterpret certain behaviors. It is one thing to interpret a youth's failure to keep his appointments as a resistance to looking at his problems, as it well might be, and another to understand that, in addition, he is being asked to make use of cognitive skills—travelling to an office, keeping track of time, understanding cause and effect and temporal sequencing—which are not in his cognitive repertoire. Such a youth may complain of being "bored in school." In addition to telling us something about his self-esteem and his attitude toward competition, he may also be saying something which should be heeded about his neuropsychological capacities.

Failure to appreciate these neuropsychological deficits and their effects on self-esteem and ego formation may also lead to a misunderstanding of the nature of the intervention needed. In many of these youths language is bypassed as a channel for expression. As Blos (1979) points out, for some adolescents "only concrete modalities of expression are found adequate for the externalization of thought, memory, affect or conflict" (p. 280). Because of a distorted relationship between action and verbalized thought or speech, concrete expression through action, too often antisocial, is often the means of communicating with the environment. Interpretations of such concrete thinking and behavior or attempts to alter it through verbal intervention are often ineffectual because "the implicit primitive, prelogical thought countermands the discrete element of language gained by the secondary process" (Blos, 1979, p. 280). Such interpretations early in treatment, when the need for practical help in learning and coping is acute, can be felt as another deprivation and may only serve to lower already impaired self-esteem. The initial stages of treatment of such patients must often be characterized by the therapist's offering help in a way the patient understands—help in some concrete form, or even, at times, through action (Jacobs, 1979). Such a response is better understood, fits better into the cognitive and perceptual mode of the patient, than "talking about feelings." This active participation in helping the youth find an adequate environment for learning within school, explaining his difficulties to law enforcement officials and courts, seeking the views of his parents and including them in his thinking, may do much to further the individual therapy.

At the Cambridge Court Clinic, a multidisciplinary approach is utilized, gathering a team including a psychiatrist, an educational psychologist, a social worker, teachers, and court officials (Jacobs and Pries, 1982). Any remedy, educational or psychotherapeutic, is designed to aid the child increase self-esteem through mastery of the tasks that face an adolescent. Such an attempt to foster further individuation often requires a combination of psychotherapy, the development of an educational setting in which the child can experience some success, and working with parents to better understand the nature of their child's and often their own difficulties. Any one of these approaches alone may prove unsuccessful, particularly with those children who have repeatedly experienced failure and whose self-esteem has been persistently lowered.

It is essential to be active in changing the environment for these children. Their concreteness in thinking and perceptual-motor difficulties foster a stronger dependency on the environment than for more mature children. Separating from the family becomes more difficult in adolescence, as it well may have been in the first separation-individuation phase, when a cognitive or perceptual-motor defect is present. To explore the environment beyond what is familiar is a more frightening venture and the inability to do so limits the youth to familiar "turf." The connection to the familiar must be protected at all costs. It may be expressed in an overdependence on family, neighborhood, or peer group. The tenacious clinging to "turf" bespeaks not only a universal tendency in human nature but also an unconscious fear, based on real impairments, of being lost, disorganized, and helpless. Whether such developmental deficits can be overcome and "the arrested internalization process carried forward" (Blos, 1979, p. 294) depends on the response of the environment as well as on biological givens and genetic history. The therapist must often be active in suggesting how the environment can foster growth for these impaired children.

In order for these children to learn and continue the process of individuation, two conditions must be met. First, the environment must actively aid in restoring damaged self-esteem. This is essential for any further development to take place. Second, an attachment of the youth to someone outside his familiar turf must develop. The following case illustrates these conditions and how they were met.

Charley was 17 when he came to see us in the mental health clinic associated with the court. He had committed many burglaries, continuing his crimes even after he was caught and awaiting trial. The repeated warnings by school and court officials that his behavior would end in incarceration had no effect. Charley had attended school sporadically, frequently getting into fights with students and teachers when he did appear. Happy when he was absent, teachers had given up hope on the "bad kid."

Despite numerous legal difficulties which threatened his freedom, Charley's main interest in coming to the clinic was learning how to read, something he could not do despite repeated attempts at special education and tutoring in the schools. The Court Clinic tutor quickly recognized Charley's cognitive difficulties. She also suggested that he talk with someone about staying out of trouble and out of jail, so that his goal of working with her and learning how to read could be met. Charley agreed to be seen in what became weekly sessions. After railing against the schools and courts in an attempt to maintain self-esteem, he admitted his terrible humiliation at not being able to learn like the others. In despair he said, "You need to read to live," and went on to tell how he had had to pretend to read birthday cards given him by his family and friends. He told of being left back three times in the first four grades. He was consequently bigger and stronger than his classmates. His way of asserting himself and restoring his self-esteem was to depend more and more on physical action rather than on language. We suggested that more complete testing might pinpoint just what his difficulties were. At the same time he could continue to talk about his problems. He agreed, particularly since the taking of tests was something concrete that he could do.

On the Wechsler Adult Intelligence Scale, Charley had an average full-scale score of 92, a dull-normal verbal scale of 84, and an average performance score of 104. His reading, spelling, and math skills were all at the third-grade level. Charley's fund of general information was extremely impoverished. He had difficulties with matters relating to time, space, and distance and a general concreteness when asked to see similarities between items. Charley demonstrated strength in one of the auditory tests, a test of sound blending. He did less well, however, on a test of sound mimicry and poorest on a test of sound recognition. When reading from the Snellin eye chart, he revealed very poor vision in his left eye. An ophthalmological examination was given and glasses prescribed. His ocular-motor control was within normal limits.

While Charley took the tests over several weeks, he talked about his family. His problems were more complicated than learning how to read. The fourth of six children, he never knew his father, who had disappeared when he was three. His mother, who was 13 when her first child was conceived, remained vague as to the father's identity, saying only that he had drunk a good deal. Charley tried to attach himself to some of his mother's numerous lovers, many of whom were underworld characters who came and went. Some met untimely deaths about which the boy eventually learned. During Charley's adolescent years, the mother lived openly with a female lover. Charley had surgery for strabismus between ages six and eight, and suffered a concussion at age seven, with subsequent headaches. Charley learned from an early age that his mother's affections could be bought with stolen objects, a toaster, a TV. "I stole to get her love," he said sadly one day. Although he did not know his father's identity, he was sure he had been a criminal. As Charley learned more in therapy about himself and his feelings about his mother, he stayed away from home more often and his impulses to steal diminished. His living situation remained unstable, however, because his mother frequently threw him out when he did return home. His way back was to bring her a stolen gift. Here, reunion with the mother and father, as well as Charley's symbolic comment on their life style, was acted upon and condensed in the act of stealing. Unfortunately, the mother was unavailable for interviews, despite repeated efforts to contact her.

It became increasingly clear that Charley needed more structure than weekly therapy and tutoring could provide. He was referred to a special school where he could learn a vocational skill as well as concentrate on improving educational skills. Charley was initially reluctant to go. School again? He had failed in the past. Only our encouragement and the insistence of the court that he be in some kind of program made him attend. Fortunately, the school's director, a skilled educator, quickly found "that something unique, something special" that made Charley different from other students: his ability to draw. In the early phases of learning, she deliberately tried to increase his self-esteem and sense of mastery by concentrating on his drawing. Once he felt appreciated for his specific and unique skills, she began to introduce tasks that were more difficult for him. When enraged or frustrated by his difficulty in learning how to read, she allowed him to take a break and to draw (to return to the more concrete form of pictorial imagery). This approach, in which self-esteem was continually monitored in the learning situation, coupled with weekly therapy, began to have results.

Charley began to change his view of who his father might have been, picking an ex-boyfriend of his mother who was now a stable and law-abiding person in the community. He would visit and talk with him but never ask him whether he was indeed his father. This also reflected a shift of allegiance from the father imagined as a criminal to the therapist (in displaced form) as father and to the values Charley perceived in his therapist.

Encouraged by his successes, Charley began to read. It was, for him, a small miracle. His self-esteem improved dramatically, and his hopes for the future brightened. He is by no means out of the woods. There remains a strong masochistic wish to submit to the mother in order to gain her love, and there is a good deal of confusion over sexual identity. At times drinking is a problem. Antisocial behavior, however, has decreased. The process by which ideas can take symbolic form has begun. While cognitive mastery of written language has somewhat enhanced Charley's self-esteem, intrapsychic conflicts no longer acted out in antisocial behavior continue to plague him and to contribute to a continuing lowered self-esteem.

Therapy alone without the wisdom of an excellent teacher could not have achieved as much. One can wonder, as well, whether teaching, talented as it was, would have made such gains without Charley's being able to explore his past and form an attachment to the therapist as a new model for identification. Had his mother been able to help in the process, still further gains might have been made. Had nothing been done, there is little doubt that Charley's identification with the imagined (perhaps real) criminal father would have led him eventually to jail and perhaps to a lifetime of crime. His ability to begin to separate from both the father he did not know and from his mother who demanded tribute through gifts could only be realized as words became more meaningful, thoughts became as real as actions, and dependence upon himself and his skills led to further individuation and free-dom from the environment.

While such changes in Charley are late and somewhat limited

in scope, they reveal how self-esteem is related to learning. Maturational arrests and lags as well as perceptual problems can only be overcome or adequately compensated for, to whatever degree possible, where there is a supportive environment. The response to the child must include not only an understanding of the deficiency from which he suffers but also the effect on self-esteem it has had at various levels of development. Each educator and parent must determine how best to maintain and raise the self-esteem of the child while asking him to overcome his fear of failure and to try tasks that have lowered his sense of self-worth in the past. To achieve this task, parents, psychotherapists, and educators must cooperate closely. Had such cooperation been available for Charley earlier in his life, his impairment might not have been so severe, his self-esteem not so fragile, and his struggle not so difficult.

Finally, it is important to note that such deficits and maturational lags need not always lead to difficulty and lowered self-esteem. Asynchronous development may also lead to the development of unique and special ways of looking at the world. Creative solutions may be born from chaotic beginnings. Our knowledge of the world and of ourselves can be enhanced by a new perspective that comes from not seeing the world in the usual way. There are even rare instances in which a maturational lag may lead to an insight which stuns the world. Albert Einstein once said:

> I sometimes ask myself how did it come that I was the one to develop the theory of relativity. The reason, I think, is that a normal adult never stops to think about problems of space and time. These are things which he has thought of as a child. But my intellectual development was retarded, as a result of which I began to wonder about space and time only when I had already grown up. Naturally, I could go deeper into the problem than a child with normal abilities [quoted in Clark, 1971, p. 27].

REFERENCES

Ausubel, P. (1954), *Theory and Problems of Adolescent Development*. New York: Grune & Stratton.
Berman, A., & Siegal, A. (1976), Adaptive and learning skills in delinquent boys. *J. Learn. Dis.*, 9:583-590.

Bergman, P., & Escalona, S. K. (1949), Unusual sensitivities in very young children. *The Psychoanalytic Study of the Child*, 3/4:333-352. New York: International Universities Press.

Blos, P. (1967), The second individuation process of adolescence. *The Psychoanalytic Study of the Child*, 22:162-186. New York: International Universities Press.

———— (1979), Adolescent concretization: A contribution to the theory of delinquency. In: *The Adolescent Passage*. New York: International Universities Press, pp. 278-302.

Clark, R. W. (1971), *Einstein*. New York: World.

Condon, W. S. (1975), Multiple response to sound in dysfunctional children. *J. Aut. & Child Schiz.*, 5:37-56.

Cozal, R., & Ronsey, C. (1968), Hearing and speech disorders among delinquent children. *Corrective Psychiat. and J. Soc. Ther.*, 12:250-257.

Critchley, M. R. (1968), Reading, retardation, dyslexia, and delinquency. *Brit. J. Psychiat.*, 115:1537-1547.

Fries, M. E. (1944), Psychosomatic relationship between mother and infant. *Psychosom. Med.*, 6:159-161.

———— (1977), Longitudinal study: Prenatal period to parenthood. *J. Amer. Psychoanal. Assn.*, 25:115-140.

———— & Woolf, P. (1953), Some hypotheses on the role of congenital activity type in personality development. *The Psychoanalytic Study of the Child*, 8:48-62.

Jacobs, D. H. (1979), Problems of mental health counseling within the criminal justice system. In: *Working with the Impulsive Person*, ed. Wishnie & Nevis-Olesen. New York: Plenum.

———— & Pries, R. (1982), ACS: A court-based program for serving learning-disabled delinquents. In: *Successful Innovations in Child Guidance*, ed. G. L. Judy. Springfield, Ill.: Charles C Thomas, pp. 334-344.

Peller, E. (1965), Language and development. In: *Concepts of Development in Early Childhood Education*, ed. P. B. Neubauer. Springfield, Ill.: Charles C Thomas, pp. 59-83.

Robbins, D. M., Pries, R., Jacobs, D. H., Beck, J., & Smith, C. (1983). Learning disability and neuropsychological impairment in adjacated, unincarcerated male delinquents. J. Amer. Acad. of *Child Psychiat.*, 22:40–46.

Sander, L. W. (1969), The longitudinal course of early mother-child interaction: Cross case comparison of mother-child pairs. In: *Determinants of Infant Behavior*, Vol. 4, ed. H. M. Foss. London: Methuen, pp. 189-227.

Weil, A. (1978), Maturational variations and genetic-dynamic issues. *J. Amer. Psychoanal. Assn.*, 26:461-491.

11

Self-Esteem in the Retarded

Frank S. G. Wills, M.D.

Articles on self-esteem in retarded people usually focus on self-image problems that are due to the retardates' awareness of their differences from others and to insensitive treatment they receive at their hands. These papers often imply, and sometimes state, that self-esteem problems are universal in this group. This paper will attempt to show that this need not be the case. It will discuss the development of self-esteem in a retarded child, implications for a theory of self-esteem development which can be drawn from observation of retarded individuals, and the importance of self-esteem considerations in the care and treatment of normal and emotionally disturbed retarded people. Aggression, as a factor which may have special significance in self-esteem development for this population, will also be discussed.

CASE 1

The case of Joe, a mildly retarded man in his mid-twenties, illustrates that poor self-esteem does not always follow upon the retardate's awareness of his differences from others and insensitive treatment. Joe was married, had no children, and had a steady job which he had held for about four years. His job and salary were appropriate for his level of skill and were satisfactory to him. He and his wife, who was of a similar intellectual level, had adequate social and money-management skills; they had a number of interested family members and supportive professionals, and they managed well. Joe smoked moderately and did not drink at all.

He had been raised by strict, religious, demonstrative, blue-collar, first-generation immigrant parents of average intellect who had accepted his limitations appropriately. The cause of his retardation was not known but was strongly suspected to be related to problems in his delivery, which his mother had said was "long and difficult." His childhood memories of his family were generally positive with one important exception—a memory of occasional episodes in which he felt, and thought he probably literally had been, "backed into a corner" by his father and "scared to death" over misbehaviors, the details of which he could not recall.

He had always had a somewhat volatile temper, which may have been partly associated with neuropathology underlying his retardation. In addition, his temper may have been an outgrowth of his identification with and patterning after his father's apparently volatile temper. Joe's temper was particularly a problem in situations in which he felt himself "backed into a corner." This was what had brought him into consultation.

His school years were often difficult, with the combined problems of slowness at learning and teasing from other kids. Joe was quite aware of his differences from others and had received a great deal of insensitive treatment in the past. Through the efforts of his concerned, supportive, and strict parents, however, and the help of knowledgeable and kind school personnel, he had learned excellent work habits and attitudes. He had also learned useful skills, including his trade, and social skills that had enabled him to get along quite well and feel proud of himself as an individual who had "made it" despite a significant handicap. This came out remarkably in the context for which he sought help.

He had gotten into a fight at work with severe enough injuries to the other man that serious consequences were being considered for Joe. As information from various sources came in, it developed that he had been "set up" by sociopathic fellow employees who knew Joe had a problem with his temper. He had been subtly goaded for some while and, finally, was literally backed into a corner one day and taunted. Touching on his most sensitive area, the situation exceeded his capacity for control, and Joe exploded.

When he talked about this later, he was able to say, with appropriate discomfort and chagrin but without unwarranted shame or self-deprecation, that temper and panic when cornered were areas in which he was particularly limited and in which he had always had to be careful. He tried to avoid such situations; this was one reason why he abstained from alcohol. He knew that there would have to be some consequences and he was prepared to pay them. His boss had reassured him about his job, and his wife, family, and friends were behind him all the way. He was clearly very regretful about the incident. He was sad and fearful about the probability of significant consequences, but nevertheless aware of his accomplishments and proud of his state of general success, despite this setback. He said he had felt badly about himself temporarily after the incident but had bounced back quickly.

Joe radiated a general sense of success in a context of adversity. He was one retardate who showed outstanding results of infantile and childhood experiences "good-enough" to provide a solid base for self-esteem. Enough "little victories" (a concept to be discussed later in the paper) had helped him to be able to appreciate success, and enough successes had helped him to maintain a positive self-image and good overall self-esteem in a situation which could have been devastating for many people with fewer apparent liabilities.

Most importantly, his parents and teachers had seen his basic humanness and worthiness as he grew up; and he eventually had begun to see it in himself. Then, in a time of severe stress, his wife and boss had again seen and supported these qualities, helping him to regain his equilibrium quickly and to feel, basically, good about himself again.

IMPLICATIONS FOR THEORY

Any discussion of such a complex process as self-esteem development in the retarded child is complicated by the lack of any universally accepted definition of intelligence, or even of cognition as one important element of intelligence. A related problem is the difficulty of determining and describing cognitive ability in terms of behaviors other than verbal. In this paper, the concept of intelligence includes "the ability to learn or understand or to deal with new or trying situations. . . . the skilled use of reason . . . the ability to apply knowledge to manipulate one's environment or to think abstractly as measured by objective criteria" (Gove, 1976, p. 600). Thus, intelligence includes fact-accumulating, remembering, analyzing, synthesizing, utilizing data for social adaptation, and even developing new arrangements or combinations from old information. It is a broad concept and includes more than the items just listed. Cognition refers essentially to the intake process, to "the act or process of knowing, including both awareness and judgment" (Gove, 1976, p. 217). Clearly, the amount and variety which one can take in and remember will affect greatly the permuting, combining, adaptive, and productive manipulating one can do.

The retarded form a "living laboratory" for the study of many developmental phenomena, since they go through the same phases in a sequence similar to nonretarded people; but the phases are prolonged and development never proceeds to the same extent as in normals. In 1966 Cobb put it this way:

> As with those of normal intelligence, the self-attitudes of the retarded are the product of experiences sustained in the developmental years. . . . In the case of retarded children many essential components of this [developmental] process are modified. The developmental stages of maturation tend to be delayed, but not uniformly for all functions; the efforts to cope with the environment are more limited by intellectual and often motoric disabilities [quoted in Balthazar and Steven, 1975, p. 44].

The prolongation of the phases permits observations of small increments of change in a gradual process, in marked contrast to the rapid development of the normal infant and toddler. Observing both normal and severely retarded children makes us realize just how rapid, in fact, normal development is. As Cobb notes and as Case 2 will illustrate, the delays tend not to be uniform for all functions. Physical and motor development often advance more rapidly than psychosocial development. Discrepancies created by unequal progress highlight particular developmental-stage behaviors and make them stand out even more than they would otherwise. A play-activity style characteristic of a two-year-old, for example, is a striking phenomenon in a normal-size 13-year-old.

It is particularly important to examine developmental processes in retarded children from early infancy; much of the development of the severely retarded may never progress beyond infantile levels. Infancy is also the stage at which much of the groundwork is laid for the development of self-esteem in the retarded, and in the nonretarded as well. The conceptualizations of normal child development of Winnicott for emotional and social processes (1958, 1965) and of Piaget for cognitive processes (1954, 1966; Woodward, 1960) are particularly translatable to retarded persons at all levels of handicap. Both Winnicott and Piaget start in great detail from earliest infancy, in contrast to traditional Freudian psychodynamic theory.

Winnicott (1965) describes the early mother-infant relationship as one in which the infant is totally dependent on the mother's ability to anticipate the infant's needs and to be empathic with the postural and behavioral cues the baby emits. The infant at this stage, he believes, not only cannot survive biologically without the mother but cannot be appropriately conceived of as a separate entity, his dependence on her is so complete. The infant and mother are a unit more than they are a pair. There is a psychological, even a spiritual, dimension to this relationship/unity. To the extent that this unity exists in a "good-enough" way to a "good-enough" degree, the beginnings of such feelings as basic security, ease, intactness, and wholeness are formed. The substrate laid down here provides underpinnings for future development as the infant gradually becomes relatively independent. The significantly retarded infant remains more nearly totally dependent longer and develops relative independence much more gradually and tentatively. The mother and other caretakers must adapt to the different pace of this development if the affectional and emotional needs of the retarded child are to be met. It is remarkable how many mothers and significant others are able to adapt. The sensitivity they demonstrate to the child's often minimal cues is certainly not purely cognitive nor mechanical. What is striking is the spiritual quality in such maternal intuition. Winnicott describes this well.

Basic biological and psychosocial developmental factors must also be included in a study of the development of self-esteem in retarded people. Both have significant implications for self-esteem developmental theory in normals as well. The primary biological issue is the neurological status of the individual. R. D. Adams (personal communication, 1980) states regarding "functional neurologic issues . . . with severe brain diseases, and profound mental retardation . . . [that] the possibility of forming a concept of self vs. nonself requires a well-functioning parietal lobe. The possibility of recognizing one's self in a mirror or photograph, as distinct from someone else, is a parietal-occipital (?) non-dominant hemisphere function. The possibility of knowing, that one is sick, abnormal, defective, or different from others, i.e., insight, is also a parietal lobe function. The possibility of experiencing affection, fear, anger, etc., towards others is a bitemporal-parietal function." As we will see in Case 2, children with severe brain damage can develop good self-esteem. Adams makes it clear that neurological status influences the process.

Psychosocial considerations include the degree of cognitive ability necessary for the development of a sense of self and a self-concept, and the degree to which verbal ability is important in this process. They also include the distinction between narcissistic hedonistic pleasure and object-related self-esteem. Still another factor in self-esteem development of the retarded is the role of aggression.

The development of self-esteem as a specific phenomenon of self-judgment is not dependent on a high level of cognitive ability and does not require verbal conceptualization, but it does require some development of object-relatedness. These arguments will be pursued in the following case example, in which aggression also plays a part. The case illustrates some of the contributions that observations of retarded youngsters can make to a developmental theory of self-esteem.

CASE 2

Fred is a 12-year 7-month-old very severely retarded boy who lives at home. He is a slim, active blond boy with dark brown eyes, who loves company. He usually either babbles ("converses") happily with his caretakers or amuses himself with simple toys. He screeches with indignation when too hungry or if he doesn't want to "go potty" or have his clothes changed. He was first diagnosed as neurologically impaired on the second day of life. He is the fifth of six children; all of his siblings have participated actively in his care and two of them are still at home. His parents are knowledgeable upper-middle-class people. The family's care is supplemented by a public school special-class program for mul-

tiply handicapped, severely retarded children, and by three res-
pite-care home aides who collectively spend about 20 hours a week
with Fred.

In addition to his retardation, Fred is microcephalic, has spastic
diplegia (he walks on his knees by himself and on his feet with
help), extreme myopia (with a focal point of about three inches;
legally blind), grand mal epilepsy well controlled with medication,
and an occult spina bifida which is asymptomatic except for some
rectal hypotonia so that stools must be kept soft. All developmental
milestones have been seriously delayed except for dentition. As
well as it can be measured, his IQ is between 15 and 25. Despite
the extensive neurological involvement, he has sufficient intact
cerebrum to have developed a number of subtle functions which
will be discussed later.

In Piagetian terms, most of his behavior is at the sensorimotor
level. There are increasing numbers of behaviors on an early
preoperational level, such as winding musical toys to hear them
play and putting together and taking apart two or three Lego
blocks as a play activity. He also moves a large building block to
stand on in order to reach over a window guard screen to drop
toys behind it. He used to think this was hilariously funny and a
great achievement, perhaps because his caretakers who had to
retrieve the toys frequently displayed frustration, at least until a
hole was cut in the screen so that Fred could retrieve the toys
himself. He continues to play this as a solitary game, occasionally,
or pulls a caretaker over to play it with him. He feeds himself with
a spoon and responds to simple commands such as "Sit on your
chair," "Throw the ball," "Get up on the bed." He has several play
skills, the most complex of which are playing "catch," taking turns
with the ball with two other people, and snapping as many as
seven Lego plastic blocks together with only verbal prompting.
His favorite play is spinning pot lids because he likes the noises
they make as they slow down and clatter to a stop. Fred often
spins his lids on different surfaces and appears to be intrigued
with the different effects. This appears to be a persistence of
behavior that Piaget labelled "tertiary circular reactions: (stage
five of the sensorimotor period)" (Kahn, 1979, p. 273), which is
consistent with the findings of detailed developmental testing
which placed Fred's skills mostly in the 12- to 18-month-old range.

"Tertiary circular reactions occur when the child, apparently intentionally, searches for novelty in the results of his behaviors. . . .
The child observes the varying results of his or her actions and
continues to repeat the behavior with modifications designed to
produce novel results" (Kahn, 1979, p. 273).

Fred has moved from a prolonged "absolute dependence"
phase, in which satisfaction of his needs depended on his caretakers being able to anticipate them or to interpret very vague or
subtle cues, to such an extent that he was totally dependent on
their empathy, to a phase of "relative dependence" (Winnicott,
1965). In this phase, he indicates his needs more specifically and
clearly, and satisfies some needs through his own actions. In the
earlier phase, there appeared to be little or no sense of separateness or self. In the present phase, he clearly has some sense of
what he can do and of what he needs another to help him with.
He is far from independent but approaches and leaves the presence of his caretakers with considerable appropriateness. He is
also moving through a very prolonged phase of negativism, much
to everyone's distress at first, especially his teachers', since they
have had to deal with him in small groups. Now, to everyone's
relief, he is becoming less negativistic as he develops more areas
of skill and of relatively autonomous functioning. There is a related sense of competence and an apparent growing self-esteem.
His gradually increasing sense of "I can" seems to be mellowing
his need for "I won't." This most recent phase of his development
will be elaborated further in the discussion of aggression.

Fred forms specific relationships in which he is demonstratively
affectionate. He distinguishes his mother and father by attitudes
which are slightly different toward each and by words, "Mum"
and "Pa-pa." He also clearly distinguishes his favorite sister and
favorite home aide. His reaction to strangers was, for a long time,
"gut reactive" to the stranger's manner, going to some as readily
as to known people whom he liked and shying away from others.
For roughly the past year, he has appeared to be anxious around
strangers in the manner typical of young toddlers. On his first
day at an overnight special summer camp, for example, he responded to his new counselor's gentle, friendly "Hi!" with a
sprightly "Hi" of his own, then immediately burrowed his face
into his sister's shoulder and only very gradually peeked up at the

counselor. He eventually went off with her and the overall separation from sister and parents went as smoothly as might be expected with a young preschool age child. Fred is a good example of the different rates of development in different functions. As indicated above, his play and performance skills generally fall into a 12- to 18-month-old range; many of his social skills are more like those of a 24- to 30-month-old child.

For a long time, Fred has been very responsive to approval and disapproval from others. His family members are demonstrative people. They recognize that he needs all the affection they can provide and also believe, to quote his mother, that "mental retardation is not an excuse for bad behavior," so limit-setting is generally clear and reasonably enforced. Caretaker approval and disapproval have consistently been the strongest reinforcers for him in all attempts at behavior training, as they seem to be for most retardates (Zigler, 1967; Bernstein, 1978). Now, despite his very limited intellect and 10-word vocabulary, Fred appears to have introjected approving others. He certainly has incorporated in some sensed way—even though not verbally conceptualized—the sequence of action, accomplishment, good feeling, and praise (from other or self). On occasion he does things specifically to elicit good-feeling responses from others *or from himself.* A number of his current behavior patterns demonstrate clear realization of cause and effect, of his ability to effect change, to influence his material and human environment, and to elicit pleasurable feelings from others and within himself by reason of his own actions. He starts roughhousing sessions with his brother, games of "catch" and "peek-a-boo." He plays with his music box and Lego blocks for self-amusement and not just stereotypic self-stimulation. He says "Hi" or "Eat" until he gets an appropriate response. The pleasure derived from some of these situations depends heavily on the response of another person. He is, after all, still in a phase of "relative dependence." Some might interpret his initiation of such interactions as mere attention-getting or as meant to satisfy dependency needs. Fred appears, however, like any other child, to get maximum pleasure most of the time from the relationship and the genuine give-and-take that he can engage in within his physical and mental limits.

Fred's pursuit of solitary activities for self-amusement or self-occupation as contrasted with stereotyped self-stimulation suggests a rudimentary element of productive thrust rather than pure idle void-filling. The implications of this for self-esteem development should be evident. Fred will sometimes look to the other for reaction and at other times will simply show obvious pleasure over his own activity. When observing him, I have asked myself if I could be seeing purely conditioned responses, but the examples are too varied and complex for such a simple explanation. One of the more dramatic ones I happened to witness was the first time he urinated in the toilet instead of in his diaper. His sister was prepared to "raise the flag and shoot off a 21-gun salute" if he went in the toilet. She had the wind thoroughly taken out of her sails when Fred, immediately upon urinating and before she had begun to react, laughed and clapped spontaneously, a response he had learned in some earlier situations. He had somehow put the elements of the situation together, knew he had accomplished something, and was proud of himself.

He often shows a similar reaction in other such situations. He does not always look at the person who is with him for approval or seek to involve that person in his self-approval, although he frequently does. He has also been observed behaving similarly while alone. He will wind his music box and put it to his ear, put a few Lego blocks together, or push himself around on a Sit-and-Spin (a toy like a lazy susan on which he can spin himself), all for self-occupation. All of this behavior was occasionally present throughout the phase of negativism, and even before, and is quite routine now.

The indications from such observations of Fred and other well-adjusted severe retardates are that self-esteem development requires a well-enough developed ego to have some sense of differentiation from others and some capacity for object relations, but requires little, or perhaps no, formal expressive language. A sense of mastery, achievement, of approving (and sometimes disapproving) meaningful others, and some developing sense of self are all clearly important.

Since this paper is about people who, by definition (Grossman, 1973), have limited formal intellectual and social adaptive capacity, it is important to reiterate the distinction between purely rote repetition of behavior for external praise or continuance of interaction (as in a dog's fetching a stick) and the introjection of rewarding aspects of the significant other so that the child goes through the entire process internally and spontaneously. The complexity and variety of Fred's self-occupying behaviors argues strongly in favor of just such introjection rather than rote repetition, and suggests that he has developed some self-concept (however rudimentary), an ability to feel good about himself and his accomplishments in relation both to himself and to others, and a prevailing sense of an "all right" self.

A related element, difficult to tease out but important for these people, is their general sense of the world—their primitive *Weltanschauung*, their sense of the positiveness, benignity, or malignancy of their environment. This general sense of others seems intimately related to and interwoven with their sense of themselves. Their general sense of the expectations of others becomes equivalent, as it were, to their estimation of themselves, and helps to develop their actions, responses, and capacities. Thus, retarded children whose experience has given them a general sense of the environment as benign or even encouraging seem more likely to feel that they can do things and gain satisfaction from doing them. Doubtless, this is partly due to the fact that the environment has permitted and encouraged exploration, experimentation, and development of capacities. In other words, the caretakers have recognized the retarded child's human worth. They have encouraged normal curiosity, striving, growth, and development. But they have also provided models of behavior, demonstrating expressions of affect and thought that the child can imitate within the limits of his ability. He can thus incorporate some of the permitting, encouraging, and guiding patterns of the environment and make them his own, a part of his self.

While at times the degree to which Fred can separate his sense of others from his sense of himself seems questionable, and at times it is difficult to determine precisely where in his interactions his sense of self-esteem lies, Fred's separation becomes more distinct as he continues to develop. Thus, he used to say "Pa-pa" only after his father spoke to him but now greets him with a smile and a loud "Pa-pa" whenever he sees him come into the room. At the same time, he is using his most highly developed skills more of the time when alone and resorts to self-stimulating behaviors much less often. It makes sense that self-esteem development in such a severely retarded child is still in a relatively early phase.

Winnicott (1958) speaks of "transitional phenomena" as occurring in the "space" which gradually expands between the mother and infant as the infant moves from absolute to relative dependence. He describes these phenomena, and certain "transitional objects," as the first of the infant's experiences of "not me." But they are not quite "they" either. Self-esteem development may be an aspect of life particularly well explained in terms of that "space" wherein Winnicott's "transitional phenomena" lie. It may be that in the severely retarded the distinctions between self and other are still too indistinct, the introjections too partial, the dependence still too great for full development of a sense of self and a prevailing self-estimation. Yet Fred demonstrates that enough sense of separateness and enough object-relatedness can develop that some particular good feelings are not purely reactive or purely narcissistic, unrelated in any meaningful way to others. They are, rather, in that realm of self-appraisal, however primitive, wherein approval of self as a replica of approval from others is becoming or has become self-esteem, related to, but not quite the same thing as, the sense of well-being. Basic trust, a sense of autonomy, and object relations to whatever degree they have developed, are clearly significant elements of these feelings.

As Ablon suggests (see Chapter 2), the key phenomenon in development of self-esteem may be mastery of affect, perhaps as much as or more than the mastery of skills. Retarded people generally have no shortage of affect although many have problems with affective control. The degree of correlation between self-esteem level and affective control would be a worthwhile subject for study in this population.

AGGRESSION

Herbert Haessler (personal communication, 1979), a pediatrician who has done a great deal of work with the retarded, recently commented, "It seems to me that self-esteem is built up by a series of little victories. The retarded don't have many victories!" He may have hit upon a critical point with his concept of "little victories." In the literature on self-esteem much is made of the importance of mastery, achievement, and success. These concepts are vaguely unsatisfying. They do not seem to go far enough. Self-esteem is a strong term, and these notions seem a bit pallid in relation to it. My old Webster's Unabridged Dictionary (Harris and Allen, 1928) lists the following under "esteem":

> To esteem is to value or prize, especially for real or intrinsic worth; it commonly implies some warmth of feeling in attachment. Respect . . . is a word of less warmth than esteem. Regard implies perception or recognition of what is estimable or admirable (p. 751)

The nuances are critical. The key nuances in "esteem," or "self-esteem," are the nuances of prize and warmth, of high valuation. That is why Haessler may have hit on a key to the understanding of its development. It is not just a matter of success versus failure. It is a matter of winning—victory—versus losing—defeat.[1]

During his period of intense negativism, Fred was learning a number of skills, including fine motor skills with several toys, toileting skills, and social skills, particularly in the area of control of aggressive affect. There were frequent horrendous scenes, with both Fred and his caretakers distraught for months. During this time, he gradually learned new cognitive skills and better control of aggressive expression. He learned to wait a little for some of what he wanted, in marked contrast to the instant gratification he had, in his own way, demanded before. Each achievement during this stormy time was far more than just a success. It was an unquestionable victory, for his caretakers but more importantly for Fred. It has been striking since, that as he has become less negativistic, he appears to be learning cognitive skills somewhat more rapidly and easily. He is doing more things more of the time by himself and getting pleasure from "doing" and from simple success. It appears that enough experiences of victory have facilitated his achievement of adequate pleasure from success without adversity or affective storm. A similar process probably goes on in milder form early in normal childhood without the struggle being so dramatic and the distinction between "victory" and "success"

---

[1] One of the problems is that self-esteem is used, often loosely, with two different and often not clearly specified meanings: one is for a high level of self-regard; the other is for the more awkward but more accurate term "self-estimation."

so clear, since the odds are not as great. Adams (personal communication, 1980) points out that "the possibility of experiencing and remembering 'little victories' requires some degree of intact hippocampal-medial thalamic functioning."

Kessler (1966) has questioned whether retarded children can pass through the stage of negativism into a phase of autonomy. Fred makes it clear that even a severely retarded child can do so, at least in certain areas of living.

CASES 3 AND 4

Planning, care, and treatment for any retarded individual must aid him to reach the point at which he is not merely having a number of observable, superficially successful experiences. He must also begin to be able to accomplish some things he has the capacity for, wants to do, but believes because of his prior experiences he cannot do. This is when success equals victory and when modest self-regard or poor self-respect become positive self-esteem.

For a program to help individual retardates actualize their potential to the maximum degree possible, it must help each one to become able not only to do everything which comes reasonably easy. It must also help the retarded person do a few things which come hard and preferably at least one or two things which they want to do and think they cannot do. To implement programming toward such a goal obviously calls for individualized treatment planning done with delicacy and care, and yet with courage.

The following two cases are both examples in which self-esteem considerations were of major importance, even though the details differ.

Karen is a 23-year-old moderately retarded woman with a pushy manner, a curvature of the spine which makes her posture different enough to attract attention, and rather coarse facial features. When I first knew her, she was usually not well groomed and was almost constantly complaining about an ache or a pain somewhere. She was the scapegoat of her group home and frequently referred to herself by saying, "I guess I'm just a bad person. I could never be a lady."

Over time, she has been able to indicate particular aspects of ladylike behavior that she would like to achieve. We have taken those as our therapeutic goal in the weekly sessions we have had for over a year. The staff of the group home have concurrently worked with her on related social skills, such as appropriate ways of getting people's attention when she needs it and table manners. Progress has been good. Recently, when a visiting psychiatrist and I were touring her sheltered workshop, we stopped at her work station and I introduced them. The visitor commented on her attractive pants suit. She responded, "Thank you. I like to dress nicely. It makes me feel good." This was a far cry from the un-kempt "bad person" who could "never be a lady." From the psy-chotherapeutic standpoint, as a result of her growth in self-esteem, Karen is now able to begin to work on issues which she had never been able to deal with before. These include her mixed feelings toward her family, the fact that she can never live with any of them, and aspects of life in the group home, including the fact that she has not yet outlived her bad reputation and still tends to get scapegoated on occasion. Her newly found more positive self-esteem enables her to withstand day-to-day difficulties better. To some extent, she can stand back to look at herself and her life circumstances, and thus work on the problems of her life with some objectivity. Karen is not a borderline or even high-level mild retardate. Her IQ is about 55. Things could not have gone so well so quickly for Karen if she had not had a core of good self-feeling, self-feeling which had become buried under layers of negativism accumulated through years of distressing experiences (Gorlow, Butler, and Guthrie, 1963). She had, after all, formed a concept of a "lady" even while she thought that an unobtainable ideal for herself.

Laurie is a 19-year-old woman who was institutionalized at a very early age on strong medical advice, despite parental misgiv-ings. The institution has been her place of residence for as long as she can remember. Her parents and siblings have maintained close ties with her and are still ambivalent about the issue of in-stitutional versus community placement for Laurie. In the present climate of medical opinion, she would probably never have been placed in the institution. While parents and siblings have all been wrestling with the issue of placement, another situation arose which seriously threatened Laurie's self-esteem. This situation brought on symptoms of irritability, overtalkativeness, anxiety, and problems with sleeping that Laurie had never exhibited before. Her parents, hard-working, first-generation European immigrants with a strong work ethic, derive much of their self-esteem from pride in their work attitudes and performance. Despite not having raised her full-time since her early childhood, her parents have instilled this same ethic in Laurie. When she lost the restaurant kitchen job she had had outside the institution for over a year—through no fault of her own; there had been a change of management—Laurie had a hard time understanding, and a harder time believing, that it was not her fault in any way.

Laurie was aware of her symptomatic reaction and agreed to come to treatment sessions. She used help readily and well for the acute situational reaction. When she began feeling better, she started, very anxiously at first, pressing for a new job, saying, "I'm a worker. I'm a good worker. I'm not a low-level who can't work or doesn't want to work." As soon as she found a job, she informed me, "I'm not coming back. I don't need you any more. Besides, you should be using your time for some of the ones who are really crazy. They need you more than anybody." She then named three residents of the institution who were psychotic as well as retarded. She refused to come back even for one follow-up visit. Her usual level of self-esteem had been regained in the arena that maintained it best, work. Now therapy threatened rather than supported her self-esteem. Our interviews would couple her with the "low-levels" and the "crazy ones." Follow-up was done indirectly through reports from staff.

CONCLUSION

Self-esteem in the retarded is an area in which much exploration remains to be done. Retardation itself, and the neurological deficits that often accompany it, make self-esteem development a difficult process. It places unusual demands on parents, for whom there are often few sources of knowledgeable guidance and support. The problems arising from the retardate's awareness of his differences from others and from insensitive treatment are well recognized. But the paucity of "little victories" in the normal course of their lives adds to their high level of risk for self-esteem problems. So too does the paucity of people, professional and otherwise, who are dedicated to helping to increase their successes and victories.

Retardates at all levels of severity seem capable of developing self-concepts and self-esteem. Joe illustrates that retarded people can develop a sense of self-esteem strong enough to carry them through difficult life crises. Fred illustrates that even very severely retarded people can develop a sense of self-satisfaction that may be a rudimentary form of self-esteem. Karen and Laurie show that retarded people can be helped to gain or regain good self-esteem.

The essential element in each case appears to be the respect for the retarded individual's basic human worth shown by parents and caretakers. Enough such caring and respect enables the retarded person eventually to develop his own sense of self-worth, despite his awareness of differences and disrespectful treatment at the hands of others.

The relative lack of highly skilled mental health professionals capable of working with retarded people means that they have to plan the expenditure of their time and skills with care. It may well be that the psychiatrist or other mental health professional can be most useful in helping to decide which specific problems to work on and what goals to work toward. Mental health professionals can contribute to the important task of monitoring progress and guiding pace so that the retarded individual is neither overwhelmed, on the one hand, nor understimulated, on the other. In this way, he will not become discouraged by lack of progress when he rightly senses he could be doing more difficult work. In starting a program, the special interviewing skills of the mental health professional can help, even while most of the program implementation will have to be done by others.

In careful collaboration with the retarded person and his caretakers, the mental health professional can identify areas of previously experienced defeat and suggest possible routes for future victory.

REFERENCES

Balthazar, E. E., & Steven, H. A. (1975), *The Emotionally Disturbed, Mentally Retarded.* Englewood Cliffs, N.J.: Prentice-Hall.

240 Frank S. G. Wills

Bernstein, N. R. (1978), Mental retardation. In: *The Harvard Guide to Modern Psychiatry*, ed. A. M. Nicholi. Cambridge, Mass.: Belknap Press, pp. 551-566.
Gorlow, L., Butler, A., & Guthrie, G. M. (1963), Correlates of self-attitudes of retardates. *Amer. J. Ment. Def.*, 67:549-555.
Gove, P. B., ed. (1976), *Webster's New Collegiate Dictionary*. Springfield, Mass.: G. & C. Merriam Co.
Grossman, H. J., ed. (1973), *Manual on Terminology and Classification in Mental Retardation*. Washington, D.C.: American Association on Mental Deficiency.
Harris, W. T., & Allen, F. S. (1928), *Webster's New International Dictionary of the English Language*. Springfield, Mass.: G. & C. Merriam. Co.
Kahn, J. V. (1979), Applications of the Piagetian literature to severely and profoundly mentally retarded persons. *Ment. Retard.*, 17:273-280.
Kessler, J. (1966), *Psychopathology of Childhood*. Englewood Cliffs, N.J.: Prentice-Hall.
Piaget, J. (1954), *The Construction of Reality in the Child*. New York: Basic Books.
————— (1966), *The Origins of Intelligence in Children*. New York: International Universities Press.
Winnicott, D. W. (1958), *Collected Papers*. New York: Basic Books.
————— (1965), *The Maturational Processes and the Facilitating Environment*. New York: International Universities Press.
Woodward, M. (1960), The behavior of idiots interpreted by Piaget's theory of sensorimotor development. *Brit. J. Ed. Psychol.*, 33:123.
Zigler, F. (1967), Familial mental retardation: A continuing dilemma. *Science*, 155:292-298.

12

A Community View of Self-Esteem

SAMUEL J. BRAUN, M.D.

Working in the same community in the public practice of child psychiatry for 17 years provides glimpses of as many as three generations in their individual and collective struggle for self-worth. This urban community is densely populated, divided about its purpose, diverse in its ethnic and religious roots, and propelled to change by technological advances beyond the grasp of most of its members. Most people think of Cambridge as the home of two prestigious universities. In fact, 95,000 people live there of which the vast majority are low-income Irish and Italian Catholics. Many of the 10,500 blacks emigrated several generations ago from the West Indies, primarily Barbados. More recent immigrants are Portuguese-speaking from the Azores; some are Hispanics (approximately 4,500) and fewer still Haitians.

How a family bestows upon its young a sense of worth and purpose is of central interest to the public practice of child psychiatry. Where that family receives or finds a source of belonging, support, and affirmation is its corollary. It is my intention to examine this process with regard to a number of different individuals who were referred to me while I worked as a consulting psychiatrist to a public school. These students were identified as having behavior or learning problems. The meetings with the students and their parents were separate, brief, and intense encounters. Particular attention was devoted to determining how children or their parents derived strength and self-worth.

I have chosen for study two families whose isolation from the larger community has crippled their capacity to function and limited their ability to thrive. Later I will describe three immigrant families in their struggles to integrate past roots with present reality. The three teenagers depicted near the end of the paper are not drawn as examples of a conventional population. Each

241

invents or creates a reference group which reflects his or her own experiences and the adult society they are about to enter in the service of finding sources of self-regard. Only one example, Laura, emphasizes the role professionals in the schools, social services, or mental health agencies play in assisting youngsters or their families. The many self-help groups in a community are but mentioned in passing.

Laura serves to remind us that sensitive people in community institutions are valuable and valued. I met Laura when she was enrolled as a preschooler in Head Start where I served as a consultant. I met her again as a 19-year-old senior in high school when we had an opportunity to reminisce about the meaning of her early experiences. When Laura entered Head Start at three and a half she was urine-drenched, clingy, whiny, demanding constant attention. Once attached to an adult, Laura literally had to be peeled away. We decided to embark on a plan to give her "intensive care" before she asked for it, making an adult lap available to her as much as possible. Also, other children were encouraged to minister to her needs and demands in the housekeeping area of the classroom. Almost immediately her whining and clinging ceased and her bathroom skills blossomed. Her need for nurturance and "intensive care" persisted over the next three to four months. In the fourth month Laura indicated mild interest in leaving her teacher's lap to join her classmates who were about to play outdoors. When her teacher commented that maybe she was feeling more like a big girl, Laura corrected her with characteristic articulateness: "I don't want to be a big girl—just a growing up girl!" Soon after, she was able to participate more fully in classroom learning and activities.

Laura recalled some 16 years later her Head Start experience. She had entered school at a time when her mother and father had separated and soon after, her mother had given birth to her fourth child in four years. Laura knew "inside herself" that she wanted to "leave home" to go to Head Start even though the prospect frightened her. She said succinctly: "I wanted, no, I needed, to find someone to take care of me." She felt a sense of desperation and panic about her plight. Her teachers filled an important need that she regarded highly; of equal value, they affirmed that her need was a valid and legitimate one—a fundamental experience in self-esteem. She still recalled her teachers by name and had carried their images with her through the rest of her schooling. She attributed her wish to become a teacher to the strong impression they had made on her. At 19 she was planning to attend a well-known college where she had received a full scholarship. She had asked to see a psychiatrist: "Now that I'm escaping the 'cycle of poverty,' I want to resolve things with my family and my past. They never thought I was or could be different. It makes me feel angry. And I don't want to repeat the experience of 'putting down' my own children someday, the way my grandmother did to my mother and my mother did to me."

There are some notable instances in which the failure to enlist support or find outside groups fosters low self-esteem. Michael was such an instance—a husky, tall, physically mature 19-year-old. His age was camouflaged by the hunting cap he wore with visor rotated to the back much like a baseball catcher. Of average intelligence, he had dropped out of school for a year; he had found it too difficult to commit himself to his school work. He would not take regular courses because he "could not go all out." To enroll without commitment was, for him, to live a lie—a humiliating experience of which he had had too many.

His family had centered its life around his mother's drinking problems. Many nights were spent with brothers and sisters assigned to keep vigil. His mother often spent the night pacing, screaming, falling down so that one was assigned to sleep with her, another to watch the door. The day was often devoted to conspiring to control her alcoholic intake at night. Fresh bottles of bourbon were destroyed or hidden; open bottles watered down. A deep sense of helplessness overcame Michael when new empty bottles were discovered each day. This pain was accentuated when Michael's father came to his room each night to discuss his own worry and concern about the mother's drinking. The father, while sipping a few beers, usually talked to Michael one or two hours. When he left the room his father often thanked Michael for listening: "It takes all the problems out of me!"

The mother's drinking was a secret. No one outside the family discussed the problem. When her drinking became a matter of public display, Michael's feelings of low self-worth and humiliation were extreme and drove him into further isolation. In sixth grade his mother arrived at school drunk to complain about a school policy. The principal ended up driving Michael and his mother home; for Michael a referral to the guidance counselor offered some relief. It was the first time he had told a person outside the family about the problem. His nightmare went unabated with each new public scene, e.g., carrying his mother home from the liquor store because she had passed out. His father's death when Michael was 17 aggravated the plight of his brothers and sisters. Michael escaped to a full-time job, his one source of satisfaction and a sense of competence.

The isolation Michael felt was not unlike that of others who struggle with a family member who is alcoholic. Feeling the moral equivalent of being outcasts, they have no support, no reference group, only the nagging sense of failure and unrelieved responsibility.

Self-help groups speak directly to the issue of self-esteem of family members; Alanon and Alateen support the spouse and children of alcoholics in the same way Alcoholics Anonymous provides a social reinforcer for abstinence among alcoholics. They offer a public forum for what otherwise is a private hell. Children of alcoholics represent a significant portion of this school population.[1]

Another facet of problems of low self-esteem can be examined by studying a different kind of family unit isolated from the community. A second grader, John, at eight and a half, had been to three different private day care centers and two public schools in five years. He never completed more than three months in any one private school. His mother, without a friend in the community and with ties to her own family deliberately broken, kept up a constant dialogue with the school about her dissatisfaction with how her son was being educated. In turn, the school made heroic efforts to enlist her help in understanding John's behavior in school. He was described as easily distracted, unable to work in-

---

[1] Much beyond age five, most children have difficulty identifying or acknowledging that their parents have a drinking problem when counseled individually. Their sense of loyalty to the parent and the shroud of secrecy are too strong. A group education approach speaks with more ease to the issues of these children. In the adjoining city of Somerville, the school system is conducting an education program beginning in first grade using the city's teachers and teen-aged peer counselors trained by the Alcoholism Unit of the mental health center.

dependently, and talking out in class at inappropriate times. He and his mother lived in a small apartment. The mother worked in a local college assembling and organizing learning materials; John often spent time with her there after school.

A tall, shy boy, he was dressed in a well-worn, stained shirt and pants held up by red suspenders. His too-small sneakers had three-inch slits cut along the inner sole to allow him to walk in comfort. John said he was lonely. He had learned to play soccer and Candyland by himself. When he played cards, checkers, chess, or any other game, he always won because he "cheated" when he moved for the other person (who was never present). He said he was trying to make friends at school but could never tell when friends would become enemies. Some of the children at school, he said, were "Southerners" and his mother wouldn't let him play with "Southerners" or go to their houses. His mother telephoned the other mothers to tell them she did not approve. "School is hard," John explained. "I do not do my work too good." He added that his mother had told him, "The more money you have, the better treatment [at school] you get." Looking puzzled, John said: "I don't really understand what she means. I really don't understand my mother. In fact, I wish sometimes she wasn't my mother. I wish I had another mother. Sometimes I wish I could turn my mother into a goat and take her to the river and drown her."

John said that he didn't like school at all and was afraid he wouldn't ever like it; he lamented that he did not know how to behave well and had no friends at school. "My friends just cause me trouble," he summarized. Unable to talk about where he lived or about his dreams, he explained, "It's a secret. She does not like me to tell people things." John had grown accustomed to making up stories, unable to tell any of his classmates truthful things about himself and his mother. As he left the office John asked if he could take something home from the office. When offered index cards, he declined; he was afraid that his mother would make "flash cards" out of them and "do math with him."

John's loneliness is well documented. He lived a life full of secrets in a bond with his mother forged out of loyalty and survival. The opportunities to affirm his self-worth were limited to experiences exclusively with his mother who, for reasons of her own, had cut herself off from the larger community. Her own deep

emotional concerns could only be imagined; she lived a life filled
with deep distrust. There are not many students like John in a
school system. Such isolated people challenge our capacity to help
them become engaged in a community of which the school is but
one representative part.

Most children and their families seek affiliations and support
from many subgroups of the larger community. In some instances
those sources are chosen by virtue of birthright, heritage, or tra-
dition passed on from one generation to another through the
aegis of religious affiliation, ethnic group, or nationality. There
must be room in a school curriculum to honor and validate such
diverse backgrounds.

In some instances a problem is posed for the student when the
school chooses not to listen. Jim was a second-grader referred
because he did not finish his work and took every opportunity to
wander from class. It had been reported that he spit at his teacher
and hit a student with a belt. His family had moved from Jamaica
to Cambridge one-and-a-half years earlier without his father
whose emigration papers were held up because of a court action
still pending in Jamaica. A religious woman, the mother found
sustenance in her church community. Her extended family helped
with child care arrangements while she worked the three-to-twelve
shift at a hospital cafeteria.

Jim was talkative and engaging, fascinated with any attention
but especially attention paid to his memories about Jamaica or his
father. No matter what topic we began to discuss, it was not long
before Jim brought the conversation back to Jamaica. No one in
his school knew of his interest in Jamaica except maybe "the boss
of the school," to whom he was often sent for his school behavior.
His teacher was too busy with workbooks and lesson plans to hear
him.

In our session, Jim enjoyed contemplating his artistic endeavors.
He drew a car—just the kind of car his father would have loved
to drive. Sometimes, he recalled, he and his brothers and sisters
drove to school. Usually they walked the three-and-a-half mile
long, scary journey. He described the bridge they crossed, fearful
of falling into the pond where he thought sharks were. Most of
all he missed the water in Jamaica: Some of it was salty, some cold,
and some sweet. Jim said he could not wait to leave school some

days so that he and his brothers could reminisce about Jamaica—the clouds, the birds, the sun, a special kite they had made.

Jim wanted to let everyone know he was from Jamaica. He could not bear to wait much longer at school. His eyes widened, his frown disappeared, and his lips parted when he heard the suggestion that he and his teacher could make and read books about Jamaica. In fact, he was ready with a plan; he would get paper and put it in a folder and. . . . Jim's pride was special and required recognition. He was diminished without the acknowledgment of his past by his teacher.

Coreen had another kind of concern about school. She was not sure what to share and what to keep secret. Having moved from Haiti two-and-a-half years before, Coreen spent the first two years of her school life in a bilingual class until her English became proficient enough to move her into a regular fifth-grade class. Her father noted that she missed their house, the yard, the ocean, and the neighborhood children. He was also aware that Coreen was filled with questions about the meaning of being black or white. She asked her father why color was so important and why life was so different here. The father tried to tell Coreen and her younger brother that fighting is a matter of respect and knows no racial boundaries. The father wondered if tensions in the marriage contributed to Coreen's shyness. Part of the marital problem he attributed to his no longer attending the Jehovah's Witness Church.

Coreen was very conscious of being a Jehovah's Witness. This was indeed her secret and she was unable to mention it to a soul in her school. Fearful of what others might think of her, she said it was hard for her to express herself in English but she sometimes thought she could tell her secret to the school librarian. When asked what a Jehovah's Witness was, she explained that " 'They' do not believe in Christmas, Thanksgiving, or any holiday. 'They' believe if you do not listen to God, He will make a hole for you to fall into." She relaxed when she described the church services; what she liked best was caring for young children.

Without a perceived ally in school, Coreen struggled with her religious and cultural differences alone. She did not dare risk identifying herself with her religious or cultural background nor dare believe her roots to be a strength. She saw herself as so different that her self-regard in school was jeopardized. Coreen's isolation was made more complicated by her perception of her church, which had also set itself apart from the community. She kept this fact a closely guarded secret, too intimate or too discordant to reveal.

Another immigrant chose still another way to cope with his past and present life. By constricting his activities and acquaintances he reinforced what was familiar and more comfortable. Paulo arrived at age nine from the Azores with his mother, father, and eight-year-old brother. Ten years later he could read and write in both English and Portuguese but was unable to tolerate the anonymity of the large public high school from which he dropped out for a year and a half. Many unexpected events in his family prompted the decision to leave school. His father required a back operation after which he was unable to return to work; his younger brother became involved with drugs, alcohol, and stealing automobiles which required psychiatric hospitalizations and court appearances. During this time his mother's father died in the Azores. The only member of the family who could speak fluent English, Paulo negotiated with hospitals, courts, and his parents. In fact, he added these tasks to the already important letter-writing function he performed for his family so that they could communicate with their relatives in the Azores.

Handsome and well-built, Paulo's eyes sparkled as he reflected on his years in America. He longed to return to the islands or the continent, where he envisioned a "better place to study." The permissiveness of the high school here was difficult for him to manage. In Portugal he believed a better system of education existed where cutting classes, pot, and alcohol were not tolerated in school. These practices both scandalized and tempted him sorely. His visions were of an earlier time: playing soccer in the fields, or cutting the horns from the carcass of a bull, fastening the horns to a board and playing bullfight with his friend. In fact, Paulo's allegiance was to the islands and not to this country. He worked daily (as did all able members of his family) through contacts made with Portuguese-owned businesses. His social life was highlighted by attending "Portuguese Feasts" in different parts of the state; at one such event, he was reunited with a friend from the island who was touring with a soccer team which played exhibition games with Portuguese-American teams.

Paulo's girlfriend was also Portuguese; he drove her to and from a local college but worried that she might "meet some pervert there." Many of his daydreams were taken up with concerns about his future: Should he study in Portugal, drive a truck, become a soldier of fortune, join the Army, emigrate back to the islands? His self-worth was not questioned as it had been in the past; he felt he was "special," destined "to do something special." During the family crisis and prior to his decision to drop out of school he was intolerant of criticism, thin-skinned, and down on himself. A remarkable young man, he had seemingly stumbled through American life mostly on his own while many of his peers went astray during high school. His continued ties to the "old world" were an obvious source of strength and affirmed his worth as a man who could work and think. He had solved problems mostly on his own without relying on others, in part, because he was the only one able to negotiate the "new world." When Paulo considered taking a regular class in the high school, he could not tolerate not knowing his classmates or not understanding the material. Both experiences lowered his self-regard.

He is an interesting contrast to Tony, a 15-year-old eighth-grader who had lived in a closely knit neighborhood all his life. An attractive dark-haired boy, Tony spoke haltingly but openly about his life, using his prominent hands to emphasize a point. What he lacked in articulateness he made up for in his ability to convey his feelings directly. He still missed his mother's old boyfriend with whom he had felt a close tie; the boyfriend had been shot to death in a gangland-style murder when Tony was 10 years old.

Since reading about a group of volunteers who "watch over the subway" in New York City, Tony felt like a "Guardian Angel." He had been "watching over his neighborhood" from the recreational park nearby. He climbed atop the roof of a lookout tower there to make certain no trouble lurked on the streets. When not there, he often patrolled the neighborhood to ensure that his younger brothers and neighborhood children were safe. Especially solicitous towards younger children, he taught them how to play ball or ride a bike. Sometimes he bought ice cream or candy for them. Being a "Guardian Angel makes me feel good," he commented.

Tony had been worrying about his temper. He had often become enraged about injustices done to others, as he had felt when his mother's boyfriend Ted had been shot. Since Tony had acquired a girlfriend of his own, he had been thinking more about Ted, who had been his own "guardian angel." Rarely a day had passed when Ted had not taught him something or bought him a cone. When Tony played sports he visualized Ted and discovered that his performance immediately improved. He could jump further or make the most difficult swish shot. Even when he dreamed about his girlfriend, "flashes of Ted" appeared until he awakened to stare out the window, fully remembering what Ted had looked like. "It makes me feel lonely. I just get sad and wish he were here," he commented. Obviously Tony still has grief work to do over the loss of Ted; still, he has used his sense of identification with Ted and found a newly created vigilante group to supplement his sense of connectedness to the past. The "Guardian Angels," a source of identity and expectations for his own life, provide him with a way to measure his activities and assess his self-esteem. His mother had requested consultation, not for problems in school, but because of Tony's temper, which seemed associated with the difficulty the family had in talking about Ted. The family had been unable to attend the funeral and had never "buried" Ted nor visited his grave.

Not all sources of self-esteem in adolescence are synergistic with the goals of the community as a whole. At 16, Frank had already had many court hearings for charges of larceny and assault and battery. Committed to several community residential programs, he managed to run away from each. Notes about him began to appear in the school record in fourth grade at the time when he and his mother moved to the area. These earlier school comments document Frank's sensitivity to criticism and the very high expectations he held for himself.

Frank observed that he became easily enraged when anyone told him what to do. Much of his energy has been directed toward avoiding his temper. When he worked in the teachers' cafeteria in the high school, he had to smoke a joint in order to "mellow to the task." With his teachers he too often felt like a "slave," a position he loathed. Running away from his anger was at least a part-time job. He has lived in more than 10 places around the country but considered his grandparents' home in another state as a place (his birthplace) to which he has enjoyed returning. His grandfather whom he resembles taught him how to play basketball, but his visits there were infrequent ones.

He felt best at the recreation park where he met his friends in the evenings to drink beer and smoke joints. On his forearm was tatooed a cross with three dots lined up above the cross. The dots stood for his friends' greeting to one another, "Take three"; the cross for the "Kay Ko Klan." The latter he explained was like the Ku Klux Klan but disavowed racial prejudice, standing only for a dislike of ignorant people.

A friend of his, Steve, also belonged to the "Klan." A curly-headed, blond-haired boy, constantly fidgeting, Steve was bright but truant. He spent considerable time watching movies on television; his mother worked two jobs and was seldom home. Steve was more attached to his grandmother who had raised him but who had died the year before. He was interested in revisiting Nova Scotia, her native land, where he had become fascinated with the evergreens and the idea of raising Christmas trees.

Steve planned to be the only member of his family to graduate from high school; he otherwise identified strongly with his brothers as "prejudiced and bigoted." The best part of his family, according to Steve, was that "no one will fuck with you"; he took pride in being from a family of "troublemakers." Considered an "average white boy," Steve was convinced that "average white boys just get screwed." Since he believed that the high school basketball team was composed primarily of blacks, he has found the "Kay Ko Klan" a way to play on a basketball team.

Both Steve and Frank are extreme examples of teenagers with low self-esteem. Their tempers are crippling; their drinking habits are a serious problem to them and to the community. Much of their bravado, criminal activities, and interest in the Klan mend what for them are a series of failures at home and at school. They view their black classmates as competitors and feel worthwhile only at the cost of being against others. When Steve was asked what he wanted to do when he graduated, he answered, "I want to be a fucking killer of the U.S. of A." He added that he feels "trapped in a city where there are too many niggers." Racial and ethnic identity based primarily on *what you are not* is, at best, a temporary solution to matters of self-esteem. Both Steve and

Frank became more relaxed when exploring their own ethnic backgrounds. Unfortunately they felt cut off from an enormous fund of positive information about their parents and grandparents.

Teenagers sink their lifelines where they can. When they fail to find groups in the community that are constructive sources of self-esteem, they invent a peer support group fashioned after an adult model that still allows some integrity with their past. Sometimes these groups have a potential for destruction. In the absence of family or community education or sanctions, drug and alcohol abuse can become a common pastime; the consumption of two six-packs of beer by an individual on a weekend night is not considered excessive. Like other public high schools, the high school these teenagers attend is a large diverse one—not a sufficiently intimate environment to guarantee subgroups that foster self-worth. It is barely a holding environment for those tempted to cut class or determined to stay uninvolved. Whether they come to school very often is seemingly of no consequence.

The two teenagers disengaged from their high schools are reminiscent of those families previously described who are isolated from the larger community. They lack the sense of connectedness that evolves from the many everyday activities that more typical families perform in reciprocity with each other and some segment of the larger community. The effects are particularly devastating to those children of isolated families who have no source outside their own family to validate, categorize, and understand the feelings and experiences they have in growing up. Roots, formal institutions, and traditions are powerful antidotes. Said in a more positive way, they can help sustain the sense of self-worth.

In the absence of formal ties to institutions, the number of support groups people choose or create are many and fluid. They can reflect political concerns, work, neighborhood, recreational pursuits, sexual roles, health concerns, or drinking habits, to name a few.

Many mothers whom I met derived a great deal of pride and satisfaction from being a part of the women's movement. Working in a construction job while raising a family and studying was an enormous undertaking for one single mother. She did so with the support of a women's group and an extended family. Others found spouses, day care, and an informal network of friends, or church groups, important. Most parents sought affirmation for themselves and their tasks as parents whether part of the women's movement or not. Few formal channels gave encouragement for what was for most a very busy and active life.

In many of the children referred, affective issues blocked communication so that the children themselves often felt isolated within their own families. They became unable either to express their feelings or to validate their hunches. This was often so for children whose parents were separated or whose parents had drinking problems. Such was the case for Francey, a fourth-grader, whose mother had left the deep rural South to separate from a father with a drinking problem. Francey's mother described herself as "stunned" for the first six months living in an urban area for the first time. She gradually found a church to which she devoted all of Sunday. But she did not become fully acclimated until she joined a group of gospel singers; this she marked as the beginning of her "new life" in Cambridge. The father moved to the neighborhood years later and his presence puzzled and disappointed his 11-year-old daughter since he seldom kept his promises to take her to the movies and the like.

Francey never spoke during the interview. She liked the idea of conducting a conversation in writing or gesture. The idea of secrecy apparently appealed to her. To a message about her father's not always remembering his promises, she wrote, "I know what you mean!" She did not know why this was. When I wrote her that some folks with drinking problems forget their promises, she responded, "That's what my father has." I replied, "You must love him very much but feel very sad and mad." She became angry and wrote back, "I get it. You want me to leave him so he can die while he drinks and hangs with another woman." We established that what Francey knew about her father she thought was a family secret. She was surprised that her mother knew. I told her that most children I knew whose dads had drinking problems were sad and lonely. She began to cry. I wrote that it was a terrible secret to keep. She agreed, writing, "I know."

Francey's mother had found a source of self-worth but that did not guarantee that Francey herself would. The school noticed Francey was quiet. She had information she felt she could not share and consequently isolated herself at school and at church, finding ways to place distance between herself and others.

Support groups, more formalized institutions or self-help groups within a community, make significant contributions to the sense of self-worth of children and their parents. The lack of meaningful communication within the family about affectively laden issues can be thought of as an individual dilemma or as part of a larger social system's problem. In a diverse and fluid society there are both opportunities and impediments to family access to valued subgroups and institutions that help validate perceptions, feelings, and activities. In contemporary life we are challenged to explore, create, and utilize whatever unique sources of self-affirmation may exist in the community. Their creation and availability to children and their families are an essential ingredient in the quest for self-esteem.

13

Education and Self-Esteem

RONALD GERATY, M.D.

Most educational programs express the goal of promoting self-esteem in their students. To work most effectively with schools, the psychiatrist or other mental health professional must understand not only the concept of self-esteem but also the educational setting.

This paper will briefly review the history of educational thinking as it relates to self-esteem. Educational literature that is consistent with the recent understanding of the development of self-esteem in children is presented; two students referred by schools because of self-esteem problems are discussed. Following a brief review of recent educational research, the paper concludes with a description of how self-esteem is enhanced in the classroom and how one particular school achieves this.

EDUCATIONAL LITERATURE

Until recently, educators have emphasized the acquisition of knowledge. Curriculum development, lesson plans, and schools of education directed the teacher toward presenting specific information in ways designed to help the student learn. Scholastic achievement and skill-building were the endpoints of successful education; self-esteem, if addressed at all, was viewed as a by-product of this process. Recently, however, educators have become increasingly aware of the relationship between self-esteem and school achievement. In a March, 1974 issue of *Learning* magazine, a popular educational journal, there appeared the following statement:

The development of self-esteem is the primary prerequisite to learning. Children must be heard if they are to feel that they

count and are worthy people. . . . When the child feels good
about himself, he can begin to invest in the world of people and
things. He can start learning something new, meeting new
friends, playing new games. But he will not risk a new venture
if he fears rejection and failure. Thus we must establish an
environment that is consistent in nurturing and honoring the
special worth and value of each child [p. 68].

Thus teachers have shifted from placing marks such as A or B on
papers to using the "happy face" logo. Instead of reading circles,
children sit in "feeling groups"; the educational purpose is to
provide "affective" education and to build self-esteem. The structured classroom, in which curriculum is the guiding force, has
changed to the entirely "open classroom," in which individual
interests and pacing reign supreme. That these trends may have
been overemphasized is suggested by the fact that some com-
munities have begun a "back to basics" movement to restore the
acquisition of knowledge to its former place of prominence.

Historically, educators, like many other theorists, have taught
that self-esteem develops in a one-dimensional fashion. Some have
suggested that individual achievement leads to positive self-image;
others have stressed that a teacher who rewards his students with
positive feedback enhances their self-esteem. These educators are
confused when faced with a child who has achieved scholastically,
been rewarded, yet appears to have a negative self-image. Purkey
(1967), a writer in educational psychology, begins a comprehensive discussion of the self by describing the influence of J. B.
Watson, a behaviorist, on educators, and placing primary responsibility for the one-dimensional theories on the behaviorists' emphasis on observable and measurable behavior. Purkey credits
Carl Rogers, a humanistic psychologist who popularized the client-
centered approach, with reintroducing the self as the central aspect of personality. Rogers proposed that the basic drive of the
organism is to maintain and enhance the self.

Purkey further describes the self as organized, dynamic, and
learned. He discusses a concept similar to "psychological centrality," according to which central beliefs have a much greater impact
on the self than peripheral beliefs. Thus, a child who has long
believed that he is a poor student (central for the child both because of its importance and the length of time the belief is held)

has greater self-esteem problems than a child who does poorly in a ceramics workshop (of peripheral and brief importance to most children). The dynamic quality of the self results from the process of actively selecting what is needed to be consistent with it; this process helps determine behavior. A student, considering himself a failure at school, will reject and distort evidence that contradicts his perceived self, no matter how positive the information appears to an outside observer.

Purkey (1968) holds that by the time a child reaches school age he has already formed his self. School experience will be accordingly accepted, rejected, or modified. But except for the home, the school, in Purkey's view, plays the most important role in the formation of the self.

Norem-Hebeisen (1976), an educational psychologist, describes both a developmental and a multidimensional construct of self-esteem based on four themes: (1) basic acceptance—a preverbal emotional acceptance of oneself originating in early childhood with components of a sense of well-being, personal autonomy, freedom of feeling, and freedom in relationships; (2) conditional acceptance—contingent on meeting standards of self and others; (3) real-ideal self congruence—the congruence between the current self-concept and the ideal self; and (4) self-evaluation—the individual's judgment of how he compares with others. Her construct, consistent with the developmental concepts proposed in this volume, stresses the role of the self and the interpersonal aspects of self-esteem.

Teachers readily accept Norem-Hebeisen's view that conditional acceptance and self-evaluation influence the development of self-esteem. Many intuitively recognize that "basic acceptance" is a psychic reality the student has had to deal with for better or worse long before he started school. But it is the concept of the real-ideal self congruence and its development that mental health consultants can best introduce to the educator. According to Norem-Hebeisen, the real-ideal self congruence is the "perceived match between perceptions of what one is and what one thinks one ought to be" (p. 560).

The following two clinical cases were referred to a psychiatrist specifically because of self-esteem issues. The therapist used the Norem-Hebeisen and Purkey concepts not only in the treatment

of the individual child but more importantly in consultations with
the school.

CASE 1

Jimmy, a 12-year-old seventh-grader living with his parents and
three siblings, was referred by his guidance counselor three weeks
after he had tearfully entered her office, refusing for the first
time to go to classes and saying, "I'm feeling upset and I don't
know what it is." He described feeling that he was not ready for
the seventh grade, that he was doing poorly in school and finding
it too hard to cope in class. Checking with his teachers, the guidance counselor found that Jimmy was in the "gifted" track of the
junior high school and excelled in all his classes. Referring Jimmy
and his family for a psychiatric evaluation, the guidance counselor
told the consultant that she was baffled as to how Jimmy could
feel he was not a good student and yet be doing so well.

Jimmy, somewhat overweight and seeming embarrassed, tearfully told the psychiatrist that he was doing poorly "in these large
classes in junior high." He could not understand how his teachers
gave him all A's in his first quarter in spite of his being absent for
three weeks. He knew that he had been doing adequately, but
guessed that the teachers were being nice to him because they had
seen him crying in class. He told of losing interest in eating, reading, and watching TV, as well as trouble in getting to sleep. He
admitted that he was sad but did not know why. Moving from
class to class for the first time in his schooling, he missed knowing
his teachers personally. In spite of always being first in his class
and a favorite of his teachers, Jimmy had always worried about
his grades; even occasional B's troubled him.

Seeing his family, the therapist noted that Jimmy looked and
acted like his father but sat beside his mother, who stroked his
neck and patted his knee when he sniffled. His father, a successful
and driven middle-aged man with a doctorate in his field, spoke
of his concerns that this "temporary setback" not affect his son's
chances for college. Jimmy's two older brothers were doing well
in college and his sister was an accomplished musician. His
mother, a homemaker, focused her time on her children and
husband and was upset that Jimmy was so sad. She had made

daily trips to the school with him and brought him home early to be with her.

They reported an unremarkable early history except that Jimmy's birth had resulted from an unplanned pregnancy and that he had been very much the "baby" of the family. His brothers and sister called him the favorite of his mother; he had always preferred to be with his mother or other adults rather than with peers. Six months previously, the father had had a severe coronary and Jimmy had been seriously shaken by this, spending most of his spare time visiting his father in the coronary-care unit. The mother spent much of her time with her husband and was not available to Jimmy to help him with homework or watch TV with him as had been her custom.

Psychological evaluation revealed a WISC-R Full Scale IQ of 131; he scored in the 99th percentile in all the achievement tests at school. On projective tests (Rorschach, TAT, CAT), he was said to have "doubts of his own capabilities and adequacies."

After meeting with Jimmy and his family, the consultant requested permission to set up a meeting with school personnel including the guidance counselor and selected concerned teachers to address these questions: How could Jimmy, with excellent test scores, be doing so well academically but believe he was doing so poorly? Since his home appeared stable, was this a temporary setback in self-esteem precipitated by depression secondary to the illness of his father? In addition, the consultant introduced Norem-Hebeisen's real-ideal self congruence concept for discussion with the school personnel.

In the behaviorist theoretical framework of many educators, the external evidence would have suggested that Jimmy had high self-esteem. But the consultant, supported by ongoing evaluation, suggested that Jimmy had internalized his ego ideal by identification with an overachieving, hard-driving father. His father, rarely at home and emotionally unavailable to him, viewed no job as completed satisfactorily. His mother, though an emotional support for Jimmy, was dependent on her son for her own sense of well-being. He was much younger than his siblings, and the last child. Unlike his siblings, who had been involved in out-of-home activities, Jimmy preferred his mother's company and provided her with the companionship not available to her from her husband. Although he had mastered his school work, Jimmy had not achieved his ideal self. Only perfection could satisfy his expectations.

In this instance, the recommended first step of learning about the school setting was unnecessary because of the consultant's prior familiarity with the school. Without this knowledge, the consultant would have tried to understand the philosophy, administrative structure, workload, and skills of the teachers, the physical setting, and, most importantly, the school's liaison person with whom he would have worked—in this case the guidance counselor. After discussion with the consultant, the guidance counselor arranged with Jimmy and his family to decrease both his classload and classroom changes. Teachers were advised to give Jimmy individual attention and to encourage him to set realistic goals for himself. The consultant met with the guidance counselor quarterly for the first year to discuss Jimmy's progress.

He was seen weekly for the next three years, with the focus of therapy being the recognition and modification of his rigid and perfectionistic ego ideal. Jimmy gradually resolved internal conflicts as he dealt with his fears about the potential death of his father. As his depression lifted, he resumed his interest in friends and school. As his therapy progressed, the consultant decreased his contact with the school and the guidance counselor decreased her contact with Jimmy. By the time Jimmy was a tenth-grader, his new school was unaware of Jimmy's earlier difficulties and Jimmy's self-image was unshaken by an occasional poor mark.

CASE 2

Jackson, an eight-year-old third-grader living with his parents and 13-year-old sister, was referred by his guidance counselor because "he obviously is having problems with self-esteem because he reads so poorly." Both his parents questioned this assumption but were willing to have Jackson seen—they wanted the best for him. Jackson had come to the attention of the guidance counselor at a conference to discuss Jackson's reading disabilities. She referred him and his family to the consulting psychiatrist.

Jackson walked into the office without hesitation, wide-eyed and eager to talk. Speaking easily about home, school, and friends, he said that he understood that he was being seen because "I have trouble reading." On an assigned pencil-and-paper task he was able to concentrate well. He appeared happy and said he was happy. There were minor "soft" neurological signs of asymmetrical associated movements and poor quality of eye-tracking but he was otherwise neurologically intact. His articulation was perfect. He read on a first-grade level and his writing was labored and of poor quality. On his Draw-A-Person, he said of the boy he drew, "He is a baseball player going to a game. He wants to win. He won. He was happy. He got home and wondered why the other team couldn't win too. He told his mother. Then he went and got his friends to play football." He said that his favorite thing to do was play sports and that he was usually captain of his team in football and baseball. He enjoyed most playing with his dad.

A meeting was held with Jackson's family. The father, a middle-aged man, could neither read nor write. He was a janitorial services manager in a department store and compensated for his lack of writing skills by keeping a full-time assistant with him. He joked about his difficulty and was upset that his son seemed to be having the same trouble. He added, "But it never stopped me so I don't see why it should stop him." His mother had been active in trying to tutor Jackson. She hoped the school would provide a tutor and asked for support in this. She took care of the finances at home and did all of the reading for her husband and son.

Jackson's birth had been abnormal. Labor had been induced; after 24 hours he had been delivered with high forceps and spinal anesthesia. He had cried lustily and had no difficulties after birth. His developmental landmarks were normal despite breaking his leg in a fall at nine months. He had started school without separation problems and had had no difficulty in first grade. During second grade he fell rapidly behind his peers in reading, writing, and spelling though he did well otherwise. His parents verified his cheerful attitude and energetic approach. He had been referred by the school in second grade to a pediatrician because of his reading difficulties and was given a trial of Ritalin. It was stopped because behavior had never been a problem and was unchanged on the medication.

Jackson's teacher described him as "an extremely sensitive child. He tries to please so hard that at times he's a bundle of nerves.

He is kind, considerate of others, and well liked by his peers. He is a diligent worker and has good concentration. He seems content outwardly, but I'm not sure what his self image is. His diligence is probably one of his greatest assets. He also enjoys drawing and is good in art." Previous year-end reports from the first and second grade stated that he had done well in all nonverbal areas. On his WISC-R he achieved a Full Scale IQ of 109 with a performance IQ of 127 and verbal IQ of 98. This significant difference between performance and verbal IQ as well as the subtest scatter verified Jackson's learning difficulties. Since the evaluation was done at the school, no projective tests were given. Educational testing uncovered a specific reading disability.

Jackson spoke about his reading difficulties, saying, "Yeah, I feel bad about not reading well, but I can already read a little. My dad doesn't read at all you know. I'm not too worried about it but I'd like to get a tutor and I'll try real hard."

As a result of the evaluation, the school provided Jackson with a tutor. The parents were seen in two sessions to clarify with them ways they could continue to build his self-esteem in a society oriented toward reading. Jackson was seen twice at yearly intervals to assess his progress. He has continued to do well emotionally and has improved educationally although he is still not reading at grade level.

In a meeting with the school guidance counselor and teachers, the consultant used the concepts of Purkey and Norem-Hebeisen to help the school personnel better understand Jackson. How had Jackson, lacking achievement in a vital school area, maintained his self-esteem? As in the previous case, his ideal self resulted at least partially from identification with his father. He saw his father as potent and successful in spite of a reading handicap, and looked forward to a bright future. Using the one-dimensional view of the development of self-esteem, the guidance counselor had expected Jackson to have low self-esteem because he was poor in reading; but there was no evidence for this. Jackson had learned to tolerate the frustration of trying and being unable to read even in the presence of many who were able to. Although not being a reader could have been a central factor for Jackson's self-image, he did not give it a negative value because of his identification with his father. More central and of higher value to him were his views of himself as an athlete.

As previously stated, these two cases appear paradoxical when viewed from the one-dimensional developmental notion of self-esteem. It is in just such cases that psychiatric consultants are often sought. Contrary to common sense, good grades do not always result in high self-esteem, nor do poor grades always result in low self-esteem. These cases also suggest that the educational literature itself can be used to demonstrate the psychiatric concepts of identification, ego ideal, and multiple causalities.

THE ROLE OF SCHOOLS IN THE DEVELOPMENT OF SELFESTEEM

By the time a child reaches school age, the foundations of the self have been formed. If all has gone well, the child enters school with the sense of basic acceptance described by Norem-Hebeisen. For many children the teacher is the first significant other he meets outside of the home. In the charged atmosphere of the first day of school, one can begin to see the transfer of influence from parent to teacher. It is in school, with the new adult and with his peers, that the child first tests his view of himself as significant and competent, two of the four sources of self-esteem described by Coopersmith (1967). A sense of significance results from interpersonal experiences such as the acceptance, attention, and affection of others. To be competent is, of course, to perform successfully in scholastic work.

From his early primary dependence on parents, the child comes increasingly to be influenced by teachers, peers, report cards, and, later, by more personal standards in college, graduate school, or in work situations. This shift mirrors how reliance on the interpersonal influences of self-esteem gradually decreases as the self develops more fully.

Teachers affect their students' self-esteem. Classroom studies show that teachers who themselves have a positive self-image affect their students more positively (Edeburn and Landry, 1977). The more children perceive their teachers' feelings as positive toward themselves, the better their academic achievement (Davidson and Lang, 1960).

Many studies have shown the correlation between self-esteem and achievement in school (Stevens, 1956; Fink, 1962; Williams and Cole, 1968; Simon and Simon, 1975). There is often a self-perpetuating circuit: Success experiences lead to a positive perception by others which in turn leads to self-esteem which in turn results in even more success experiences. Unfortunately the opposite is also true, with self-devaluation leading to experiences of failure, negative perceptions by others, and poorer self-esteem. Even in later grades, however, improvement in self-esteem leads to improved reading skills and educational achievement (Sweet and Burbach, 1977).

It is important to note that gifted children do not have self-esteem indicators significantly different from average children unless they are *identified* as gifted (Dean, 1977). On the other hand, children who have been identified at random as high-ability students actually improve to meet expectations (Rosenthal and Jacobson, 1968).

PRACTICAL CONCEPTS FOR CONSULTANTS IN EDUCATIONAL SETTINGS

Beyond evaluating and treating individual students with difficulties, the consultant must know the educational setting and the realistic restraints on the educational system as they affect students and their teachers.

First, of course, parents and children must give the mental health professional permission to contact the school. Parents and children should be encouraged to ask questions about the limits of the consultant's involvement and issues of confidentiality. When parents understand how important the school is to the evaluation and treatment of the child, they usually give permission readily. When it is given, a call can be placed to the guidance counselor.

Depending on size and philosophy, schools use personnel differently. Larger schools have guidance offices with the capabilities to evaluate and treat; smaller schools assign the role of individual assistance to the principal or even the teacher. The consultant should ask to have the structure of the school explained to him so that he can understand both its impact on the child and the individuals with whom he should be in contact. The way a consultant works with an organization has been discussed extensively elsewhere (Caplan, 1963, 1970; Hirschowitz, 1971; Beisser, 1972;

Berlin, 1977), and the theoretical implications will not be discussed here. They should, however, be reviewed and understood. The consultant should be flexible in his approach based on the needs of his patient and the needs of the school.

As described in the clinical examples, the consultant may evaluate patients and accept them for treatment or make suggestions to the teacher which will aid in the maintenance of self-esteem. In some situations both interventions are needed; in other situations, the school personnel may be used as co-therapists. In certain instances, the consultant may act as a teacher himself and suggest to school personnel an integrated theory of the development of self-esteem and the impact schools have on it. Some schools have requested the involvement of child psychiatrists when philosophy is being formulated or reviewed.

No sound method is incorrect in consulting with schools; still, the consultant must be careful to avoid such countertransference pitfalls as assuming the role of the "good parent" or the "knowledgeable teacher." Parents may wish to transfer their authority to the consultant in dealing with schools; this must be carefully avoided. Consultants need to remember that teachers are trained educators and though they may require consultation, they must be treated as colleagues.

Beyond the role of evaluating individual students, the consultant must be prepared to evaluate the schools and how they influence a child's self-esteem. Purkey (1970) discusses the atmosphere a teacher must create in the classroom. His discussion may be used as a reference point for evaluating the classroom or school program.

The teacher must allow himself to become an important person to the student, recognizing and utilizing the concept of transference from the "good parent." The teacher must be aware of the "bad parent" transference as well and not let this interfere with his effectiveness. A teacher who accepts himself is more likely to be accepting of his students. The teacher needs to offer opportunities for successful performance. By providing a challenging atmosphere geared individually to the student's past experiences and expectations, the teacher allows chances for success. Multiple small successes are as valuable as big successes, if not more so, because they are easier to accept and integrate into self-views without feelings of being overwhelmed. Knowing the student well so that "central" beliefs are validated is important. Whenever possible the teacher can help the student identify with a successful group. An individual self-view is thereby strengthened by having it consensually validated.

Positive comments on work should be made specifically and accurately. Inaccurate positive feedback is recognized as such and sweeping praise is usually felt as condescending. The "happy face" drawn by the teacher on each paper or the comments "well done" on all work are not helpful and suggest the one-dimensional view of the development of self-esteem I have criticized earlier.

The teacher should help students develop self-evaluation skills. When a student asks for the teacher's evaluation of work done, the interchange can be used first to ask for the student's evaluation, thereby teaching both the skills and value of self-evaluation. Subsequent feedback should then be accurate and comments should be directed not only to the work but to the self-evaluation itself. It is important for the teacher to recognize that students are *active* recipients of external influence, accepting or rejecting feedback to maintain self-esteem.

Though the teacher should be in firm control of the classroom, the students should feel a sense of freedom to experiment. The freedom to explore and make mistakes is crucial to learning. Mistakes can be interpreted as a natural byproduct of the scientific method rather than as failure. Intense competition, in contrast, usually inhibits learning. Grading and games based on competition always demand that where there is a winner, there must be a loser as well.

The consultant must be realistic in what he expects the school to provide for its students. Schools, like their students, must esteem their own teaching programs. Ideal programs are rare, but can be found. The school I shall now describe illustrates certain concepts which foster the development of self-esteem. This school is located in the inner city and made up of 35 students aged five through twelve in an ungraded, large classroom with four teachers. In an initial visit to the school the visitor sees student and teacher work on the bulletin board. On one wall is a display of the "Artist of the Week," with a retrospective study on one of the student's artwork. Multiple ethnic and socioeconomic groups are represented by varied dress and appearance. There are no assigned desks but cubbyholes where students store their work. There are large multistudent areas and small cubicles with individual study areas. Some students study on their own, others play in the dress-up area, others are with teachers.

The program has a flexible, student-directed, though teacher-planned, curriculum and an individualized learning program. The child is given assignments at the start of each school day and is responsible for completing them. Parent involvement in the classroom is expected.

The brochure describing the school states that it "seeks to help children develop the skills and strengths they will need to lead effective and personally satisfying lives in a complex and changing world. Some of these skills are academic—reading, oral and written communication, mathematics, and logical thinking. Others are self expressive—music, art, drama and movement. Some are personal—feelings of self worth, confidence, and motivation. Others are interpersonal—the ability to work and play with concern for others, and a willingness to share in the responsibilities of a learning community." The school stresses that children grow and learn differently. Each child is allowed to develop at his own rate and is encouraged to pursue individual interests. Children of different ages interact daily, teaching and learning from one another.

The physical design of the school, a single "open classroom" used by all the children, facilitates this approach. Separate areas for math, reading, art, science, and other activities are equipped with materials and suggested activities appropriate for different ages and skill levels. The children explore and use the resources of the classroom, independently learning to select and initiate their own educational experiences.

The staff plays an active role in guiding the child's experiences. Small group activities are planned to bring together children of similar interests and ability or to structure a peer teaching experience. While traditional techniques are often used to introduce academic skills, project-centered skill development is emphasized. Activities through which the child learns about the world are structured to include practice in a variety of academic skills. The child thus perceives the skills as useful and complementary tools in the pursuit of current interests. Projects may spring from a particular interest of an individual child or may be initiated by the teacher and designed for a group of children. Students may elect to join a variety of study groups throughout the year to investigate particular topics in depth.

Though not necessarily applicable to every school, this program demonstrates an attempt to integrate and foster the development of self-esteem in an educational setting.

CONCLUSION

Psychiatrists and other mental health professionals usually evaluate and work with the inner world of a child. When consulting with schools, the psychiatrist must be prepared to understand and work with the child's outer world as well. The consultant can be most effective when he is prepared to understand not only the individual child but also the teacher, the classroom, the school, and the pressures on the educational environment.

REFERENCES

Beisser, A. (1972), *Mental Health Consultation and Education.* Santa Monica: Institute Press.

Berlin, I. N. (1977), Some lessons learned in 25 years of mental health consultation to schools. In: *Principles and Techniques of Mental Health Consultation,* ed. S. C. Plog & P. I. Ahmed. New York: Plenum.

Caplan, G. (1963), Types of mental health consultation. *Amer. J. Orthopsychiat.,* 33:470-481.

——— (1970), *The Theory and Practice of Mental Health Consultation.* New York: Basic Books.

Coopersmith, S. (1967), *The Antecedents of Self-Esteem.* San Francisco: W. H. Freeman.

Davidson, H. H., & Lang, G. (1960), Children's perceptions of their teachers' feelings toward them related to self-perception, school achievement, and behavior. *J. Exper. Ed.,* 29:107-118.

Dean, R. S. (1977), Effects of self-concept on learning with gifted children. *J. Ed. Res.,* 70:315-318.

Edeburn, C. E., & Landry, R. G. (1977), Teacher self-concept and student self-concept in grades three, four, and five. *J. Ed. Res.,* 69:372-375.

Fink, M. B. (1962), Self-concept as it relates to academic underachievement. *Cal. J. Ed. Res.,* 13:57-62.

Hirschowitz, R. G. (1971), Mental health consultation to schools. *Mental Hygiene,* 55:237-241.

Norem-Hebeisen, A. A. (1976), A multidimensional construct of self-esteem. *J. Ed. Psychol.,* 68:559-565.

Purkey, W. W. (1967), The self and academic achievement. *Florida Educational Research and Development Council Research Bulletin*, 3:3–10.
————— (1968), The search for self. *Florida Educational Research and Development Council Research Bulletin*, 4:10.
Purkey, W. W. (1970), *Self-Concept and School Achievement*. Englewood Cliffs, N.J.: Prentice-Hall.
Rosenthal, R., & Jacobson, L. (1968), *Pygmalion Effects in the Classroom*. New York: Holt, Rinehart, & Winston.
Simon, W. E., & Simon, M. G. (1975), Self-esteem, intelligence, and standardized academic achievement. *Psychology in the Schools*, 12:97-100.
Stevens, P. H. (1956), An investigation of the relationship between certain aspects of self-concept and student's academic achievement. *Dissertation Abstracts*, 16:2531-2532.
Sweet, A. E., & Burbach, H. J. (1977), Self-esteem and reading achievement. *ERIC Reports*, ED 137756.
Williams, R. L., & Cole, S. (1968), Self-concept and school adjustment. *Personnel and Guidance Journal*, 46:478-481.

14

Self-Esteem of Parents of Disturbed

Children and the Self-Esteem of Their

Children

PAULA SCHNEIDER, M.S.W.

The self-esteem of children is partially shaped by the self-esteem of their parents. Children develop self-esteem in the reciprocity of the parent-child dyad, through identification with their parents and by how they experience subjectively their parents' views of them. Children also incorporate an identification with the cultural values of the groups in which they function. The extent to which they conform to these norms will have a bearing on self-esteem.

All parents struggle with diminished self-esteem during child-rearing, but the parents of emotionally disturbed and learning-disabled children are particularly vulnerable. As do others, they partially base their self-esteem on appraisals derived from direct reflection, but also on fantasies of how others perceive them. The parent internalizes his or her worth relative to the significant community (Rosenberg, 1979).

This paper examines the particular issues that affect the self-esteem of parents of disturbed children and how the self-esteem of their children is affected as a result. A social work educational group was used as the major treatment modality, seeking to elevate these parents' levels of self-esteem and increase their feelings of

My thanks to Todd Smith for functioning as co-leader of the Parents' Group; to Miriam Vale for serving as observer and recorder for the group sessions; and to Edward Boyd, Ed.D., the Director of the Gifford School in Weston, Mass., where the work which this article describes took place, and from whom I received much support and encouragement.

My thanks as well to those parents who provided the inspiration for this paper, and who contributed to my knowledge of this particular aspect of self-esteem in children.

competence through cognitive understanding, with the goal of enhancing their potential for empathic interactions with their children.

ISSUES FOR PARENTS OF DISTURBED CHILDREN

"Disturbed" children are those who chronically display one or more of the following characteristics: an inability to learn commensurate with their intellectual, sensory, motor, and physical development; an inability to establish and maintain adequate social relationships; an inability to respond appropriately in daily life situations; a variety of excessive behaviors ranging from hyperactive, impulsive responses to depression and withdrawal (Love, 1970).

Those of us who work with these troubled children and their parents know that their pathology interferes with the mutual pleasures and satisfactions available to less disturbed children and their parents. These parents and children experience a number of negative feelings and responses which lower self-esteem. Parents feel guilt, disappointment, hostility, anger, self-pity, pity for the child, sorrow, and at times empathy—the feeling most important for parents in relating to their children. Each of these feelings has an effect on the self-esteem of both the parent and the child. Some parents accept and resolve the conflicts generated by the recognition of their child's difficulties. They learn to empathize with their children to overcome day-to-day difficulties, and to accept that they have a child with special needs. One mother expressed this when she said that she felt that her son had given her a gift; his special needs required her to increase her understanding of him. But when she is viewed by someone in the community as an extension of her child's problem, she feels battered. This mother's self-esteem is enhanced or diminished by external sources.

At times the child's emotional disturbance originates in the family, and at all times it has consequences for the family. In both instances it elicits grave disappointment and guilt. Those who have brought psychological strengths and maturity to the role of parent frequently feel depressed and inadequate as they absorb the recognition of their child's disturbance. Because parent and child are so enmeshed with one another, the well-being of one is dependent on the well-being of the other. Of course, the affect of stronger parents is not as vulnerable to the fluctuations in behavior and self-esteem of their children as it is in parents with serious emotional difficulties of their own.

These parents have difficulty coping with the daily demands of caring for their children. Often, their low self-esteem is confirmed by their awareness of the child's flaws and their inability to separate their own emotional problems and feelings from the child's.

Parents of emotionally disturbed children experience two major kinds of guilt. The first is the guilt aroused by the fact of their child's problems. The parents try to understand what they did wrong before having the child—during pregnancy, perhaps—which could have created their child's problem. Not uncommonly they wonder if they have violated some religious principle or moral code for which they are now being punished. The second kind of guilt is connected with how the parents deal with their child's behavior. Parents wonder if they have caused the problems and are continuing to contribute to them. This uncertainty about how responsible they are for their child's disturbance has further ramifications. They feel less certain about their positive feelings and then feel guilty about the negative side of their ambivalence. This may lead to inconsistent discipline and limit-setting, lack of affection, or compensatory defenses such as excessive control and protectiveness. In families with parents who have other psychological vulnerabilities, there is chaos—yelling, physical abuse, and hostility directed toward other family members as well. Expressions of anger lead to further guilt, helplessness, and an inability to respond empathically to the child. Ornstein (1976) suggests that the child's sense of helplessness creates similar affects in the parents, reminiscent of their own childhoods. The parent defends herself with anger at the child for having exposed her to this renewed sense of helplessness. In both parents and children, diminished self-esteem produces the need to provoke and retaliate.

ATTITUDES OF OTHERS

Parents of disturbed children must also cope with the real or imagined judgments they perceive others to have about them and their children. Society reinforces the fantasy, based on a misreading of psychoanalytic theory, that parents are totally responsible for producing an emotionally healthy and well-functioning child. Negative judgments which exacerbate the parents' feelings of failure may emerge when parents seek help with their child's problem behavior. For some families there is a feeling of relief when a professional confirms a serious maladjustment. The problem has been identified and the first step has been made in dealing with it. Other parents are profoundly saddened and develop the idea that they have produced a faulty product. Parents of an aggressive child, for example, were asked to come to his school to discuss their child's argumentative behavior with his teacher. The principal was understandably critical of the boy. His final comment, "An apple doesn't fall far from its tree," left the parents sad and angry. One wonders what feelings the parents communicated to the child after this encounter and how the child's behavior was affected in school and at home. "Negative appraisals not only reduce the pleasures of the present but they also subvert or eliminate realistic hopes for the future. The corrosive drizzle of negative appraisal presumably removes the job of today and anticipation of tomorrow" (Coopersmith, 1967, p. 130).

For some individuals self-esteem depends more on external rather than internal variables, on social comparisons. Rosenberg describes two types of social comparisons: "One marks individuals as superior or inferior to one another in terms of some criterion of excellence, merit or virtue. Smarter or duller, weaker or stronger, handsomer or homelier are comparative terms requiring a relative judgment both of others and of the self. . . . The other type of comparison is normative, and refers primarily to deviance or conformity. Here the issue is not whether one is *better* or *worse*, but whether one is the *same* or *different*" (Rosenberg, 1979, p. 68). Both these types are important in considering the experience of disturbed children.

When children and their parents compare their achievements and characteristics with normal children or parents of normal children, they frequently form a negative self-image, the most obvious example being the case in which academic grades do not reflect real ability because of psychological impairments. At an early point in a child's educational career, deficits become apparent to both parent and child. The extent to which self-esteem suffers depends largely on the significance the family places on academic excellence. Poorly educated parents are often thrilled when their children do above-average schoolwork. Those who witness failure are somewhat saddened but communicate an attitude of "how could I have expected more—I didn't complete the eighth grade."

Normative comparisons are particularly difficult for parents; the child who is too aggressive in school may not seem like a menace to empathic and competent family members who find ways to engage his energy at home. The teacher with a class of 25 children to teach, however, may feel overwhelmed and angry with the confusion which the aggressive pupil creates in her classroom. In her eyes, the child is deviant. Thus families of disturbed children suffer from both kinds of comparisons. During periods when behavioral norms are ambiguous, as in the turbulence of the 1960's, nonconforming children do not have as much impact on the self-esteem of their parents. The time in history, as well as the social context, affects the self-esteem of parents and, ultimately, their children.

INTERVENTION WITH PARENTS

Working with parents of troubled youngsters requires a warm, respectful attitude which encourages parents to develop competence, mastery, and heightened self-esteem. A critical ingredient is the enhancement of parental empathy for the child's anxieties, conflicts, and narcissistic vulnerabilities. This can only be accomplished if the professional people with whom parents come in contact become significant to them and convey an "appreciation of the parents' attempt to interrupt the downward spiral of increasing distance and antagonism between themselves and their troubled child" (Ornstein, 1976, p. 18). Although the treatment interview may not be able to meet the psychological or social needs of parents, the therapist must convey his awareness that these needs require attention if the important persons in the child's life are to create a nurturing environment for the child. A mismatch between a family's needs and the external support systems puts pressure on the family which may increase pressures on the disturbed child. The therapist must be alert to these kinds of burdens. Many parents use a variety of defenses when referrals have had a coercive quality. A frequent defense is to place blame for the child's difficulties on the mental health system, or the school system, or on a particular teacher or diagnostician, allowing the parents to deny some responsibility for their problems. Parents with low self-esteem feel so hopeless about their quandary that they find it difficult to participate in therapy unless they can imagine some potential for change. At times, preventing further deterioration of the situation is tantamount to improvement. Feelings of isolation, hopelessness, and a paucity of ideas and information continue to plague parents of difficult children in spite of their efforts to use collaborative or family treatment.

GROUP WORK

Group work for parents of disturbed children is a modality which can address the issues of self-esteem in more ways than is possible with the traditional child guidance approach (of a therapist for the child and a separate therapist for the parent) or family therapy techniques. A group offers the appraisals of several others, a multiple reflection rather than the single reflection of the patient-therapist dyad. Since the group participants are faced with people with whom they have much in common, and can empathize with one another, the reflected appraisals can be seen as positive. Other esteem-enhancing qualities as well as several therapeutic factors will be mentioned below.

Members support one another as the group functions to provide feedback which members can use to increase their understanding of themselves and their children. It provides knowledge, guidance, resources, and identifies tasks which members have in common. This task-sharing has a bonding effect which dilutes the transference, countertransference, and authority issues inherent in other treatment modalities. The group can be a refuge for those who are exhausted from the strain of perceiving themselves as deviant in a normal environment; it provides a chance for people to participate in ways comfortable to them. Some individuals can derive a great deal from listening, others from speaking. It is often too uncomfortable for certain individuals to talk only with a therapist for an entire session. Most important, the empathic environment of groups may result in parents' increasing ability to maintain an empathic home atmosphere. This was a primary reason for choosing group work for these parents.

Yalom (1970) describes the curative factors which can exist in every type of therapy group. Based on research, clinical experience, and a review of the work of others, he divides therapeutic qualities into ten primary categories: those which arise from the group's ability to impart information, instill hope, communicate the universality of problems, express altruism, correctly recapitulate the primary family group, develop socializing techniques and imitative behavior; and those which arise from the group's ability to offer interpersonal learning, group cohesiveness, and catharsis. Different kinds of group therapies favor the operation of different clusters of these characteristics. The factors are interdependent; they neither occur nor function separately and they have differing significance to different group members. According to Yalom, behavior and attitudinal changes frequently take place coincidental with the patient's participation in group therapy and are frequently traceable to some aspect of the group experience. There is often improvement in family relationships or increasing success with work. With a higher reservoir of real accomplishments, self-esteem is raised. The benefits which the group provides for parents may be indirectly passed on to the children.

THE GROUP PROCESS IN A PARENT EDUCATION COURSE

A parent education course was developed to provide a therapeutic group experience for parents of children with emotional disturbances and/or learning disabilities at a private school for such students between the ages of eight and 18. The need for this intervention was recognized by the director, principal, and social workers who interacted daily with the parents. As family/school coordinator, I had helped to organize a parent association with a small board of directors so that parents would have some input into school-wide issues. In that capacity, I learned about parental concerns. I heard accounts of hurt and anger, isolation, loneliness, and uncertainty as to where to turn for comfort, resources, and advice. There were anecdotes of parents describing how they or their children had been mistreated by neighbors, clergy, mental health professionals, and educators. One mother summed it up by saying, "We all hear a great deal about parents who are abusing their children. What about parents who are abused because of their children?"

A mutual support group with professional leadership (as contrasted with self-help groups like Alcoholics Anonymous) was made available to any parent who wished to join. The two leaders and the observer-recorder considered the building of self-esteem to be a major goal. We strived to build on the parents' strengths and their potential for mastery, presenting the group as social and educational rather than therapeutic. We planned to impart information and to create a warm and altruistic environment. The presence of both a male and female leader would facilitate identification with a same-sexed parent figure. We were also aware that as members identified us with their parents there could be negative transferences. Still, we believed that these transferences would be of minor effect as compared with those encountered in individual work.

Parents received a letter inviting them to participate and were told in broad terms what could be expected: "a course in parenting in order that you can develop more skills in communicating with your child or children while sharing some of your thoughts and ideas with others 'in the same boat.' We shall concentrate on the following areas: listening within the family; building self-esteem; sensible rules and roles."[1] Parents had a clear choice about participation; we offered rather than urged. Cost was not a major factor because of a sliding fee scale. These parents had often been coerced into decisions; now we wanted to increase their sense of control over their lives. We used adult education principles based on the premise that adults bring their own knowledge and life experience to each situation and can therefore take responsibility for their own learning (Knowles, 1970). We thought of these parents as having capacities to acquire knowledge, although we recognized that they might be too neurotically involved with certain feelings to change. We suggested several topics, giving them some

[1] Areas to emphasize were suggested by John Caplan of the Cambridge Guidance Center.

idea of what to expect and then solicited their participation in deciding priorities.

To do this, the parents talked about their feelings about their children and described incidents and situations which they wanted to understand better. At first we could hear that they were angry and depressed. Expressions of these feelings abated as the parents realized that they were not "unique in their wretchedness." They began to experience a sense of relief which then permitted them to explore other feelings and ideas. We labelled and conceptualized the various behaviors, feelings, and situations, which enabled the parents better to understand and formulate cognitively what had happened in their families, rather than merely reacting to their experiences. Much of this was an outgrowth of the "universality" factor described by Yalom (1970).

We discovered in those early sessions that there were signs that self-esteem was already beginning to rise. The gap between ego ideals and realistic functioning began to narrow. This may have resulted as the parents lowered their expectations of themselves, having heard from parents with similar difficulties. In later sessions the gap may have narrowed further because of slight improvements in the other direction, as parents began to function more realistically with their children.

The ways in which the parents shared their feelings led to mutual support and the beginnings of group cohesion. As leaders, we called attention to the fact that each of the 10 families, with one exception, had other children without special needs; we wanted to help promote a view of themselves as parents who could produce normal children. We attempted to reduce the narcissistic injury which parents suffer when they think of themselves only as the parents of particular problem-ridden children attending a school for troubled children.

Group members and leaders affirmed the idea that it was alright to produce a child who was not perfect. The child has intrinsic value despite his problems, and parents have value in spite of their negative feelings toward parenthood. These kinds of attitudes were reinforced by sensitive listening and understanding, warm and respectful responses. Group members helped one another appreciate the positive aspects of their children.

Incidents vibrant with affect contributed to group cohesion.

One of the mothers, describing her family to the group, began to cry, saying of her 15-year-old, "He's a very bright boy but a miserable kid and makes our life miserable." Through her tears, she said to a father who had spoken previously, "I like your answer, you're very positive about your son. I hope we get there some day." The "positive" father may never have had his tentative statements of pleasure received with this kind of appreciation in another setting. The desperate mother was allowed a glimmer of hope. This hope may have improved her self-esteem (Yalom, 1970); but, equally important, it seemed to increase her desire to cope, which now was translated into her being more reflective and patient with her son.

We focused on what a statement like "I hate you" means to both parent and child. Parents seemed so relieved, even at the first meeting, to be able, without reprisal, to confess to having made such statements, and, in fact, to receive empathy for every aspect of the situation which had led to it. Initially, we had no way of knowing in what ways this support from peers was permitting parents to be more empathic with their children. The group sharing of ideas and feelings was only a first step. Parents expressed empathy in areas which evoked sad and/or angry feelings—their child's sense of isolation, their feelings of being stigmatized, their inadequacy in learning. At times there was an overidentification with the feelings of the child.

One mother described an incident in which her 15-year-old boy refused to do his religious-school homework. She immediately intervened with the teacher on his behalf. With the group's help she realized that her distress about his learning disability had interfered with her ability sufficiently to distance herself from her child so as to allow him to grow by working out his own solution. This mother used the group to gain support for her efforts to separate from her son. As long as her own emotional energy was focused on his academic deficiencies, she was unable to choose a proper course of action. On a subsequent occasion she allowed her son to find his own solution to a different problem and was able to say with obvious pleasure that she had felt better about her own response.

We discovered that initially parents were able to be empathic about those areas toward which they had similar feelings and responses. We hoped that the parents could also become empathic about feelings which they did not share with their children; we discovered by the fourth meeting that this was beginning to happen. In the previous three meetings we had emphasized through mini-lectures and discussions—"Behavior as a Statement of Feeling," "Sensitive Expressing" (Riley, Apgar, and Eaton, 1977)—the idea that communication could improve relationships and that improved relationships between parents and children could result in some behavioral and environmental changes. Parents described how they had become aware of changes in the inflection in their voices when they became anxious or angry and how they had known that this must have had an effect on their child. They talked about their tendency to blame their children for things they may not have done because of previous wrongdoing and how hard it was to "stick up" for their children in the neighborhood when their children were blamed for something that was not their fault. They were able to say that their past suffering with their children's problems made it more difficult to handle current situations. Further evidence of their efforts and beginning successes emerged as they described changes in dinner conversations and ways of dealing with situations between siblings.

One couple, after describing the hyperactivity and aggressiveness of their son, told of how they had found a new response to his behavior. In the middle of a rage he had told them how it felt to be rejected from play by his sister and her friends. With heightened consciousness about his feelings, the parents were able to intervene successfully in helping their son rejoin the group of children and play with them peacefully. They had been able to "hear" their son and engage the sibling's cooperation.

Parents were helped to see the benefits of reviewing such pleasant experiences with the child. The group members discussed the effect on the child's self-esteem when parents were able to point out to the child how he had bettered his own play situation with more controlled and generous behavior. The group experience had enabled this couple to respond more empathically to their child. It also provided a secondary consequence—more confidence in their parenting decisions.

Parents who tended to be somewhat ambivalent and indecisive were helped by the group to become more assertive with their children. Some of this new assertiveness may have derived from the group's support, but part of it may also have developed from an appreciation of the reasonableness of the approaches expounded in the meetings.

Our leadership efforts included attempts to facilitate cognitive mastery of those situations which parents described in the sessions, and guidance for efforts they might make to change family behavior patterns. In the discussions which followed the mini-lectures, group members were encouraged both to express their feelings and to expand each other's views of the situations. With the leaders, the members provided clarification and explanation when appropriate. Needless to say, understanding has the potential for reducing fear and anxiety and a sense of powerlessness.

We also prepared the parents for disappointment. With our knowledge that each new change in the families could trigger a minor crisis, we were cautious in encouraging them to make changes. We encouraged them to make efforts and to be patient with the slowness of change. The group model of interest and empathy, allowing for a rehearsal of difficult situations, facilitated the maintenance of self-esteem even when things went wrong at home.

A dominant theme of the meetings was the feeling of being "out of control" and powerless. The parent of a younger child who had temper tantrums and the parents of adolescents who had stolen money shared these feelings. Their ambivalence, uncertainty, and fear of how their children would retaliate led to their being inconsistent and permissive. Coopersmith comments that children with higher self-esteem come from families in which clear regulations are firmly enforced (Coopersmith, 1967).

Through the group process, parents were helped to expand their conception of those situations which had led to out-of-control behavior. They had a chance to look at the usefulness of anticipating behavior and were able to report the ways in which anticipation could mitigate what might have been in the past a difficult encounter.

Another dominant theme was separation. The parents, who often related destructively to their children, also savored their affection and the occasional pleasures of warmth and closeness. They often had developed few interests outside of parenting and often felt bereft when their children seemed to need them less. This was complicated even further when the psychological boundaries between a particular parent and child were too ambiguous to permit appropriate separation. The group dealt with one mother's problems of separation by encouraging her to begin a new career and by encouraging her to support her son's efforts to move away. Members suggested other ways of maintaining her connection with her child—by helping him obtain a job, for example.

One parent would communicate the view that another parent's child had what it takes to be successful. To hear such a statement about their own and their child's competence was clearly different from what they had heard from their own parents: "Why is our grandchild so difficult?" Because this person valued a group member's opinion of her child, the compliment raised her self-esteem.

The parents of troubled youngsters may have had poor relationships in their own families of origin, and their difficulties may continue to intrude upon the extended family. Grandparents, for example, may find it difficult to be supportive of their grandchildren. Parents feel isolated. The group has provided the support that had not previously been forthcoming from relatives.

In written unsigned evaluation sheets, members commented on the course's usefulness. Universality was one of the most significant factors. They all mentioned how helpful it had been to know that they were not the only ones with these kinds of problems. A majority of them stated that they had found the session in which we discussed self-esteem to be the most enjoyable. Most of the parents responded that their self-esteem had been raised by the course. A few indicated that it had stayed the same. One person said it was lowered at moments, "depending on my control." The implications of that comment are important. The feeling of being in control and effective both as a group participant and a family member is crucial to the self-esteem of both the parent and the child.

Optimally, it would have been useful to discover whether there were any changes in the child's self-esteem concurrent with the parents' participation in the group. In the absence of such information, we had to rest content with the knowledge of improved self-esteem in the parents.

Before participating in the group experience, parents of these emotionally disturbed children were angry, hostile, and at times depressed. They frequently felt emotionally injured by their acting-out children and by the community. Their responses to both were immediate and vengeful and resulted in further distance and distrust between parent and child or parent and school or agency. The group process, by encouraging their expression of feelings and their understanding of what had taken place, provided parents with an opportunity to screen their own responses. They were then ready to deal with their children in a different and more beneficial way.

CONCLUSION

Self-esteem is inextricably interwoven with the vicissitudes of the parenting role. Parenting is the critical task of the generativity phase of life development; bearing and rearing normal children are considered indicative of individual mastery.

The self-esteem of parents with an emotionally disturbed child is usually diminished, especially if the child requires special handling at home and special arrangements for schooling. While it is uncertain whether shattered self-esteem damages a parent's capacities for empathy and competence, or whether the reverse is the case, we have addressed self-esteem as a critical component to which we should direct our treatment efforts in any event. Both individual or group work with parents can promote an empathic environment which builds self-esteem and which can be translated into a home environment beneficial to the self-esteem of the child. Individual work provides parents with an opportunity to understand themselves more deeply in relation to their children. It can also more easily unearth the unconscious roots of the child's feelings and behaviors. But it does little to reduce the parent's sense of isolation and his feeling of having produced a faulty product. The group thus has several advantages. It has the potential to create an atmosphere conducive to positive trials directed toward new adaptations. And by providing an empathic environment, the group may enable parents to acquire new insights about their relationships with their children.

The self-esteem of the parents, diminished by guilt arising from their having produced a disturbed child and their negative feelings about him and the parenting role, can be addressed in this group situation. At the affective level, parents express their despair and their anger and experience warmth, support, and empathy in return. At the cognitive level, there is an exchange of perceptions, advice, and information. Empathy from and acceptance by the group's leaders and members allowed parents to communicate a similar empathy to their children and to increase their skill in handling difficult moments.

REFERENCES

Coopersmith, S. (1967), *The Antecedents of Self-Esteem*. San Francisco: W. H. Freeman.

Knowles, M. (1970), *The Modern Practice of Adult Education*. New York: Association Press.

Love, H. D. (1970), *Parental Attitudes toward Exceptional Children*. Springfield, Ill.: Charles C Thomas.

Ornstein, A. (1976), Making contact with the inner world of the child. *Compr. Psychiat.*, 17:3-34.

Riley, D., Apgar, K., & Eaton, J. (1977), *Parent Child Communication*. New York: Family Service Association of America.

Rosenberg, M. (1979), *Conceiving the Self*. New York: Basic Books.

Yalom, I. D. (1970), *The Theory and Practice of Group Psychotherapy*. New York: Basic Books.

15

Concluding Remarks

STEVEN L. ABLON, M.D.

Rather than review the papers in this book, I have chosen a classic children's story, "Beauty and the Beast," to convey our message as to the differing and interrelated aspects of self-esteem development and sustenance. Myths and fairy tales are compelling not only for children but also for adults. In symbolic terms they show us children's developmental conflicts, their fears, wishes, and aspirations. They express our efforts to gain and maintain self-esteem as well as our attempts to overcome injuries and restore a sense of worth. In our culture and history, myths and fairy tales are powerful spotlights on our conflicts and on our chances for growth.

"Beauty and the Beast" is one of a series of beast marriage stories that have been popular throughout world literature. One of the earliest, from the second century A.D., is the story of Cupid and Psyche in *The Golden Ass* of Apuleius. By the end of the 19th century, Ralston had collected from Norse, German, Sicilian, Cretan, Indian, and Russian sources numerous stories in which girls marry goats, monkeys, wolves, and bears which eventually become human (Opie and Opie, 1974). One tale describes how a crocodile turns into a handsome man when his bride agrees to lick his face. The classic text of "Beauty and the Beast" was translated from a story by Madame Leprince de Beaumont, the first English translation appearing in 1761. "Beauty and the Beast" has undergone a number of translations, been adapted for theater and cinema, and been retold in novel form. Well-known versions include Jean Cocteau's full-length movie in 1946 and Robin McKinley's recent novel *Beauty* (1979).

"Beauty and the Beast" tells of a very rich merchant who had three sons and three daughters and devoted his resources to their education. All of his daughters were very attractive but his young-

est daughter was particularly admired and came to be called
Beauty. The older sisters gave themselves ridiculous airs and
turned down good suitors, wanting to marry a duke or an earl.
Beauty spent most of her time reading good books. She told her
suitors she was too young to marry and chose to stay with her
father a few years longer. Suddenly the merchant lost his fortune,
and the older sisters were abandoned by their suitors. The people
were glad to see the older sisters humbled, but were concerned
for Beauty, who was charming, sweet-tempered, kind, affable, and
obliging.

When the family had to move to a country house, Beauty
worked hard to clean and prepare meals. Although unaccustomed
to this work, she grew stronger and healthier. After living about
a year in the country, the merchant received a letter that a ship
with his possessions had arrived safely in port. The older sisters
begged their father to buy them gowns, headdresses, and ribbons.
In order not to condemn her sisters' conduct, Beauty also asked
for something—a rose. The father journeyed to take possession
of his merchandise; but after much trouble, he returned as poor
as he had left. On his way home the merchant found himself in
a terrible storm. He discovered a house with no one around, but
where hay and oats were ready for his horse and fine meals were
prepared for him. The merchant slept in a grand apartment,
magnificently furnished. In the morning, preparing to depart,
the merchant passed an arbor of roses. He remembered Beauty's
request, and picked a branch. Immediately he heard a great noise;
a frightful Beast appeared saying that although he had saved the
merchant's life, the merchant had stolen his roses and would die
for it. The merchant begged forgiveness. Finally the Beast agreed
to let the merchant go, if one of his daughters came willingly to
suffer for him. The merchant did not intend to sacrifice his daughters, but wanted the comfort of being home and seeing his children
once more before he returned to die.

When Beauty's father returned home and told of his dreadful
adventure, the older sisters accused Beauty of causing their
father's terrible fate. Beauty said she would go to the Beast in her
father's place, happy to be able to save her father's life and prove
her tender love for him. Beauty insisted on this plan, and her
sisters were happy because they were envious of her virtue and

fine qualities. Beauty and her father returned to the Beast's palace. When the Beast appeared, Beauty was terrified at his appearance. The Beast asked her if she came willingly; trembling, Beauty replied that she had. The merchant agreed to leave the next day. That night, in a dream, a fine lady came to Beauty and said that Beauty's good will and good action would not go unrewarded. When her father left, Beauty wept, feeling convinced that the Beast would eat her that night. But when Beauty saw a special apartment, a large library, and a harpsichord prepared especially for her, she felt reassured. In a book she opened, Beauty read:

Welcome Beauty, banish fear,
You are queen and mistress here:
Speak your wishes, speak your will,
Swift obedience meets them still [Opie and Opie, p. 145].

At dinner that evening the Beast asked Beauty if she thought him ugly. Beauty replied that she did, for she could not lie, but that she also found him very good-natured. The Beast said that besides being ugly, he was poor, silly, and stupid. Beauty was so pleased with the Beast's kindness that she hardly noticed his ugliness. Beauty told the Beast that among mankind "there are many that deserve that name more than you, and I prefer you just as you are, to those, who, under a human form, hide a treacherous, corrupt, and ungrateful heart" (p. 147). After supper the Beast asked Beauty to be his wife. Beauty refused. The Beast sighed, hissed frighteningly, and left. For three months the Beast came to visit Beauty after supper at nine o'clock and Beauty looked forward eagerly to his visits. But every night the monster also asked Beauty to be his wife. Finally Beauty said that she would always value the Beast as a friend, but could not consent to marry him. The Beast replied that since he loved Beauty so much he would be happy if she would just stay with him and promise never to leave him. Beauty asked if she could first see her father again. The Beast said that she could remain with her father if she wished, although he would die of grief without her. Beauty loved the Beast too much to be the cause of his death and promised to visit her father and return in a week. The next day Beauty was happily reunited with her father. Beauty's sisters had meanwhile married. The eldest had married an extremely handsome man; but he was so fond of himself he neglected his wife. The other sister married a very witty man who used his wit to torment everyone, especially his wife. The sisters were terribly jealous of Beauty. When they heard her story they plotted to detain Beauty from returning in a week as she had promised.

Beauty stayed longer than a week, but worried about the Beast. She dreamed she saw him lying in the grass dying, reproaching her for her ingratitude. Beauty returned to the Beast's palace but could find him nowhere. Finally she remembered her dream and found the Beast lying in the garden almost dead. Beauty "threw herself upon him without any dread" (p. 149) and brought him water. The Beast said he would die satisfied, having seen her once more. Beauty both begged him not to die and to be her husband. Beauty told the Beast she thought she had felt only friendship for him but her grief convinced her that she could not live without him. At this moment the Beast became the prince he had been before a wicked fairy had transformed him. The beautiful lady of Beauty's dream reappeared and brought Beauty's father and family to the palace. She also turned Beauty's sisters into statues standing before the palace gate until they recognized their faults. Beauty's family was transported to the prince's land where they lived happily for many years.

"Beauty and the Beast" can be read as a psychological document in which each step in the story reflects the development and sustenance of Beauty's self-esteem. Fairy tales give us the inner life and conflicts of their characters, not directly, but in symbolic and metaphorical language. Story, action, behavior, relationships, and ideals can be linked to the characters' inner-life conflicts and sense of self. Of course, on an obvious level, "Beauty and the Beast" is concerned more with what we value in others than with how we feel about ourselves. But what is valued in the characters of fairy tales are also externalizations and projections of what generations of children and adults value and struggle with in themselves.

A central theme of "Beauty and the Beast" is marriage. The marriage of the beautiful and the bestial reverberates on many levels, bringing together mind and body, the spiritual and sexual, civilized and uncivilized, ego and drives. Our potential for love, happiness, and mature self-esteem depends on how we blend and integrate these two sides of ourselves. As Beauty grows and develops, this marriage, or progressive integration, of ego and drives is central to her self-esteem. At first Beauty's self-esteem is supported by her physical beauty. Her narcissism is nourished by everyone's admiration; people observe: "The youngest, as she was handsomer, was also better than her sisters" (p. 139). This underscores how people link physical beauty and worthiness. These external sources also value her other qualities such as personality, temperament, and her interest in reading good books. No effort had been spared in Beauty's education, contributing to her competence and effectiveness, strengthening her self-esteem and helping her cope assertively with the conflicts and crises that ensue. The sisters of Beauty serve as a contrast to her; their narcissism fails to develop and to modify. Continuing to be exhibitionistic, superficial, and unable to tolerate and sublimate affects such as jealousy and rivalry, they are unable to cope with the crises in their lives. When Beauty chooses to stay with her father a few more years while her sisters pursue marriage, she reveals another aspect of her developing self-esteem. The reciprocal love between Beauty and her father highlights the importance of strong early parent-child attachments, and how only gradually, but inevitably, this love is transferred from parent to wife or husband. Although strong parental attachments have become associated with unresolved oedipal conflicts and interpersonal difficulties, a strong oedipal attachment is a positive force when transferred successfully to adult love.

In "Beauty and the Beast," Beauty's mother is absent, except, perhaps, as she is represented by the "fine lady" who appears in Beauty's dream and reassures her that her "good will" and "good action" will not go unrewarded. The same beautiful lady brings Beauty's father and her family to the castle when the Beast is turned into a prince. This lady symbolizes the role of internalized objects in sustaining self-esteem. The lady can be seen as representing an internalized good parent and also an ego ideal both of which allow Beauty to be brave and competent. When the beautiful lady turns the sisters into statues until they recognize their faults, we see a metaphorical expression of loving parental limits in the development of self-esteem. The other side of the oedipal mother, competitive and jealous, is represented by the sisters.

When the merchant loses his money, Beauty has to work hard caring for the house, an opportunity for successful adaptation and mastery of adversity. Her confidence, ability to tolerate adversity, to be flexible, industrious, and to master new situations all lead to increased self-esteem: She grows "stronger and healthier than ever" (p. 140). When Beauty's father leaves to look after his newly arrived merchandise, Beauty asks for a rose, the symbol of the loss of virginity. Beauty now has to contend with puberty and the upsurge of sexual and aggressive impulses. It is the rose that causes the trouble between the merchant and the Beast, just as dawning sexuality and growing womanhood strain the closeness between father and daughter. On one level, the story then becomes an unfolding of how Beauty struggles to transfer her love for her father, paternal and pure in appearance, to the Beast, who at first looks fierce and aggressive. From the beginning, however, the Beast's kindness, gentleness, and thoughtfulness are apparent.

Beauty's steadfast refusal to marry the Beast represents her unwillingness to accept not only her sexuality but also her aggression, for to marry the Beast and accept her sexuality means to Beauty the destruction of her relationship with her father. Once Beauty can acknowledge and accept her sexual and aggressive wishes, marriage and sexuality no longer seem bestial, but loving. Throughout the fairy tale, Beauty is represented only as virtue and goodness: "She was such a charming, sweet-tempered creature, spoke so kindly to poor people and was of such affable and obliging behavior" (p. 139). Marriage to the Beast symbolizes an ultimate acceptance of the selfish, aggressive, and sexual "beast" side of herself; this acceptance is represented by her refusal to give up the Beast—and thus the beast in herself—and her ability to grieve for her idealized, all-virtuous view of herself. In this context, the process of grieving and competently handling a range of affects such as anger, disappointment, anxiety, and sadness are essential to Beauty's future. She successfully negotiates the oedipal and adolescent periods of psychosexual development and emerges with intact self-esteem. In her decision to marry the Beast, Beauty realizes what we all struggle to understand: The selfish, aggressive, and sexual, and the good, loving, and altruistic must be acknowledged and wedded together. In this way we modify and sublimate our aggressive affects and direct our behavior in the world. What we feel in the dark side of our hearts is not what governs and matters most. Beauty asks herself, "Why did I refuse to marry him? I should be happier with the monster than my sisters are with their husbands; it is neither wit, nor a fine person, in a husband, that makes a woman happy, but virtue, sweetness of temper and complaisance, and Beast has all of these valuable qualifications" (pp. 148-149). When Beauty loves the Beast and sees him as beautiful—when she sees him in terms of her esteem for him—he is free to become himself, the handsome prince he was before. The liberating power of Beauty's love is centrally important to mature love as valuing and as enhancing of self-esteem.

In this book we have explored the different roots of self-esteem; how people achieve high self-regard and how they may lose it. Self-esteem is puzzling, being more than a catalogue of its parts. It is more than an outgrowth of parent-child relationships, more than a sense of confidence and effectiveness, more than a balanced sense of self, satisfied narcissism, or an ability to communicate and handle affects. Self-esteem is all of these and more. Many of us endure great personal or group tragedy and maintain a solid sense of self-esteem; while others, despite apparent success and happiness, feel poorly about themselves. Love, security, pleasure, comfort, fame, money, success, and admiration are no guarantees of self-esteem. Over the years each person must struggle with the shifts in his feelings of self-worth.

Indeed, in writing this book, our individual and collective self-esteems were challenged by the difficulty of the subject, and buffeted by hours of discussion, editing, and revising directed toward making explorations in this thick wood easier to follow. What has been clear from the beginning is that we have travelled only part way into the territory. Our hope is that our effort will encourage others to make these explorations, to travel into new areas, and so to go beyond what at best are only initial base camps. It seems that we can rest assured that self-esteem, even in these days of genetic engineering, will always be more than the sum of its parts and will always leave a great deal to be understood. But this only highlights another crucial expression of self-esteem—the pleasure of seeking itself, like a newborn looking for challenge, the pleasure of learning, of searching, and of insight.

REFERENCES

McKinley, R. (1979), *Beauty*. New York: Pocket Books.
Opie, I., & Opie, P. (1974), *The Classic Fairy Tales*. London: Oxford University
    Press, pp. 139-150.

Name Index

Abel, T. M., 104, 120
Abelin, E., 163n, 175-176
Ablon, S. L., 24, 79-89, 234, 285-292
Abraham, K., 190, 205
Adams, G. R., 108, 119
Adams, R. D., 227, 236
Adler, A., 124, 148
Alexander, J., 22, 38
Allen, F. S., 235, 240
Allport, G. W., 128, 148
Anthony, E. J., 91-92, 99, 101, 119
Apgar, K., 280, 284
Arnheim, R., 91, 102
Arnold, M., 45, 76
Ausubel, D. P., 128, 130, 148, 211, 221

Bach, S., 176
Bahnson, C. B., 103, 119
Balthazar, E. E., 226, 239
Barocas, R., 108, 119
Basch, M. F., 29, 38, 80, 88
Bate, W. J., 27, 39
Bateson, G., 7, 39
Beck, J., 210, 222
Beezley, P., 142, 149
Beisser, A., 264, 268
Belfer, H., 27
Belfer, M. L., 27, 103-121
Bergman, A., 92, 102, 128-130, 149, 153-154, 157, 162, 207, 222
Bergman, P., 209, 222
Berlin, I. N., 265, 268
Berman, A, 210, 221
Bernstein, N. R., 230, 240
Berscheid, E., 108, 119
Bibring, E., 81-82, 88, 192, 205
Binstock, W., 3, 39
Black, H., 108, 119
Blanck, J., 130, 141, 143, 148
Blanck, R., 130, 141, 143, 148
Bledsoe, J. C., 141, 148
Blos, P., 138-140, 148, 215-217, 222
Bonime, W., 192, 205
Bowlby, J., 45, 76, 105, 119
Braun, S., 11, 241-254
Brazelton, T. B., 29, 37, 39
Breger, L., 126, 135, 141, 148
Brenner, C., 80, 88

Broucek, F., 155, 162
Bry, A., 104, 120
Burbach, H. J., 264, 269
Burland, J. A., 176
Burlingham, P., 163n, 176
Butler, A., 237, 240

Caplan, G., 264, 268
Caplan, J., 277n
Carpenter, G., 89
Cavior, N., 108, 119
Clark, R. W., 222
Clifford, E., 103, 106, 108, 119
Coazal, R., 210, 222
Cobb, S., 226
Cocteau, J., 285
Cohen, A. S., 119
Cohen, F., 105, 108, 119
Cole, S., 264, 269
Condon, W. S., 210, 222
Conger, J. J., 47, 77
Converse, J., 103
Cook, S. W., 104, 119
Cooley, C. H., 124, 148
Coopersmith, S., 81, 88, 122n, 124, 127-128, 134, 148, 164, 174, 176, 263, 268, 273, 281, 284
Cotton, N., 13, 29, 122-150
Cotton, P., 122n
Critchley, M. R., 209-210, 222

Dare, C., 21, 25, 27, 39
Darwin, C., 45, 76
Davidson, H. H., 263, 268
Dean, R. S., 264, 268
Demos, J., 3, 39
Demos, V., 3, 24, 38-39, 45-79, 89
De Saussure, J., 23, 37, 41, 197, 205
Deutsch, H., 28n, 39
Dion, K., 107-108, 119
Dokecki, R. R., 108, 119
Dornbusch, S. M., 107, 120
Dowling, S., 90, 102

Eason, J., 280, 284
Edelburn, C. E., 263, 268
Edgerton, M. T., 103, 110, 120
Ehrlich, S., 122n

293

Subject Index